STALEMATE

* Onyx, 1994, co-written with John Donnelly
** Bantam, 1997, co-written with Patricia Sierra

STALEMATE

**A SHOCKING TRUE STORY OF
CHILD ABDUCTION AND MURDER**

JOHN PHILPIN

Bantam Books

NEW YORK•TORONTO
LONDON•SYDNEY•AUCKLAND

STALEMATE

A Bantam Book / October 1997

ISBN 0-553-56999-6

Published simultaneously in the United States and Canada

Bantam Books are published by Bantam Books, a division of Bantam
Doubleday Dell Publishing Group, Inc. Its trademark, consisting of
the words "Bantam Books" and the portrayal of a rooster, is
Registered in U.S. Patent and Trademark Office and in other
countries. Marca Registrada. Bantam Books, 1540 Broadway, New
York, New York 10036.

PRINTED IN THE UNITED STATES OF AMERICA

OPM   10   9   8   7   6   5   4   3   2   1

For Amanda, Amber, Angela,
Ilene, Jennifer, Michaela, Polly,
and too many others . . .

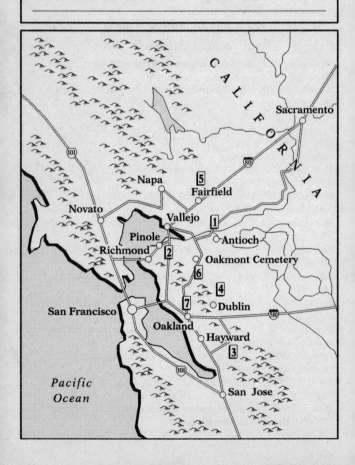

1   Angela Bugay, abducted and murdered 11/19/83

2   Amber Swartz, abducted 6/3/88

3   Michaela Garecht, abducted 11/19/88

4   Ilene Misheloff, abducted 1/30/89

5   Amanda Campbell, abducted 12/27/91

6   Oakmont Cemetery

7   Timothy Bindner, residence

TIMELINE

November 19, 1983—Angela Jane Bugay disappears—
Antioch

November 26, 1983—Angela Bugay's body found—Antioch

December, 1984—Bindner begins visiting Angela's grave in
Oakmont Cemetery

June 2, 1988—Bindner sends letter to Susan Bugay,
Angela's mother

June 3, 1988—Amber Jean Swartz disappears—Pinole

June 6, 1988—Bindner arrives at Swartz residence offering
to help search for Amber

June 15, 1988—Dogs track Amber's scent to Angela's grave

November 19, 1988—Bindner fails firefighter's agility test—
Hayward

November 19, 1988—Michaela Joy Garecht kidnapped—
Hayward

November 20, 1988—Bindner begins two-week search for
Michaela Garecht

January 30, 1989—Ilene Misheloff disappears—Dublin

February 11, 1989—Bindner searches for Ilene Misheloff

May 22, 1991—Bindner attends Oakland A's baseball game,
sees Sheila Cosgrove

May 23, 1991—Sheila Cosgrove receives first letter from
Bindner—Fairfield

December 27, 1991—Amanda "Nikki" Campbell
disappears—Fairfield

December 30, 1991—Bindner calls Nikki hot line to offer
help

January 1, 1992—Dogs track Nikki's scent to Angela
Bugay's grave

January 11, 1992—Dogs find Bindner's scent at Oakmont
cemetery

January 15, 1992—Dogs track Bindner's scent to a hill
above Sheila Cosgrove's home

December 9, 1992—Fairfield Police search Bindner's house
and find nothing

June 9, 1993—Bindner files $25 million claim against
Fairfield and Harold Sagan

April 24, 1996—Larry Graham arrested for the murder of
Angela Bugay

May 2, 1997—Fairfield agrees to settle suit with Bindner for
$90,000; the city admits no fault

CONTENTS

ACKNOWLEDGMENTS

Many people assisted in telling this story.

In Vermont, CBS Winter Olympics sports personality Paul Robbins helped with video and other media-related matters.

Psychologists Stephanie Case, Neil Marinello, and Marion Wedell offered their insights and advice. Captain Michael LeClair of the Vermont State Police once again gave me the perspective of a law enforcement professional who stuck with it for more than twenty-five years. Chief Joseph Estey, of the Hartford Police Department, as usual was generous with his time and advice.

Steve Philpin spent his Bennington College Field Work Term editing and critiquing earlier versions of the manuscript, as well as managing the more than ten thousand pages of material synthesized in this work. He also continued to provide the sound track for my life.

In California, Harold Sagan tolerated the intrusive researcher and writer. He is the consummate detective. He is also an educator—and a person to whom I will remain indebted.

Thanks also to Fairfield Police Chief Douglas Milender, Deputy Chief Jerry Walker, Sergeant Chuck Timm, and Detectives Joe Allio, Barry Hom, and Mel Ferro.

Also: Fairfield FBI Special Agents Kimton Zane and David Heinle, San Francisco FBI Special Agents Larry Taylor and Tim Bezik, and Sacramento FBI Supervisory Special Agent Don Pierce.

Daracy Kopf shared her experiences and insights, as did Bob Penkivich, California Highway Patrol (Retired), who serves on the board of the Amber Foundation. Clay Haswell, former managing editor of the *Contra Costa Times*, offered his observations on the cases.

A special thank-you is due Dale Myer and his bloodhound, Friday. The Bay Area is fortunate to have a man of Dale's skill, temperament, and dedication.

Equally important were the contributions of sources affiliated with other Bay Area law enforcement agencies. They know who they are and how they helped. Many thanks.

Kim Swartz is a person of great strength, grace, and intelligence. Through the nonprofit Amber Foundation in Pinole, she provides for others who suffer the loss of children to stranger abduction.

Timothy Bindner has not been charged with any of the crimes described here. He gave hundreds of hours of his time in open-ended, occasionally troubling interviews. He was not paid for his story, nor did he ask to be.

I owe a debt of gratitude to Sierra. I am fortunate that the Ohio office had such liberal hours.

As always, many thanks to my agent, Elizabeth Knappman of New England Publishing Associates.

My editor at Bantam, Katie Hall, has been a never-ending source of enthusiasm and advice. Her wit, keen eye, and sharp pencil keep me on my toes.

JOHN PHILPIN
Reading, Vermont
September 1996

AUTHOR'S NOTE

This story is true, and it continues to unfold in the communities of San Francisco's Bay Area. Because most of the cases discussed remain open, some changes were necessary to protect the integrity of ongoing investigations.

With the exception of the victims, the names of all minor children and their families have been changed. Despite previous exposure in the media, the names of surviving victims of abduction and abuse have been changed; privacy is necessary to their healing.

One person requested anonymity out of fear. I have respected that person's wishes.

Where conversations are reported, they are based on the recollections of one or more of the participants, official documents, transcripts, media accounts, audio or video tape recordings, and personal notes.

The lengthy italicized quotes attributed to Timothy Bindner are based on telephone conversations and personal interviews with him from November 1993 to May 1997.

AUTHOR'S NOTE

"As silent as a mirror is believed
Realities plunge in silence by . . ."

—HART CRANE,
"LEGEND"

"A man feared that he might find an assassin;
Another that he might find a victim.
One was more wise than the other."

—STEPHEN CRANE,
"THE BLACK RIDERS"

ONE

THE VANISHING

1

A little girl walked alone through the fading winter light on Salisbury Drive. She was wearing her Santa Claus earrings, a pink nylon ski jacket, purple pants, and white sneakers trimmed in pink. They were bright colors against the gray landscape of her middle-class Fairfield, California, neighborhood.

Amanda "Nikki" Campbell scuffed along like any four-year-old, oblivious to the chill and the light rain. She had come outside between three and four o'clock to play with some of the other kids, and it was getting late now. Her mother would be home from work soon.

Her friends still played elsewhere on the streets. She might have heard their voices—sound carries on the moist air—but she couldn't see them. And they didn't know where she had gone. One minute she was there, and then she wasn't.

2

Rain. There had been days of rain. And when it wasn't raining, fog.

Christmas lights wore halos in the mist. Garlands on the outdoor holiday trees drooped with the weight of dampness. Now, in the late afternoon, clouds slid across a darkening sky. What had been a light, intermittent rain threatened to become steady. The temperature dipped into the low forties, frigid for northern California's delta region.

When the weather goes wet and cold, the locals don't come outside unless they have to. The cops, however, have no choice. Detective Harold Sagan and the Fairfield investigative team had arrest warrants to serve in neighboring Vallejo. That meant a sweep—and confrontations.

A gang member had shot two kids at a local mall—one a targeted victim, the other a bystander. Both survived. It was the kind of incident that gave the city its reputation as "The Little Oakland of the North Bay."

Harold Sagan likes the city, and he enjoys his job. "We're not subtle here," he is fond of saying. "If you did the crime, you're going down. We'll sort it out later."

Despite the bulldog attitude, he is more polished than most of his big-city peers. He holds a master's degree in public administration and is at work on a doctorate in education—training that he uses when he is teaching college and graduate classes in the investigation of crimes against children.

Long days are routine for the 6'1" detective, whose crop of gray hair makes him look older than his forty-three years. He's been a cop for twenty of those years—a cop with the veneer of laid-back California. His eyes reveal his determination, his intensity. He resents it when the bad guy gets away.

On the evening of the twenty-seventh, Sagan was losing patience with the other members of the investigative team, but that was nothing new. He had worked with these guys—Detective Sergeant Chuck Timm and Detectives Joe Allio, Barry Hom, and Mel Ferro—for years. Sagan always tightened up when the time for a major bust approached. The others were loose, joking around, taking their time. They were all good cops, but each had his own style. Sagan grew thoughtful, focused, determined; his colleagues bantered with one another, kept it light, until the moment they went into action. Then they were all business.

As he walked to his car late that afternoon, Sagan could feel the dark dampness, taste the saturated air. He hated this time of year. The cop drove out onto Webster Street and headed for Highway 12. He noticed the dashboard clock as he reached over to switch on his headlights and adjust the windshield wipers to intermittent speed. It was 5:00 P.M.

By 8:30 P.M., the almost flawless sweep of Vallejo was complete and Harold Sagan was merging his car into the light traffic on the highway, headed back toward Fairfield. He was thinking over what had gone down—the coordination with the Vallejo department, the arrests. He considered what still needed to be done—booking, interrogation, paperwork. As he drove over the last big hill outside town, just before the Sunnyside Dairy, he was thinking about the one shooter who had eluded them.

The chatter of a talk radio station buzzed softly. Then the voice of a Fairfield dispatcher cut through the background noise with a missing child broadcast—an all-points bulletin for a four-year-old girl named Amanda "Nikki" Campbell, last seen by her friends wearing a pink jacket and purple corduroy pants on Salisbury Drive.

Alone on the dark highway, driving through the cold rain, Sagan listened to the end of the broadcast and felt a wave of nausea. This was more than just a kid wandering down the street to some neighbor's house. She was only four, and already had been gone for hours.

It was difficult to shake himself out of his thoughts about the child, but he didn't have time to dwell on them. He had one remaining arrest warrant, and by now, the shooter they had missed would know that his friends had been arrested. Sagan had to figure out what approach to use, how he was going to snag him. He knew he was in for a long night.

———————

At 4:00 A.M., Sagan took a short break. He walked into the atrium that was at the center of the administrative offices and the investigations unit. He asked if anyone had found Nikki Campbell yet.

No, he was told. They hadn't located the child.

As he worked on his reports through the early morning hours, he overheard bits and pieces of conversation. Nikki went out to play. Mom was at work. Dad was home with the kids. The child knew her street, knew her neighborhood. She hadn't wandered off before, hadn't gotten herself lost. It looked as if someone had grabbed her. No witnesses. No nothing.

Four years old, Sagan thought. Two days after Christmas. A little girl not even old enough to start kindergarten. Now she was a case number: 91-18747.

There was something about the child's Salisbury Drive neighborhood that struck Sagan as familiar. Working at his desk through the night and into Saturday morning, he felt as if something were escaping him, some important piece of information that skirted just beyond the reach of his consciousness. Whatever it was, it would have to come in its own time.

By mid-afternoon Sagan was finally finished with the last of the paperwork. He walked out through the atrium to the command center, next to the chief's office. He hadn't slept, but he knew that the search for Nikki Campbell was continuing, that dozens of people had volunteered to help as the scope of the investigation spread out beyond the immediate neighborhood.

"Where do you need me?" he asked. "What do you want me to do?"

The late December afternoon was cold and overcast as Sagan drove into the Salisbury Drive neighborhood. Into the night, he combed through an orchard searching for Nikki. As he waded through the tall, damp grass and among the power line towers, elusive, half-formed thoughts continued to nag at him, but he couldn't put his finger on what he was trying to remember.

He took a break for a couple of hours, slept and showered, then returned to his office at 5:00 A.M. Sunday. At his desk, he could hear muted conversation coming from the command center, but his mind kept drifting. He thought about the search, the neighborhood, the little girl.

On the basis of what the kids on the street had told investigators, and the timing of the search begun by Nikki's father and brother, the police estimated the time of her disappearance to be 5:00 P.M. If they were right, she had disappeared at the same moment Sagan had glanced at his dashboard clock on his way to Vallejo. While he was busy complaining to himself about the rain, and the cold, and the early darkness, little Amanda "Nikki" Campbell was disappearing into it.

Then it hit him. He had been in the Campbells' neighborhood six months earlier to check out an Oakland man in his forties who was sending strange letters to a twelve-year-old girl. The look and feel of the first letter caught her mother's attention. The envelope contained something round and solid, something metal. There was no return address, just a printed message on the back: "i think if they had climbed through the looking glass they would have found you, Sheila."

Sheila Cosgrove—that was the kid. Her mother's name was Liz. Sagan pulled the file.

3

Liz Cosgrove opened a strange letter that someone had
sent to her daughter. Two coins fell out—an Indian
head penny and a silver dollar. She stared at them,
puzzled, then pulled out the letter and unfolded it. The
printing looked like gibberish, but she had been a kid
once herself. She knew the trick. She held the paper in
front of a mirror and began to read.

> Dear "Sheila"
>   The "peace" type silver dollar was first made
> in 1921 to celebrate the end of the war, and in
> hope that there would never be another one, and
> that the eagle's wings could remain folded (sadly,
> they haven't). The coin has little intrinsic value;
> it is to convey good luck and hope for a commit-
> ment to peace and non-violence.
>   I wish you the best.
>   TJB

A few days later, Liz was back in front of the mirror with a second letter:

Dear Sheila,

You can read this if you stand on your head and climb through the mirror. This would be a good way to begin a day, don't you think?

The peace dollar was a hope, and the Indian penny is always a wish for good luck.

If you or your parents want to ask me anything, please write like this, other wise I might have to stand on my head and climb through the mirror to read it.

I dare not send you a hug and a kiss, so instead I send you one-third of a hug, and two-millionth of a kiss, and thirteen dodecillian dreams.

Your friend,
Tim

Liz Cosgrove knew there was something wrong. No one Sheila's age had sent the letters, and they certainly weren't from any relative. Nor were they a joke.

She looked at the postmark. Oakland. They didn't know anybody in Oakland, and she didn't know anyone named Tim. If her child was in danger, Liz Cosgrove was going to do something about it. So she went to the police. She wanted an investigation, an arrest.

A cop tried to calm her down. He agreed that the letters were frightening, but explained that no crime had been committed. There was nothing threatening in the letters, nothing sexual. He said it wasn't against the law to write letters or send gifts to little girls.

None of that mattered to Liz. This guy could be watching the house. He could be stalking Sheila.

She didn't have long to wait for the third letter to arrive. This one had a return address—a post office box in Richmond, California. It was a greeting card with Bible verses hand-printed on it. The writer had underlined certain phrases, words that terrified Liz.

From the book of John: "Ye have not chosen me, but *I have chosen you*"; "Father, I will, that they also, whom thou hast given me, *be with me where I am*."

On the facing page was a poem:

> *Never seek*
> *to tell thy love*
> *that never told*
> *can be*
> *For the gentle breeze*
> *ever moves*
> *silently,*
> *invisibly.*
> *i love you*
> *Sheila*

When the Cosgroves got no satisfaction from the police, they hired a private investigator. They wanted a name and a face for the man who was writing to their child. They wanted to know if he was dangerous. And they wanted the letters stopped.

The investigator had no difficulty tracking the man, but the information he turned over to the Cosgroves offered no comfort. The letter writer's name was Timothy Bindner. He lived in Oakland and had been generating suspicion in the law enforcement community for years. Cops knew that Bindner approached children. Once they had arrested him and charged him with annoying two little girls, a violation of the California Penal Code, Section 647.6, Crimes Against Children. But the charge was dropped and no jurisdiction had convicted him of anything.

When Liz Cosgrove came to Harold Sagan with her bizarre story about a man, a stranger, sending letters, poems, and gifts to her daughter, he listened. Then he started inquiring about Timothy Bindner.

Within a few days of starting his investigation,

Sagan received a call from Special Agent Mary Ellen O'Toole, the FBI's resident West Coast profiler. O'Toole had heard about the detective's inquiries, and she knew Bindner. She'd had extensive contact with him during her investigation of a child's disappearance in 1988. O'Toole told Sagan that Bindner was extremely intelligent and suggested that the two of them interview the Oakland man together. Bindner could run circles around any one cop. He was shrewd—and capable of getting more information from an interviewer than what he gave, the agent said.

Sagan prepared for the meeting by gathering more background on Bindner. He learned that the man indeed was bright, yet had gotten nowhere in life. He hung out in cemeteries, did volunteer work repairing gravestones, and had once worked in a crematorium. But one thing stood out: All the cops who had investigated Bindner over the years agreed that he probably had an unhealthy interest in children.

In 1985, Bindner was fired from his job as a claims processor at the Social Security Administration in Richmond, California. His superiors caught him using the agency's computers to collect the names, addresses, and birth dates of little girls in Colorado, applicants for Social Security benefits. He sent each girl a gift of $50 on her fourteenth birthday—almost $2,000 out of his own pocket. The *National Enquirer* picked up the story and placed it on page 2.

In media interviews, Bindner said the inspiration for his cash giveaway was the 1950s TV show *The Millionaire*. At the start of each episode, a man arrived at someone's door with a check for a million dollars—a gift from a stranger. Bindner said he thought of his giveaways as a touch of magic for the kids. But some of their parents considered the gifts alarming. They feared that a strange man would turn up at the door, so they went to police and postal authorities, filed complaints, and Tim Bindner lost his job.

It took him sixteen months to get rehired. His union, the American Federation of Government Employees, fought the firing. He even received a letter of support from U.S. Representative Pat Schroeder. When an arbitrator found that there was no "just cause" for Bindner's firing (he hadn't used the Social Security records for personal gain), he was reinstated.

Harold Sagan wanted to meet with Agent O'Toole to discuss Bindner, but O'Toole, after urging that Sagan not interview Bindner without her, put him off. Finally Sagan called Bindner's home. His wife, Sandra, answered. She said her husband was at work, but she would let him know that the detective had called.

Two days later another letter arrived at the Cosgrove house addressed to Sheila.

On the envelope, Bindner had written: "Sheila: if you do not want me to write you any more just let me know. i did not mean to scare you!"

Liz Cosgrove took the letter to Sagan. He held it up to a light and began to read, starting at the bottom and moving up the page:

Dear Miss Sheila,

The cops called, but i don't know why, i wasn't here. i wish you or your parents had, so I could have explained, + got to know them. Anyway, I could never do harm to a child!

The coins were meant for you to keep, for good luck. I am not a threat to you, and never will be.

"God is love! For this is the message that ye heard from the beginning; that we should love one another." 1 John 3:11

My love to you all.
Tim

He enclosed another poem.

Joy
For a child or two
A fresh cool breeze

> *Or mystery gifts*
> *That come in threes.*
>
> *The view after climbing*
> *To a mountain top*
> *And knowing that love*
> *Will never stop.*
>
> *A heart that can cry*
> *Yet be strong and bold*
> *While reaching out*
> *For a hand to hold.*
>
> *I wish you the best*
> *As i sign good-bye:*
> *I may not have touched,*
> *But i sure did try.*
> *(To Sheila from a friend)*

Harold Sagan had questions to ask Bindner. Why was he writing to Sheila Cosgrove, a twelve-year-old he didn't know? Did he realize that he was terrorizing her entire family? To get some answers, the detective called Bindner's home a second time. Again the man's wife answered. She agreed to convey the message, but Bindner never returned the call.

Sagan doesn't like it when someone stonewalls him. Tired of waiting for a return call, Sagan prepared an affidavit alleging a violation of the California Penal Code, Section 647.6, Crimes Against Children.

The district attorney kicked it back. There was nothing sexual in the letters, he said. Nothing threatening. No *intent* to do anything illegal.

Sagan disagreed. In the letters, Bindner declared that he loved Sheila and wanted her with him. The man had to be sick. Sagan's training told him to suspect pedophilia, a persisting sexual interest in children. But his hands were tied. The D.A. wouldn't budge.

4

Before dawn on that Sunday morning in December, two days after Nikki Campbell's disappearance, Harold Sagan riffled through his file, searching for the Cosgroves' address, then ran from his office out through the rear exit of the building and slipped behind the wheel of his car. He drove fast and reached the neighborhood in minutes.

He slowed to a crawl, measuring the distance from Sheila Cosgrove's house to Nikki Campbell's house on his odometer. Only four tenths of a mile.

That was enough to convince Sagan that he had a substantial lead. Tim Bindner lived forty miles away from Fairfield, but he had been writing to Sheila Cosgrove, who lived only blocks away from the site where a little girl had disappeared. In a metropolitan area of five million people, what were the odds? The child interested Bindner, and he had some bad baggage—an unusual history when it came to young girls.

He'd sent them gifts of money and been fired from his job at Social Security for it. Although the matter was dropped, he'd been arrested once for annoying kids.

Sagan felt a surge of guilt, a sense that somehow he was responsible for Nikki Campbell's disappearance. He knew that wasn't rational. Nobody was even certain that she had been abducted, nor did Sagan know that the man from Oakland had played any role in whatever had happened to her. But that didn't matter. For the detective, the truth was that he should have pushed harder on the Cosgrove case. Maybe if he had handled things differently back then—just maybe—Nikki Campbell wouldn't be missing now.

Sagan reversed direction and returned to Sheila's house on Nephi Drive. The neighborhood was asleep. A few colored lights shone in windows where Christmas wreaths still hung. Sagan sat there, alone in his car, in the first gray light of morning. He studied the street, the sidewalks, the houses. Then he looked up at an undeveloped hill across the street, directly opposite the Cosgroves' house.

A man standing on that hill could easily see Sheila's house, Sagan thought. He would have a perfect view of the neighborhood streets and of anyone walking on them. Especially a little girl dressed in pink and purple. She would almost glow in the fading light.

This had to be more than coincidence. Bindner had been trying to scope out Sheila Cosgrove, Sagan thought. He had written letters to the kid, and now he wanted to be closer. From the top of the hill it's a stone's throw to Sheila's house, but it's also in the line of sight of where Nikki was wandering around. He's already psychologically pumped up by the thought of seeing Sheila. He's excited. Aroused. He sees this girl. It's drizzling, late afternoon. Nobody's around. Commuters haven't started coming home yet. Talk about opportunity, Sagan thought.

Sagan drove back to the office, grabbed his report on the Cosgrove case, and walked into the command center. The only one there was the lead FBI agent, called in because it looked as if they had a kidnapping on their hands.

"Here," Sagan said, offering him the report. "I think you need to take a look at this."

The agent nodded and went back to what he was doing.

Detective Barry Hom walked in, and Sagan told him the story. He described clocking the four tenths of a mile that separated the houses. "We need to look at this guy," Sagan said.

They were already looking at everyone else. Investigators were out getting registration slips from every motel in Fairfield, Vacaville, and Vallejo. They were going through parole lists, sex offender registration lists—anything they could think of. Those investigative techniques were by the book, but they were shots in the dark. This lead, the letter writer, looked solid.

When the FBI agent got around to looking at the Cosgrove file, he agreed. By 6:00 A.M. he was saying, "We gotta do something about this guy here. We gotta look at him."

———

The search effort continued through all of Sunday, with more volunteers covering an ever-widening area. Media people were everywhere. Inside the house on Salisbury Drive, Nikki's mother, Anne Campbell, was in shock. But she had to give the interviews and answer reporters' questions. She had to get the story out there and keep it in front of the public. People needed to know what had happened, who the child was. They might have seen something. They might know someone.

So Anne Campbell sat with her son on her lap, and a photograph of Nikki behind her, and answered the questions. She pleaded with whoever took her daughter to bring the child home. And when they took the cameras away, Anne remained in her chair.

Neighbors and friends brought food to the house. The women congregated in the kitchen; the men stood inside the open doorway of the garage, away from the rain. Media people moved among those in both groups.

Volunteers were already walking through the neighborhood posting and distributing flyers that had on them a picture of the smiling, chubby-cheeked, little blond girl. "Missing. Reward offered. Amanda Nicole Eileen Campbell. Nikki."

All Harold Sagan knew was that Nikki Campbell had disappeared. One minute she was there, then she was gone.

When a child vanishes it hits home with everyone. People identify with the loss. They relate to it because they have children, and their children have children. For the investigator the pressure is immediate and unrelenting. He feels an urgency to solve the case for the child, the child's family, and the community—even for himself. He knows that, with the passing of time, there is a decreasing likelihood of finding the child. The earth has tipped a bit on its axis. He questions his own competence, wonders if he's capable of handling the investigation.

There was no witness, no weapon, no body, no physical evidence. The only trace of anything was a pair of socks—blue, in a child's size—found on the street when officers moved the mobile crime lab. No one knew whose they were. It was the kind of case where detectives generate theories and work backward from them. Who takes a child, how, and why?

It was still raining in Fairfield at 9:30 P.M., when the dogs and their handlers from the Contra Costa County Sheriff's Department Search and Rescue Team arrived on Salisbury Drive. The rain helps their work. Moisture holds a scent on the ground, keeps it alive. These large, black-and-tan bloodhounds with long ears and loose skin have an acute sense of smell. Their ability to track humans is uncanny—and innate.

Dale Myer, a fifteen-year veteran dog handler, scented Friday, his 120-pound bloodhound, with Nikki Campbell's Christmas dress. Friday pulled Myer from the Campbell home down Salisbury Drive toward the intersection with Larchmont. When the big dog arrived at the corner, he tore up a patch of lawn, marking the area.

Friday went out Larchmont Circle, then returned to the corner lot and marked it again. It was a scent pool. The dog was telling Myer that something happened there. It was a probable abduction point. That was as far as Nikki got on foot.

Myer can tell when Friday changes from following a foot trail to following scent that has drifted from a vehicle. He moves faster. Some dogs just stop, as if they're saying "This is where she got into the car." When a person on foot is dropping skin rafts, the scent is so strong it almost overwhelms the dog's sensitive nose. He slows down because there's so much he needs to examine. Once Nikki was in a car, there was less scent emitted—only whatever managed to leak out through air vents or an open window—and that trail was the easiest for Friday to follow.

The dog pulled his handler to the end of Larchmont, then south on Oliver, where he doubled his speed. In the prevailing breeze, the scent had drifted into the northbound lane, so the handlers, deputies, and Fairfield police were running into the traffic as they headed south.

Friday covered a mile and a half to the McDonald's, where he paused at the microphone and speaker box in the drive-through. It made sense. The driver would have opened his window to place his order, and more of the child's scent would have poured out.

The dog ignored the eastbound I-80 on-ramp. Instead, he crossed Travis Boulevard and headed for the westbound on-ramp, where a green highway sign

directs travelers to Oakland and San Francisco. Dale
Myer stopped the dog there.

———————

On Monday morning the investigative team held a
meeting of representatives from all the Bay Area agencies that were working on unsolved cases involving
child abduction and child homicide. Detectives arrived
from the Antioch and Pinole departments. FBI Agent
Larry Taylor was there, and so were Special Agent
Mary Ellen O'Toole and FBI polygrapher Ron Homer.

Barry Hom, Chuck Timm, and Harold Sagan represented Fairfield. Hom, the lead investigator, began by
sketching out what little they knew about Nikki Campbell's movements through her neighborhood late in the
afternoon of the twenty-seventh. He mentioned the
blue socks and noted the similarities between this case
and a little girl's disappearance in Pinole in 1988. Other
investigators followed, offering brief sketches of their
own cases, pointing out similarities and differences.

Harold Sagan felt a spirit of cooperation in the
room, a sense that the various jurisdictions were
working together. Were any of these cases related?
How could they pool resources? What had other agencies learned from their investigations that might help
Fairfield? Was there any link among the cases?

The gathering of local and federal cops hadn't
been under way for more than fifteen minutes before
the participants identified one element that all the
cases had in common. A name: Timothy Bindner.

TWO

THROUGH
THE PAST DARKLY

5

The rain settled on northern California. It was oppressive—overcast, unrelenting.

On that dreary Saturday afternoon, twenty-three-year-old Susan Bugay and her two children were visiting neighbors in their apartment complex at 3915 Delta Fair Boulevard in Antioch, thirty miles east of Pinole. Angela Bugay was five. Her brother, Billy, was two and a half. Susan and the kids planned to stay for dinner, but Billy wanted his rain boots. At 5:00 P.M., Susan allowed Angela to take Billy back to their apartment to get them. It was getting dark, but the kids had to travel only fifty feet along a concrete walk, past other apartments.

Susan was a single parent trying to make a life for herself and her kids. Her own mother had died when she was eight. Her father was murdered when Susan was thirteen. Things couldn't get any worse. They had to get better.

Within a few minutes, Billy was back at the neighbor's door. "Angie wouldn't wait," he said.

"Where is she?" Susan Bugay asked.

Billy pointed toward Delta Fair Boulevard. "She went off. She wouldn't wait."

Susan Bugay stepped out onto the walk. There was no sign of her daughter. She went to her apartment, checked inside to see if Angela was there. Not finding her, Susan moved through the complex calling Angela's name and knocking on doors.

It didn't make any sense. Angela liked to tease her brother, to play tricks on him, but she wasn't the kind of child to wander off. Besides, she was afraid of the dark.

Friends and neighbors joined Susan's search through the sprawling complex of more than two hundred apartments. Angela was nowhere to be found. She hadn't gone to any of her friends' apartments. She wasn't out playing in the wet, foggy night.

Susan Bugay called the Antioch police department. She couldn't find her child, she said. Little Angela was gone.

Within two hours of the child's disappearance, Antioch police, neighborhood volunteers, and the Contra Costa County Sheriff's Department Search and Rescue Unit and its dog handlers had organized a full-scale search. Police dispatchers broadcast the child's description. They were looking for a little girl three-and-a-half feet tall, forty-six pounds, brown eyes, with a blue ribbon tied around her blond ponytail. She was dressed in a pink leotard, blue pants, and black shoes, and was carrying her red Strawberry Shortcake umbrella.

During the first forty-eight hours following her disappearance, one hundred volunteers and fifty-five law enforcement officers searched four square miles in the rain. They started in the complex, then moved out through the neighborhood knocking on doors, prowling through fields, examining every corner of a nearby shopping mall, scouring the grounds of Los Medanos College and the fairgrounds, and checking out the drainage ditch behind the apartment complex. Helicopters from the California Highway Patrol and the East Bay Regional Park District hovered in the overcast skies.

The dog handlers worked their animals, but there seemed to be little point. They weren't picking up the child's scent. It was as if someone had lifted the child off the face of the earth.

The rain continued through the week, hampering search efforts. Each day, Susan Bugay went to the Turner Elementary School, where Angela attended kindergarten, hoping that someone would drop her child there. No one did.

Members of the search and rescue unit found the child's umbrella on the southeast side of Somersville Road, about a mile from the apartment complex. It was lying between the road and a barbed wire fence, five feet from the curb. They worked a grid search from there, walking three feet apart through the flat grassy fields, down into a ravine strewn with old washing machines, bedsprings, and mattresses. They didn't find anything, but no one wanted to go home.

On Saturday, November 26, at 3:00 P.M., one week after Angela's disappearance the searchers were within minutes of quitting. Evan Hubbard wanted to push through one more field, so the group moved on. Then Howard Mendelsohn, another member of the search unit, noticed a piece of clothing sticking out of the dirt. The area around the clothing had recently been disturbed. The site was at the base of a hill near the end of Nightingale Avenue. It looked as if someone had loosened dirt from the hillside and pulled it down into the gully.

This was a new residential area, sparsely populated, with construction going on throughout the neighborhood. Jogging and bike paths were already in place, and there was a cabana on the other side of the road.

Antioch detectives began the slow process of moving the dirt away, being careful to preserve the site. First they uncovered the pink leotard and the blue pants—then, beneath the clothing, they found the child's body. The blue ribbon was still tied around Angela Bugay's blond ponytail.

Myer and the other dog handlers worked the site with their bloodhounds. One dog moved away from the grave site, ran under a guardrail, then stopped on a short side road off James Donlon Boulevard. Angela's scent went no farther than the pull-out road—the route probably used by the child's killer.

By 7:45 P.M., after the investigators and the dog handlers had finished their work for the night, the story hit the media. People gathered at the end of James Donlon Boulevard along the Somersville Road. They stood in silence in the rain and watched.

Detectives and forensic specialists preserved what little evidence they had. An autopsy revealed that five-year-old Angela Bugay had been sexually assaulted. The medical examiner listed the cause of death as asphyxiation and the manner of death as homicide.

Early attempts at criminal profiling based on the nature of the crime and analysis of the crime scene suggested an offender who felt inferior to other people—one who was terrified of rejection and harbored great anger. He hated happiness, innocence, and decency, and was exacting vengeance on a world that had mistreated him.

The Antioch detectives who worked the case believed that the killer had to be a local—someone familiar with the apartment complex and the surrounding area. One suspect scrutinized by police lived in the complex. Larry Graham had dated Susan Bugay. He had a prior charge involving a child, and he was involved in a bitter divorce.

But the leads went nowhere, and within weeks the investigation sputtered to a halt.

The case, number 83-5525, remained unsolved.

6

Tim Bindner was three-fourths drunk.

The long-haired, bearded thirty-six-year-old was on a bus, on his way home from a baseball game. He had his scorebook with him, and he was blitzed, or close to it.

In the three months since it happened, that kid was on his mind—Angela Jane Bugay. He couldn't seem to get rid of the thoughts. Five years old. Kidnapped. Raped. Murdered.

He followed the story on TV and in the *Oakland Tribune*.

Angela disappeared so close to her home, just two doors down. *Fifty feet.*

People had gone out there searching for her. Bindner had wanted to search, but he had no car. He looked at AAA street maps of Antioch, constructed a search plan. Maybe his ideas were vague, he'd say— amateurish, even. But you have to start somewhere.

Then searchers had found Angela's body. She was
in that culvert with her clothes piled on top of her, the
dirt pulled down over her. Bindner looked at his maps
again. He might have searched that area. He might
have walked out that road. He could have been the one
to find her.

The day's consumption of alcohol and the rocking
of the bus finally got to him.

He fell asleep. He dreamed.

In the dream, he knew that he saw Angela Bugay,
but she was ghostlike—indistinct and ill-defined. She
needed help, and Tim Bindner was supposed to be
there to offer that help. She was dying, but he couldn't
get to her. It was as if this child were reaching out from
the grave, telling him that he had to do something.

In reality, she had been taken in a drizzly rain, after dark, in an enclosed area, while walking the short
distance from one apartment to another. Who would
even think to go looking for kids that age at night in
bad weather? "When does a little child ever get abducted after dark?" he wondered.

Bindner had saved pictures of Angela that he had
clipped from the *Oakland Tribune*—and he thought
about a man waiting in the damp, dark night. A guy
that patient and methodical probably had done it before, he reasoned. There was the way he had disposed
of the body. It was ritualized. He'd folded the clothes
and put them on top of the body. It's more difficult to
bury something that way. Bindner had worked in cemeteries, had buried bodies, so he knew. It would take
more dirt to flatten out something soft like clothing.

Bindner read and reread the articles. He saved
them in files. And he thought about the man who took
Angela. Why would he be out in that weather looking
for little girls? Or had he targeted her? Was he looking
specifically for her?

Bindner didn't consider his interest in Angela Bugay
an obsession, although others through the years would
call it that. But it was personal, he said, something that

touched him. He wept over the child, had a difficult time adjusting to the idea that she was dead.

> *I got caught up in the news reports of this kid kinda personally. Like, I wanted to find out what happened to her, what—where's she at? Who did this? I want to help. I had this vague feeling like that. Most people when they read the news, it's just a detachment. This is the story. You read a story about somebody getting shot down on the corner. It's just a story. Then you go on and read the sports. Who won the game today? But this particular story kept growing on me, and kept becoming something that I felt. Something is really wrong here. Something should be done. I wish I could do something, but I can't. It was just kind of a feeling that grew with me.*

Under one picture of Angela, he wrote some of the lyrics from the Jim Morrison song "The End." It was a tribute, his way of saying "I know I'll never know you. I'll never see you."

There was more to the song than a trippy '60s lyric. Bindner felt everything was in the song—the preparation of a killer who gets up before dawn and goes about his homicidal business. John Wayne Gacy was in the song. Ted Bundy. These were the things that really happen in this world. People kill people. Strangers kill strangers, and some of the victims are children.

Tim Bindner wrote a letter to the Antioch police department. In it he suggested that investigators look at other cases, consider the possibility that there might be a serial killer at work in the Bay Area. He reminded them about Suzanne Bombardier, the fourteen-year-old who had disappeared in Antioch in 1980 and had lived in an apartment complex near Angela's. And he mentioned one or two others, children who had disappeared in the high desert country in southern California, not far from where Bindner had grown up.

All he got back was a perfunctory letter thanking him for his interest and advice.

Bindner was working at Social Security in Richmond in the early '80s. Flextime. Punch in anytime between 6:30 and 8:00 A.M., put in your eight hours, and leave. He was in transition at that point—trying to sell his place in San Pablo while living in Richmond. He was breaking off one relationship and starting another.

He remembers that Saturday night, November 19, 1983—the night Angela Bugay disappeared. He remembers it because of the weather—a dense fog, covering everything like a damp blanket—and the steady, cold, drizzling rain.

Bindner could picture a man sitting in his car in the parking lot at Delta View. He is the kind of guy who would sit, and watch, and wait. If the weather is ugly, he loves it even more, because everybody hunkers down in their houses. He just bides his time because he knows that eventually he's going to get something. And he does.

The killer had cased it out, Bindner reasoned. He knew where he was, and he knew how to get out. He sat there and watched, and waited, thinking, "I'm gonna get me one. If I don't get me one tonight, I'm gonna get me one tomorrow night. Maybe I'll sleep here in the parking lot tonight and pick one up in the morning."

Then Angela came down the walkway.

Bindner figured that the umbrella was probably in the guy's way. Maybe it was getting his leg wet, dripping all over the car, so he threw it out the window. That could be how it ended up on Somersville Road.

The dream had stayed with Bindner. At odd moments at work, or while he was jogging through one of the many cemeteries he liked to visit, he thought about Angela Bugay, about his dream on the bus, and about the man in the shadows at Delta View. He said he wondered if the man would strike again.

Later that year, in December 1984, Tim Bindner drove to Oakmont Cemetery in Pleasant Hill to visit

Angela's grave. The flat headstone was in place, and a small picture of the child was mounted on the brass plate. Her hands were folded and pressed to her smiling face. Her blond hair was cut in bangs.

> *I guess the fact that Angela's got a pretty little picture on her gravestone, and that her picture was in the paper so many times—probably if you can't see their face, if it's just a name—but, yeah. I fell in love with Angela. . . .*
>
> *It was like a personal thing. I fell in love with her. You're not supposed to be in love with a dead girl.*

On the first of his many visits to her grave, Bindner remembers that he made a promise to Angela. "If there's any way I can find out who did this to you," he said, "I'm gonna do it. If there's any way I can find out how to get this guy, keep him from doing it to somebody else, I'm gonna do it. I promise you that."

This was the start of a mission in life for Tim Bindner. He would discover what happened to Angela, and he would search for other missing children.

Angela was real to Bindner—like the other little girls he visited in other cemeteries. He loved her. After that first visit, he made the trip to Oakmont more than eighty times, sat at Angela's grave, and talked to her. Sometimes he brought flowers. He always tidied the area.

Two years later, still thinking about Angela, he drove to the Delta View Apartments in Antioch. He said he wanted to get a feel for the place, to sit in the same area where Angela had been abducted, to see if he could develop any sense of what had happened to her.

> *With Angela, I'm really haunted by her face—a beautiful face—and the fact that she was safe, fifteen seconds from her front door, before she died.*

He was haunted by her face—an image that sent thoughts and ideas careening around in his head—the face of a child taken in the night, sexually assaulted, destroyed.

That day at Delta View, Bindner watched two young children play in the open hatchback of a car in the parking lot. They appeared to be Angela's age, but there were no adults supervising them. Three years earlier someone had grabbed a child here—raped and murdered her. Now these kids were playing in the same area, taking a risk, he thought.

7

Kim Swartz woke her kids—seven-year-old Amber and her older brother—and helped them get ready for school. New neighbors had moved in across the street the day before, and Amber walked over and introduced herself. She played with the baby boy, and Pam, the new neighbor, invited her to come back. Amber was thrilled, and intended to visit again that afternoon.

And Kim was thrilled at how easily and joyfully Amber embraced life. Eight years before, on August 19, 1980, Kim gave birth to Amber Jean Swartz. It made the local paper; Amber's policeman father had been killed in the line of duty three months earlier.

At Amber's first birthday party Kim took the required picture: a little girl covered with cake asleep in her high chair. Kim's mother had one just like it—a sleepy little year-old Kim, a demolished cake.

But Kim had no illusions that life was going to be easy for her and the kids. By the time Amber was

learning to walk and talk, Kim knew there was something wrong. She wondered if the little girl was able to
hear her. Once Amber was walking across the room
looking over her shoulder at her mother.

"Watch where you're going, hon," Kim said. "Turn
around."

Amber walked into the wall.

Another time it was a doorjamb or a table. Because of Amber's obvious hearing impairment, her
speech suffered. Kim began the process of hearing
tests and speech evaluations—an ordeal that took
three years before doctors agreed that Amber had suffered a bilateral high-frequency loss and would benefit
from a hearing aid.

But those years of struggling with a disability, with
the doctors and their tests, were also filled with what
life is like for any little girl. Amber and her mother
played dolls together in the child's room; Amber dressed
Jennifer and bald Fred, whose hair she had removed
because she didn't like it. She made sure the dolls were
comfortable on her bed, then pretended to read Bible
stories to them.

If Kim had garden work to do, Amber was there to
help. She worked the soil, planted the seeds, watched
the vegetables grow, then went out with her mother to
pick radishes and lettuce and cucumbers.

She watched *Snow White*, fascinated when the
deer gathered around the heroine and birds landed on
her hand. Amber wanted to be like Snow White. Kim
could see the expression of awe on her daughter's face.
"That could be me," Amber said.

Problems with her hearing and speech didn't inter-
fere with Amber's love of music. She loved to sing. She
would wander through the house making up songs and
singing them in her high-pitched voice. The more "op-
eratic" she became, the better she could hear herself.
Her brother wasn't as fond of her arias as she was, but
it didn't matter. The same year that Amber discovered
her opera voice, Kim made her a Halloween costume
complete with a funny hat that had musical notes all

over it. Amber was the song girl, and she sang her way through the neighborhood while filling her bag with treats.

Any day could be a dress-up day. Even Kim often joined in—wearing a clown outfit. Together, mother and daughter would dance and sing their way through the house with Jennifer and her dolly, Fred, serving as their audience.

Indeed, Amber laughed her way through life—and brought laughter into the lives of all those around her.

———————

On that day, June 3, Kim dropped the children at school, then returned to Savage Avenue. She spent the day working around the house, paying bills, and doing some yard chores until it was time to pick up the kids. As she was leaving, she noticed that Pam's car wasn't there and thought that Amber would be disappointed. But she did have some errands to run, so maybe Pam would be back by the time they got home.

Kim and the kids stopped at a 7-Eleven to get some snacks, then went on to the bank and the post office, then up to Hilltop Mall to buy new tennis shoes for Amber and her brother.

When they arrived back on Savage Avenue, at about 4:00 P.M., Pam still wasn't home. Amber's brother went out with some friends, and Amber had nothing to do. She asked her mother if she could borrow her brother's leather jump rope and play out front until Pam got home.

Kim didn't allow Amber outside alone very often, but jumping rope in front of the house sounded safe. Kim knew that she was overprotective because of Amber's hearing impairment. A car had once hit her, and though she'd lived through it, Kim was afraid that the next time she might not.

The headaches started soon after the accident. Migraines. Amber didn't understand why she was having them, but she seemed to know when they were going to happen. Colors flashed in her eyes. "Mom, I'm getting another one," she'd say, and within minutes she would be throwing up.

The doctors prescribed Fiorinal. If they gave her the medicine in time, the pain was less severe—and sometimes it didn't come at all. But there were times when Amber was crippled with pain. One night Kim didn't hear her calling out. Amber couldn't even lift up her head. She crawled down the hall on her hands and knees, her forehead pressed to the floor, trying to talk, trying to tell her mother about the hurt.

It had been a long haul, but in so many ways it had been an education in a child's love. After the accident, Amber had gotten her hearing aid. The school system assigned her to a special program for hearing-impaired students. That first day she and Kim were standing by the side of the road when the school bus came to pick her up. The driver opened the door and it squeaked. Amber stared. "What was that?"

The driver understood, and opened and closed the door several times. Amber smiled. She was hearing the world for the first time. "It squeaks," she said, and mother and daughter laughed.

When Amber arrived home that day she told her mother about a horse trotting along the street. "I heard the horse," she said. "Clop, clop, clop."

The world was coming alive for her. She was amazed as she looked up into a tree in the front yard. "Birds," she said. "They sing."

She stared at the mockingbird in the branches; it was singing—just as Amber had sung when she was younger. It was like that day after day. The blond, blue-eyed child would come home and say, "Guess what I heard today?"

That afternoon in June, Amber had removed her hearing aid and left it in her bedroom. She got the jump rope from the hall closet and went out to the front yard. Kim caught a glimpse of her as she disappeared through the door. Amber looked cute in her purple corduroy pants, pink socks, and pink-and-white

L.A. Gear tennis shoes. She had on a short-sleeved top, white, with teal-colored bands around the bottoms of the sleeves and the bottom of the shirt. On the front of the shirt there were pictures of multicolored pairs of sunglasses.

Amber could be rough-and-tumble with her brother, but she preferred her patent leather shoes and dresses with five layers of slips underneath. When the church held its *Cinco de Mayo* celebration, Amber wore her prettiest dress and danced in place near her mother. She wanted to be a mariachi dancer like the young Hispanic girls. "I want to learn how to do that, Mom," she said.

She tried to copy it, to get it right.

Of all the images that come and go, the one of Amber going out the door with the jump rope is the most vivid for Kim Swartz.

At 4:15, Amber's brother and his friends climbed a neighborhood hill. Looking back down at Savage Avenue, they saw Amber. "There's my sister," he said. "She's jumping rope. She looks like a bug from up here."

They all laughed about that and decided to go back down and tell Amber she looked like a bug. But by the time the boys got to the street, she was gone.

At 4:30, Kim's friend Deb and her daughter, Jenny, walked through the front door. The two women talked as the little girl wandered through the house.

After a few minutes, Jenny approached Kim. "Where's Am?" she asked.

"Oh, she's outside. She went out to jump rope."

"We didn't see her when we came in," Deb said.

Jenny went back out through the front door. She still couldn't find Amber, so Kim stepped outside to take a look around. Amber wasn't there.

Kim went down the front walk and called her daughter. There was no response. She ran out to the sidewalk and looked to her left. There was the street, houses, a few parked cars. No Amber.

Down the street to her right there was a two-and-a-half-acre vacant lot. Amber sometimes went there looking for bugs or rocks, treasures to tuck away in her toy chest. She might be there now and not hear her mother because she wasn't wearing her hearing aid.

But Amber wasn't there either.

Kim Swartz stood in the tall grass and looked around at the empty field. She felt a rush of hopelessness wash over her. It was like the panic she'd felt almost eight years earlier when her husband Bernie left the house and never returned. She knew that her daughter was in danger, but she didn't know what to do first.

She ran back into the house. Deb looked up, startled. Kim was crying.

"What's wrong?" Deb asked.

"Amber's in trouble."

Kim grabbed the phone and called the only two neighbors Amber might have visited without asking permission. There was no answer at either place. Kim started to crack.

"Oh, my God. Somebody's taken my little girl."

She ran out the front door screaming Amber's name just as Pam pulled up.

"What's wrong?" Pam said, getting out of her car.

"Amber's gone," Kim said. "Somebody's taken her."

"Oh, no, no," Pam said. "She's got to be around here somewhere."

The two women split up, each moving in a different direction through the neighborhood, pounding on doors, begging people to check their houses, to come out and help with the search. Kim ran through backyards, looked in swimming pools, in bushes.

At the end of the street, a neighbor who had been searching on his bicycle rode up and asked Kim if she had called the police yet. She hadn't, so she ran back to the house and placed the call. By then, about forty-five minutes had passed.

Uniformed officers from the Pinole police department arrived within minutes. They began their own search: the house, the yard, the vacant lot, a shed at the back of Kim's property. They crawled up into the attic, then did it all a second and third time.

Finally Kim said, "You guys are wasting time. How many times can you search my house? What is wrong with you? She's not here. I'm telling you, she walked out my front door and she never came back in."

It was dark by the time the police brought in the Contra Costa County Search and Rescue Unit and their bloodhounds. They asked Amber's brother to show them the places along the creek behind the house where he had taken his sister—places she might have wandered back to on her own.

By late evening the street was crawling with reporters, satellite dishes, minicams, lights, and people tramping through yards, the vacant lot, the baseball field. Lights, shadows, people, and noise. One dog handler shook her head. "No way. I'm not doing it."

She would wait until the crowd thinned, when the activity in the area would be less likely to distract the dogs.

Much later, in the early hours of the morning, the handler scented the bloodhound with an article of Amber's clothing. The big animal went directly to the front door of the Swartz home, then down the sidewalk to the right side of the house. She walked to the curb and whined, circling that one spot on the sidewalk. The child's scent went there from the house, but no farther.

Dale Myer was working as a runner for some of the other handlers. When he got the call on the evening of the third, all he knew was that a child was missing. Once he arrived in Pinole and drove up to Savage Avenue, he knew that it was Bernie Swartz's daughter, the child Kim had been pregnant with when James Odle killed Bernie.

Myer also remembered his experience in Antioch, working the Angela Bugay case. Like Angela, Amber never had a chance. Whoever the abductor was, he walked right up, grabbed Amber, and put her in a car. But that was speculation. Dale Myer is meticulous in

his work and conservative in stating his opinions. All
he and the other handlers could tell anyone was that
Amber had been on the sidewalk, and then she was
gone.

At dawn, Savage Avenue was again saturated with
people—searchers, volunteers, the media. By 5:00 A.M.
an organized search began, with the police and sheriff's deputies using the nearby Ellerhorst School as a
staging area where horses, motorcycles, and helicopters could be coordinated.

It was all a blur to Kim Swartz. Sometime on Saturday, police brought her a pair of pink socks they had
discovered near the baseball diamond by the creek
that flows behind her house.

"They brought them to me," she said later, "and
asked if they were Amber's, could I identify them?
There was a spot, it almost looked like a blood spot, on
one of them. I panicked. I told them I couldn't be sure
they were hers, but it was possible. I mean, pink socks.
How many kinds of pink socks are there? They looked
like what she had been wearing, but I couldn't be
sure."

When the searchers had worked their way through
the area by the ball field and creek the night before, no
one had found the socks. Kim wondered if someone
had placed them there during the night.

She spent her time reacting to the media, answering detectives' questions, jumping every time the
phone rang. She made the decision to put in a second
line. That way, if Amber tried to call home she would
be able to get through.

Kim looked into the minicams, spoke into the
microphones. She described the blond, blue-eyed seven-
year-old and what she had been wearing when Kim had
watched her walk out the front door with the jump rope
in her hand.

Amber is hearing-impaired, Kim said. She wasn't
wearing her hearing aid. She has a speech impediment. She suffers from migraines. Doctors and hospi-
tals should watch for her. Someone might take her for

medical treatment. One of her front teeth is missing. She's quiet. She's shy.

Kim looked directly into the camera. "We love you, Amber, and we want you home."

Shortly after 5:00 P.M. on the day Amber disappeared, George Ellwin took his daughter out for ice cream. He stopped his car near the gate to Alvarado Park, at the northernmost end of the Wildcat Canyon Regional Park, so they could eat their snacks. There he saw a man take a small, blond girl by the neck and the seat of the pants and throw her into the front of a car. The man forced the child to the floor on the passenger side of the car and drove away.

Ellwin figured it was a father and his little girl, but he didn't like the rough way the man had handled her. He asked his daughter to get a pen and a scrap of paper out of the glove compartment. Ellwin wrote out a description of the man, the girl, the car, and what he could remember of the license plate. He put the paper in his shirt pocket and drove on.

Ellwin spent the weekend visiting his sister in Mariposa. Late Friday night he saw on the news that someone had abducted a child in Pinole, not far from where he lived. He knew that Alvarado Park was only ten minutes from the neighborhood they were talking about on TV. He told his sister what he had seen that afternoon, and she urged him to notify the police.

When he returned home, Ellwin went to the Pinole police department and talked with an investigator. "The guy was rough with the little blond girl," he said. "He tossed her into this large, light blue-and-gray car and drove out of there."

The guy Ellwin had seen had sandy hair. He was clean-shaven, and he might have been wearing a baseball cap. The main thing that stuck in Ellwin's mind was the wild look in the man's eyes—like he was crazy, totally out of control. He had stared at Ellwin—glared, really—with absolute defiance. It was as if, with his eyes, the wild man had been warning George Ellwin to stay away.

Ellwin gave the cop the scrap of paper with the descriptions and the partial license number.

Five years would pass before Kim Swartz knew of the existence of George Ellwin or the wild man at Alvarado Park.

8

Amber Swartz had been missing for three days when a man in a light blue Dodge van with the California license plate LOV YOU drove up to the Swartz house on Savage Avenue.

He knocked on Kim's door in the afternoon, told a family member he had heard about Amber's disappearance and wanted to assist with the search. He seemed jumpy, nervous. He was wearing a button that said I LUV KIDS, and he signed his name in a logbook the family was maintaining.

Tim Bindner.

Kim's impression was that he was more than jumpy. The guy was wired, in tears. "I tried to save her," he said. "I couldn't. I looked everywhere. I did everything I could to save Amber."

He had maps, a list of places he had searched, and more that he thought someone should be searching. While others voiced hope about the child's safety and assured Kim that Amber was out there somewhere and they were going to find her, Bindner said flatly, "You realize that we're looking for a dead body."

His demeanor hadn't changed, but he wasn't talking about places to find a living, injured child. He was talking about burial sites.

Bindner says that when he first heard about the child missing in Pinole, he thought it could be another case like Angela Bugay's. The same person who had abducted and killed Angela might have taken Amber.

The child had disappeared, abducted by person or persons unknown, and he was going to try to find her. He hoped she was alive, prayed she was alive, prayed that he would find her—perhaps injured, but alive—so that he could return her to her mother. But even if Amber was dead, he reasoned, someone had to find her. Her mother needed to know.

When Bindner walked out of Kim Swartz's house that day, he looked at the quiet street, the windows of the houses. He glanced down at the empty field below the house, the ridge overlooking Ellerhorst School.

Bindner allowed his mind to drift. "An abduction would be so easy here," he thought.

He says he tried to put himself inside the mind of the man who took Amber away. "Well, I've got her," he thought. "Now what do I do with her?"

He surveyed the neighborhood. The house was the last one on Savage Avenue before the vacant lot that overlooked the school, then sloped down to a creek. It had been a daylight abduction. This was a quiet street with houses to the north of Amber's and across from it. It had been early, around 4:20 P.M. on June 3, before most of the people on the street were home from work. But the kids were out of school by then.

Ideal for an abduction.

The guy was careful, made sure no one was watching, then snatched the child and disappeared into the valley. He wanted to get away from everybody.

The only other possibility required the abductor to drive back through the center of Pinole to the freeway. That didn't seem likely. Even if he had risked the city's main street at rush hour, the freeway northbound led to a tollbooth at the Carquinez Bridge, and southbound into the congested metropolitan areas of Richmond, San Pablo, Berkeley, and Oakland. No, he almost certainly would have taken the child into the valley.

Bindner climbed into his van, drove to the end of Savage Avenue, and had just turned onto Pinole Valley Road when a patrol officer put his lights on, pulled him over, and asked to see his driver's license.

The officer looked inside the van and stared at the pictures of children, mostly young girls, stuck on the inside walls. "What are you doing?" the officer wanted to know.

"I'm going out to look for Amber," Bindner said.

"I thought you told the family you were going to the police station to pick up some flyers."

"I did tell them that," Bindner said, "but I decided to come out here first to do some searching."

Bindner sat in his van while the cop ran a check on his driver's license and a search for any outstanding warrants. He knew he was clear. After a few minutes, the cop returned with his license.

"I just love kids," Bindner said. "I want to help. But I have a feeling she's been kidnapped, raped, and killed by some pervert."

He focused his attention on the valley, stopping at roadside pullouts, looking for trace trails—evidence that someone had trampled through the brush. He checked under bridges and in ravines. He walked creek beds. And as he searched, he scavenged for recyclable aluminum cans.

He remembers being agitated, almost in a state of

rage those first few days. He searched the roads, scanned hillsides, prowled down through canyons. He was fired up, but able to think clearly at the same time.

People were lazy. They'd be more likely to walk downhill, especially if they were carrying sixty pounds. They'd be more likely to walk where someone else had walked or where the terrain naturally made it easy to walk.

He took vacation time from his job at Social Security and kept searching.

The Pinole police department and the FBI took a critical view of Bindner's wandering the roads with a shovel and a metal probe. The "suspicious person" calls they were getting about the guy were annoying. Usually he was outside city limits, so the local cops had to get the sheriff's people to respond.

Federal agents who were working the case wanted to talk with the spindly-legged stranger who had taken such a strong interest in Amber Swartz. If he had anything to do with her disappearance, it wouldn't be the first time that an abductor had participated in the search for his own victim.

Pinole Valley Road winds east from I-80 through the center of the city, then out among rolling hills and canyons. Three miles out it becomes Alhambra Valley Road. Developers have claimed a few areas, but mostly it's farm country and wilderness. Five miles farther out, near the entrance to Briones Regional Park, the road veers north toward Martinez. Reliez Valley Road continues east, then south into Lafayette, past the Oakmont Cemetery, where Angela Bugay's grave is.

Tim Bindner has always had rescue fantasies. When he was younger, he wanted to be a California Highway Patrol (CHP) officer and thought about applying to the police academy. He still has a picture of a CHP officer on the wall in his living room; the picture is surrounded by the faces of missing, abducted, and murdered children.

He could see himself as a cop, cruising the roads and catching criminals, doing good, saving people. As he did with other fantasies, he acted on this one, and was always ready to give a stranded motorist a helping hand.

He had a fantasy about Amber, too. In it, he was wandering through the valley, searching, and he found the little girl down in a ravine. Her leg was broken and she was hungry and in pain. He held her in his arms, took her home, and gave her to her mother. He could see himself telling Kim Swartz, "Your daughter has a broken leg. Call the hospital."

On Tuesday, June 7, at 3:00 P.M., Contra Costa County Sheriff's Deputy Judey Bloodworth-Winter was driving east on Alhambra Valley Road on her way to the Richmond substation. She noticed a light blue Dodge van parked near where the road intersects with Castro Ranch. The van had banners on each side of it that said YES I AM FROM OAKLAND. She pulled in behind it and walked up to the driver.

Tim Bindner introduced himself. "I'm looking for Amber, the missing child," he said. "I searched between Martinez and Bear Creek Road yesterday. I'm using my vacation time. I just want to help, and it seems like everyone else has given up searching."

He also told the deputy that he had stopped at the Pinole police department to check in and let them know what he was doing before driving out into the valley.

Besides the Oakland banners, Bindner also had missing person flyers about Amber taped to the outside of the van. Inside, the deputy saw photographs of young girls, all children about seven to ten years old, taped to the dashboard, the visors, and the windshield. Some were school pictures; some were snapshots.

"I hope I don't find her now," Bindner said, "because I don't think she'd be alive after this many days."

It had been four days since Amber disappeared.

Bloodworth-Winter thought the man seemed nervous. She called the Pinole police to check on his story and to tell them about the photographs in the van. Pinole turned it over to the FBI, and an agent interviewed Bindner at the Pinole police department soon after.

Bindner told the female agent that he had read about Amber's disappearance in Saturday's *Oakland Tribune*. He had been packing his van to drive to Reno that morning—he was getting married—and left between 10:00 and 11:00 A.M. He returned Sunday night, then drove out to Pinole for the first time Monday.

She took all the usual background information, focusing on his whereabouts the previous Friday afternoon, when Amber disappeared.

Bindner told her about his hobby of visiting cemeteries, repairing gravestones, cleaning up the places. After work he often went to St. Joseph's Cemetery in San Pablo, and probably had done this when he finished work at around 4:00 P.M. on Friday. Whatever he did, he was home by 5:00 P.M. he said, because he remembered seeing some of the Oakland A's game on TV.

Later, Bindner's wife would tell police that she thought her husband had returned home closer to 6:00 P.M. Investigators considered his story vague and inconsistent. He had no verifiable alibi.

As they walked out of the police department in Pinole to inspect his van, Bindner told the agent, "I just want to look for Amber. I know I might arouse suspicion walking along the road with a shovel and a probe. I know that might alarm people who see me. But I just want to help."

Inside the van, the agent saw pictures of children,

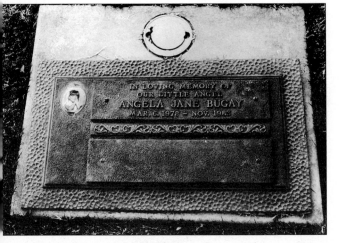

The grave of five-year-old Angela Jane Bugay at the Oakmont Cemetery.

View from Angela Bugay's grave. Bloodhounds tracked the scents of both Amber Swartz and Nikki Campbell from Angela's grave to the mausoleum in the background.

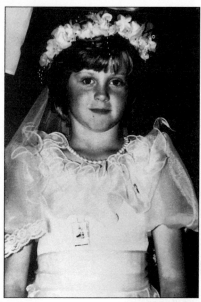

Amber Swartz, age six, at her First Holy Communion.

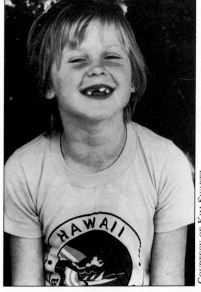

The last photograph taken of Amber Swartz before she was abducted in June 1988.

Kim Swartz,
Amber's mother.

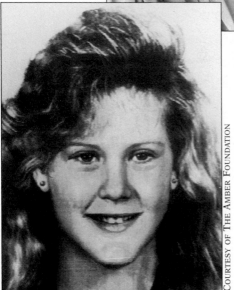

Age-enhanced photo of what Amber
Swartz would look like at age fourteen.

MISSING

Stranger Abduction
Amber Jean Swartz
aka Amber Swartz-Garcia

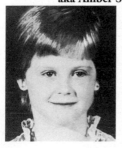

Over one million of these flyers were distributed after Amber was abducted.

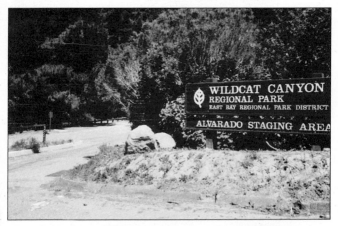

The entrance to Wildcat Canyon, where George Ellwin believes he saw Tim Bindner struggling with a young blond girl thirty minutes after Amber Swartz disappeared. This site is a ten-minute drive from Amber's house.

Tim Bindner at the ballpark
adjacent to Amber Swartz Park
(below).

STRANGER ABDUCTION

Abducted Child   **Suspected Abductor**

MICHAELA JOY GARECHT

White Female
Age: 9 years D.O.B 1-24-79
Hair: Blonde (Ponytail)
Height: 4'8"
Weight: 75 lbs. (thin)
Last seen wearing a white T-shirt
with "Metro" across the front and p
pictures of people near the mid-
section, denim pants rolled above
the knees, flesh colored nylon
stockings, white anklet socks and
black shoes, wearing 3" long pearl
or white earrings resembling feathers.

DESCRIPTION

White Male adult
Age: 18 years to early 20's
Hair: Dirty Blonde-Shoulder Length
Slender Build
Pock-marked or pimpled face
Wearing a white T-shirt

VEHICLE

Older model large (full size) vehicle,
possibly four doors, gold or tan
colored, run down condition.

Descriptions of Michaela and suspected abductor most likely have changed.

Date of Abduction: 11/19/88   Time: 10:15 A.M.

If you have any information about Michaela, please call:

911 or
HAYWARD POLICE DEPT. 800-222-3999 Case No. 88-11-2127

or
San Francisco FBI 415-553-7400

AMBER FOUNDATION FOR MISSING CHILDREN, P.O. Box 565, Pinole, CA 94564
FAX 510-758-0319
TOLL FREE 1-800-541-0777

This is the flyer distributed after Michaela Garecht was abducted from the Rainbow Market in Hayward. The composite of the suspect was later revised.

KIDNAPPED

COMPUTER AGED PICTURE

$95,000 REWARD

ILENE MISHELOFF

D.O.B.:	3-12-75	Eyes:	Brown
Age:	19	Height:	5'3"
Hair:	Brown	Weight:	115 lbs.
	Braces on teeth		

Case Number: 89-D-0252

Ilene was last seen in Dublin, California on Monday, January 30, 1989. She was wearing a charcoal gray pullover polo sweater, a horizontally striped pink and gray skirt, black low-top keds, and carrying a dark blue back pack.

NCIC Number: M-342301497

If you have any information regarding this missing child, please call the Dublin Police Services at:
(510) 833-6670 or 1-800-635-6306
or the FBI (415) 553-7400

Kidnapped when she was fourteen years old, Ilene Misheloff is shown in this flyer the way she would look at age nineteen.

Friday the bloodhound and his handler, Dale Myer.

messages scrawled in crayon on the walls, and a drawing of a grave marker inscribed TOMBSTONE TIM.

The next day, Wednesday, June 8, Deputy Bloodworth-Winter was parked on the Alhambra Valley Road when Tim Bindner stopped his van. She noticed that many of the photographs she had seen in the van earlier were gone.

"The FBI took them," Bindner explained. "They also photographed and searched the inside of the van."

"Did you ever help search for any other missing children?" the deputy asked.

Bindner said no. He wanted to help in the search effort for Angela Bugay, but his car wasn't running at the time and he couldn't get up to Antioch.

"Have you found anything?" she asked him.

"Not unless you count a dead cat and a dead dog," Bindner said.

On Thursday, June 9, when Bloodworth-Winter and another deputy were patrolling Carquinez Scenic Drive, north of Pinole, they spotted the blue van again. They followed from a distance, then stopped behind a parked school bus when Bindner pulled over to the side of the road. They watched him leave his vehicle, wandering down over a bank. The deputies waited.

In a few minutes, Bindner came up from behind a fence on the north side of the drive. He was holding an open beer and carried three more cans, unopened, on a plastic holder.

The deputies walked over and asked him if he'd had any luck with his search. He said no, adding that he had taken most of the week in vacation time to search. He'd go to the Social Security office early, wrap up some work, then head for Pinole.

When Bindner climbed back into his van and drove slowly down Carquinez Scenic Drive, the deputies walked to the hillside area on the north side of the road. Adjacent to the Alhambra Cemetery, in a gully twenty feet from the road, they saw a piece of clothing sticking out of some freshly turned dirt. Bloodworth-Winter's partner pulled at it and removed a child's sweater.

There was more—a small red-and-white polka-dot nightgown, a pink shirt, and a red-and-white polka-dot skirt. Almost five years before, Howard Mendelsohn had discovered the body of Angela Bugay in the same way. But the deputies knew the description of the clothing that Amber had been wearing when she disappeared. This stuff was different.

It had rained lightly earlier that day and showered briefly on each of the previous two days. The clothing seemed fairly new—and it was dry. A woman who lived on the drive told the deputies that she had seen the light blue van parked in the same area at least four times in the last few days—once at 6:00 A.M. A neighbor said he had passed it on his way to work.

Just beyond the buried clothes, against the hill, there was a small, crude, wooden cross. West of the cemetery there were two more crosses with empty holes recently dug at the bases of them.

The deputies contacted Pinole and, again, FBI agents responded. They said they wanted marked units kept out of the area. They would provide surveillance of Bindner and, with officers from Pinole, would search the cemetery and adjacent fields the next day.

Bindner drove his van about three hundred yards west of the cemetery, parked, and, with his shovel, walked down a hill beside the road. Within a few minutes he had moved the van again—seventy-five yards this time—and was sitting in the van with a map.

When a sheriff's cadet on litter patrol approached, the van was empty. He looked in from the driver's side window and, on the center console, saw a brown folder with Amber's name on it. There were other scribbled notes—and the name "Dep. Bloodwell."

The cadet spotted Bindner coming up out of a ravine carrying a shovel. "Any luck?" he asked.

"Not yet," Bindner said. "But if I find anything, it's probably going to be dead."

Bindner opened the back of the van to put the shovel away. The cadet noticed milk crates filled with empty bottles and aluminum cans. He also saw the kids' writing in crayon on the walls and the remaining photographs of young girls. He asked Bindner about them—two cute, little blond kids.

"They're dead," Bindner said.

He explained that he had taken the pictures from a gravestone he was working on and had them reproduced. "I like doing that sort of thing," he said.

"Why are you searching on Carquinez Scenic Drive?" the cadet asked.

"Just a hunch," Bindner said. "It's the first time I've been out here."

Bindner's beloved A's had won fourteen in a row. He was getting married. All was right with the world, he said. Then Amber Swartz disappeared.

Bindner had started his search for her about a mile out Pinole Valley Road. He figured the cops and volunteers had already searched everything inside that distance.

On Carquinez Scenic Drive, he explored a cave off the road. In some places he went a quarter to a half mile out, especially if there were signs that someone had been out there recently.

He looked at his AAA map, marked Savage Avenue, and examined the few roads—main and subsidiary—that cut through or surrounded the valley. Bear Creek Road. San Pablo Dam Road. Franklin Canyon. Cummings Skyway. Carquinez Scenic Drive.

The guy snatches the child, takes her out in the valley, does something to her, and drops her off in a creek bed or on a hillside, a trail, in a field full of haystacks, an orchard, or at his own preselected safe spot where he goes with his sexual fantasies. Where?

Bindner had to feel his way along. He had never planned out and conducted a search before. He was working at getting himself focused.

He remembered the female deputy who stopped at some pullouts and looked around. There were some bicyclists who walked their bikes for a while and looked down over the embankments. But people should have been doing more during that first week. Bindner doesn't mind being alone. He prefers it—whether he's walking through a cemetery or driving around in the valley. But the valley is immense—miles of countryside with thousands of places to dispose of a child.

On a roadside search, he could cover a quarter mile to a mile an hour. Sometimes he would spend two or three hours in one location if there were trace trails, culverts, bridges.

By the second or third day he knew the police were getting calls about his wandering around the valley. So he stopped at the police station in the morning and told them where he would be searching. When he finished for the day, he stopped at Kim's house and reported what he had done.

He knew that he was under surveillance. Sometimes it was the sheriff's deputies. Most of the time it was FBI. They didn't stop him, but those dark sedans kept going by—somebody in a suit and shined shoes checking on him.

The FBI agents were interviewing many people who lived in the area, had some connection to the family, or were assisting with the effort to find Amber. Bindner was right. Agents were watching him, and they did want to talk to him again.

What only Bindner knew then was that on June 2, 1988, the day before Amber vanished from the sidewalk in front of her home, he had been conducting a different kind of search—accessing Social Security files, the same thing that had resulted in his firing in 1985. This time he had tracked Susan Bugay, Angela's mother, and wrote her a letter.

He mailed it the day before Amber Swartz vanished.

9

In the first days following her daughter's disappearance, Kim Swartz transformed her house into a command post. She made Amber's bedroom the center of the activity—the child's dolls still on her bed, her hearing aid on the bureau where she had left it that Friday afternoon. Friends and neighbors worked as volunteers, and the phones rang twenty-four hours a day.

A man with a British accent thought he might have seen Amber in the freight terminal at the San Francisco airport.

A young woman and her boyfriend thought they had seen her at the beach.

She was with an old man. She might have been with a young couple.

A woman who claimed to be a psychic said Amber was near water.

Each time the phone rang there was the promise

of a chance, a possibility, that this might be the call that led to the recovery of Kim's daughter.

Kim walked into her daughter's room, touched Amber's dolls, ran her hand across the child's pillow. She was beginning to feel as if she had lost her ability to concentrate. Thoughts and memories raced through her mind.

Kim remembered some of the other parents in town talking about anonymous calls they had received—threats that the caller would abduct their children. But until June 3, no one had grabbed any child.

She struggled to remember all the details she could. She wasn't sleeping much. She would wake at odd moments, recalling information that was probably insignificant, but she would jot it down anyway so she would remember to tell the police. Sometimes she drifted while awake, in a half-conscious state, forgetting that her life was any different. Then it would all come back like a sharp, rude slap in the face.

One night, in the black silence of her room, she heard Amber calling her. Kim got out of bed and listened. Amber was crying, screaming, "Mommy."

Kim ran from her room to the front of the house, certain that someone had dumped Amber on Savage Avenue. She ran outside, but there was no one anywhere. No car. No taillights of a car screeching around the corner. Nothing.

She walked to the end of the sidewalk and looked into the field. She couldn't hear the haunting cries anymore.

Kim wasn't eating. She was losing weight. But she kept up with the phones—the tips and the leads—and with the media.

She welcomed the cameras and the lights, the TV interviewers, the newspaper reporters into her home. She talked about Amber, about June 3, about Amber's hearing impairment, the speech impediment, and, always, she made certain that her daughter's image was in front of the cameras.

During the first few weeks, the media people were

a constant presence. Sometimes they were intrusive. They draped cables across the dining room table or over the back of the sofa, adjusted the lighting in the room. But they were the only link she had, or her daughter had, with the community. She tolerated it. But she hated that it had to be done. Kim moved from one interview to another, one camera to another. "She's seven years old, four feet two inches tall, and weighs sixty-three pounds," Kim said so many times.

"No one has seen or heard anything," she told one interviewer. "No one knows anything. There's got to be somebody out there. We *know* there's somebody out there that knows something, has seen something."

TV sets throughout the Bay Area carried Kim's pleas: "We know that she's out there. Please help her to come home to us."

"It's a nightmare that's become reality," Kim said on another news broadcast. "Every time the phone rings you pray that it will be the call that somebody has actually found her, has her, and is going to bring her to you."

Police arrived daily with questions, but Kim soon learned that getting anything out of them was impossible. They were investigating any possible connection with James Richard Odle, the man who had killed Bernie Swartz. On May 19, 1988, the California Supreme Court had upheld Odle's death sentence for the murder, and the story had made the papers. The police also acknowledged that the man who had come to the house on June 6, Tim Bindner, was a suspect in Amber's disappearance, but he was only one of many they were looking at. Besides, they told her, Bindner had been off in Reno getting married when Amber was taken. That erroneous belief would haunt the investigation for the next eight years.

Kim never knew who any of the other suspects were. The police didn't share that information with her.

On Monday, June 6, someone had grabbed another little girl, this time in Sacramento. A four-year-old had been playing with friends outside her apartment building on Q Street. A bearded man got out of a blue compact car, snatched her, and drove away.

Pinole and Sacramento police compared notes on the cases and saw no basis for linking the two crimes.

What was happening? Someone was grabbing kids off the streets in front of their own homes. Something crazy was going on. Media interest shifted to Sacramento, then back to Pinole.

Kim Swartz is an articulate, attractive woman in her thirties. In the weeks following her daughter's disappearance, she established the Amber Foundation, a nonprofit organization that is still in operation today. Working closely with law enforcement, the foundation assists families, distributes flyers, and cooperates with other similar organizations nationally to combat the epidemic of child abductions through education and prevention.

What started in Amber's bedroom with a couple of toll-free lines soon moved to a room at the Pinole police department, then into its own quarters at 2550 Appian Way in Pinole. Kim and her volunteers handled five hundred calls about Amber in the first few weeks.

When Tim Bindner arrived at her house on June 6, Kim glanced at him as he talked with one of the family members who was screening visitors. He was scruffy, had the beginnings of a beard, with medium-length, sandy hair. This physical description, like the question of Bindner's whereabouts on June 3, 1988, would become a contested issue, and served only to confound the investigation.

Tim Bindner gave Kim the creeps. She couldn't explain it. He was nervous, jumpy, frazzled, and even in just those few moments when he was standing inside her door, he seemed to be studying her.

He had strong opinions about how to conduct a search, and said that he was more qualified for that task than the police. And he said the words that Kim

had never wanted to hear: "You realize that we're looking for a dead body."

She avoided the man after that. Whenever he
stopped by the house to report on his search activities,
she asked someone else to deal with him. Something
wasn't right about him. She felt as if he were watching
her reactions, watching her squirm—as if he had come
there not to search but to study a mother's pain.

The volunteers, who met at the Ellerhorst School,
noticed Bindner hanging around—not participating,
just looking on. Then they saw him out in Pinole Valley
carrying a shovel and a metal probe, and walking
along the side of the road. Several commented about
the weird guy with the blue van and the LOV YOU license plate.

Although Kim tried to stay out of his way, she did
allow Bindner to come to the house. She didn't like
him, didn't like the way he made her feel, but because
police considered him a suspect in her daughter's disappearance, she wanted to know what he had to say.

Bindner acknowledged that police were investigating him. He was a stranger to Pinole and didn't expect
people to grant him immediate trust. He was sticking
his nose into an investigation. He hadn't done anything, he said, and no one would find any evidence
that he had because there *wasn't* any. But he could
understand their wanting to check him out.

Kim Swartz never knew all of what the police
knew. As the months and years passed, Kim discovered numerous bits and pieces of information that
those she had come to consider "her detectives" had
never shared with her.

She threw herself into foundation work—tracking
down leads on her own child's disappearance, offering
support to other parents suffering through the loss of a
child, and educating the public about the abduction of
children by strangers.

On July 1, 1988, there was a prayer vigil for Amber at the church she had attended, St. Joseph's in Pinole. The Reverend Paddy Bishop asked those who could not be at the service to "flood the heavens with prayer" for the missing child. Other churches in the community held similar services.

Tim Bindner felt awkward in the church. He wasn't a traditionalist when it came to religion. He was making the transition from being an atheist unwilling to consider the possibility that God exists to a Christian willing to consider the possibility that He doesn't exist.

After the service he sent Kim a letter. "I pray that the person who took Amber will be brought before the judgment of God, and of man," he wrote, "and will be made to see the ugly blindness of his evil, and will find his sight, and his soul, and will atone and repent for his action."

It was a prayer he hadn't felt comfortable saying at the vigil.

He added a postscript. He said he would like to be a part of the foundation and its work. His attorney had advised him to wait, but Bindner wanted to start at the earliest possible time. He was about to lose his job at Social Security for the second time and for the same reason.

When he returned to work after his first firing, he figured, "What the hell. Y'all fired me already. I'm gonna do whatever the hell I want with your computer system here. As long as I feel it's right, and as long as I can be a nice guy to the world, why, I'm just gonna do what I want."

Bindner picked up where he had stopped with the birthday cards to fourteen-year-olds in Colorado. He also looked up an old girlfriend he hadn't seen since she was fourteen. She was thirty-five by then. They had dinner together.

He experimented with a system for tracking down runaways, kids who were old enough to have Social Security numbers and might find jobs after leaving home. Even if they used fake names, the numbers would give them away.

"This is like late '87, or early '88," Bindner said later, "and here comes Amber. She gets kidnapped. I get investigated. They audit all my computer records. They fire me again."

There was also the search on Susan Bugay, and another case of a missing child police had recovered. Luis "Treefrog" Johnson and Alex Cabarga had kidnapped a two-year-old girl from a parking lot in Concord on February 6, 1982. Police found the child in Johnson's van on December 18; she had suffered ten months of sexual abuse by the two men.

Bindner read an article about the case, and about how the state was paying for Cabarga's psychotherapy while the victim's family couldn't afford to pay for hers. The article provided the address of a bank for those who wanted to contribute to a fund to help the child. Bindner didn't want to do it that way, so he tracked the family with his computer at Social Security and called them.

Bindner also called Kim Swartz. On the morning of July 7, there was an article in the *Oakland Tribune* about a possible link between the abduction and murder of Angela Bugay and Amber's disappearance. Bindner didn't subscribe to the paper, but someone dropped three copies at his house. He figured it was the FBI.

During the call, he told Kim Swartz that when he began searching he was looking for a living child. But he had considered the possibility that Amber, like Angela, was dead. "I saw the connection a month ago," he said, "and I told the FBI that there might be a connection."

He described seeing the news that Friday night and turning to Sandra and saying, "My God. I hope that's not another Angela. I gotta go out and look for that kid when we get back. I think I can find her. I know where to look, how to look."

Bindner was candid about his status in the investigation. Yes, he was a suspect. "They're still checking for evidence on me," he said. "But of course they're never going to find anything because there's nothing to find."

Tim Bindner said he hadn't read Dostoyevsky's *Crime and Punishment*, but he knew the psychological essence of the story and explained it to Kim. A man named Raskolnikov commits a murder. He doesn't come forward. He doesn't tell anyone. He's racked with guilt but also consumed by fear of being caught. So Raskolnikov begins hanging around the investigation, asking questions, dropping hints. People like this fictional character do or say something that causes the authorities to realize that he is the one who committed the murder.

Maybe the cops thought he was like Raskolnikov, hanging around the fringes of the Amber investigation. They would be waiting for him to make a slip, but of course that couldn't happen.

10

Six weeks after the Sacramento child's abduction, police in Sacramento responded to a report of a man grabbing an Asian child and driving away with her. A witness supplied a partial license plate for the blue compact car, and police tracked down Kenneth Alvin Michael, a handyman at the Elk Grove United Methodist Church. The Asian child was in a cardboard box in the back of Michael's small Ford hatchback. The child Michael had abducted six weeks earlier was found in a crawl space beneath the church, alive.

All Kim Swartz knew was that police had recovered a child. Later, she told a reporter, "Obviously I hoped that it was Amber. At that point we didn't know if the child was dead or alive. We weren't told that. Just that there was a child found that had been kidnapped."

Police found no connection between Kenneth Michael and Amber's disappearance.

Kim was grateful that two little girls were going

home. It gave her reason to think that her daughter might be next.

––––––––––––

On July 30, Sheriff's Deputy Kirkbride saw Bindner's van parked by a creek bed on Vaqueros Drive in Rodeo. There were missing person flyers about Amber hanging both inside and outside the locked vehicle. Bindner walked up from the creek carrying a plastic bag and a shovel. He introduced himself, explained that the van was his, and said that he was looking for aluminum cans. Kirkbride asked about the shovel.

"Well, when I'm looking for cans," Bindner said, "I'm also looking for Amber Swartz. The creek area's a place she might be."

Kirkbride asked if he could look through the van. Bindner refused.

On August 9, a complaint came from Hillside Drive in El Sobrante. A man carrying a shovel got out of a vehicle and walked down into a creek area. The caller thought this was the guy who was a suspect in the Amber Swartz disappearance. Word was getting around.

On August 16, it was Highway 4, across from Yellow Freight—a report of a suspicious person digging in a field near the Franklin Canyon Golf Course. When the deputy arrived, Bindner was sitting in his van. He said he was searching for cans and that he used the shovel to retrieve cans from hard-to-reach places. "You never know what you can find," he said.

Bindner reasoned that law enforcement people would look closely at someone like him. He wasn't related to Angela or Amber. He didn't even know the children. But he was spending his time and effort trying to find Amber, and he had told them how emotionally invested he was in Angela, that he had been haunted by what happened to her. They would investigate him because of that.

On August 17, two days before Amber's birthday, Bindner was on Cummings Skyway. He found a pile of plastic garbage bags and checked them out. Whatever they contained smelled bad, like something decomposing. He opened a bag and discovered a brown mass that he figured could be human.

He brooded about the find for two days. He knew he had to report it. He had been searching for ten weeks, and now he finally had found something. But if this came from a human body, he was sure they'd try to nail him with it. Since he thought it might be evidence of a homicide, Bindner says, he did go to the Pinole police on the nineteenth to report his find. Pinole contacted the sheriff's department.

Bindner told Deputy Trojanowski he thought the bags might contain Amber's body parts. He said he had been looking for Amber and just picking up cans for extra money. He told the deputy he wasn't suspicious about the bags until he had thought about it for a couple of days.

Bindner thinks the date of his report, Amber's birthday, might have had some significance for the cops.

> They think you play games with them all the time. Maybe they thought that was another game. I don't know. It wasn't. I couldn't do it before that because I was scared shitless.

The same day he found the bags, he mailed a letter to Kim. "You asked me if I knew where your daughter was," he wrote. "I came into your life a stranger, so there is really no reason I should expect you to trust me. Obviously there are many people who don't. No, I have no idea at all what happened to Amber."

Despite being harassed by the police, he told her, he would continue to help with the effort to find Amber. He didn't mention the bags of decomposing material.

A later analysis of that material showed that it was not human.

On August 19, Amber's eighth birthday, Kim's volunteers organized a celebration and fund-raiser at St. Joseph's School in Pinole. It was for the Amber Foundation and was the first annual Amber Day, an effort to increase public awareness of the abduction of children by strangers. Parents brought their kids to be videotaped and fingerprinted.

Kim stood by a wall of pictures of her daughter, a collage one of the volunteers had put together. "I tried not to think that today was the day I was in the hospital having her," she told one interviewer.

Then there was a different microphone, a new camera: "My birthday wish for my daughter would be to have her back with me so I could hold her, and have her back where she belongs."

She looked directly into the camera and talked to her daughter. "Know that we are looking for you, that we love you and want you back, regardless of what anybody might be saying to you."

There were more media events, interviews, and talk shows into the fall. Then the reporters didn't come around as often. Kim had to go after them. She wanted Amber's face and her story in front of the public, and she was willing to travel anywhere to accomplish that.

In September, she was at the airport in San Francisco returning from an appearance on *Oprah* when she heard that the FBI was investigating a new lead. A clerk at an ice cream shop in Calaveras County, 130 miles to the east, believed she had seen Amber with a man and a woman. The child was quiet, the witness said. It didn't look as if the couple were holding her captive, but she did seem subdued and disoriented, and she had a speech impediment.

It was the second sighting near the Sierra foothills in as many days. The news brought a moment's hope, then the familiar, crushing sadness when the lead went nowhere.

The investigation was fading rapidly. Amber Swartz was becoming just a case number: 88-1501.

On November 14, 1988, Tim Bindner wrote to Kim.

I have learned many valuable lessons and made some decisions in the last few months. One of the lessons is that only I can decide what is the proper course of action for me to take, and one of the decisions is that I must not let fear of possible consequences ever deter me from actions conceived in love and compassion and a desire to help.

Kim Swartz didn't know what to make of the letter.

———————

There was a light rain falling on the evening of November 15. At 8:15 P.M., Donna Davidson drove through Oakmont Cemetery on a security check before leaving work for the day. As she came up the hill, she saw a bearded man dressed in shorts and a T-shirt walking through the Meditation area toward the grave of Angela Bugay.

Davidson recognized the man. He was the one the FBI was investigating in the Amber Swartz disappearance. It might not have hit the papers, but people who lived in the towns around the valley knew it. He always seemed to be up there at Angela's grave. One time he'd even applied for a job at the cemetery.

Davidson called the sheriff's department. The deputy she talked with wasn't sure what Tim Bindner's status in the investigation was anymore. He checked with the FBI. The response was terse. Tim Bindner was still a suspect. Direct any reports about him to Agent Dave Knowlton in Concord.

It was a combination of policy and strategy to withhold information about suspects in any investigation. But people in the valley couldn't help knowing about Bindner. He was everywhere, and people were talking.

The official silence about Bindner went deeper and revealed a problem that would haunt the child abduction investigations in the Bay Area. Law enforcement agencies weren't keeping each other informed, and they were suffering from linkage blindness.

The Pinole police willingly took their direction from the FBI, but the federal agency was notoriously silent when it came to divulging what they were doing and why. Both agencies treated the sheriff's department as a convenience. The sheriff's office had jurisdiction in the valley, beyond Pinole's city limits, so they could run errands out there until the special agents arrived in plain clothes and unmarked cars and told them to clear the area. Although the FBI reacted to the possibility of a connection between the Angela and Amber cases, and went public with it, the Antioch police continued to focus on Larry Graham, and, indeed, would later indict him for the murder of Angela Bugay. He was the local man who had dated Susan Bugay.

These interagency conflicts—the politics, the jealousies, the turf protection, and, later, the fear—prevented law enforcement from ruling Tim Bindner in or out. It was the seed from which a stalemate was sprouting. No one failed. No one succeeded.

But children continued to disappear.

11

SATURDAY, NOVEMBER 19, 1988

At about 9:30 A.M., Tim Bindner walked out of the Hayward Fire Department on West Winton Avenue, two miles north of the Rainbow Market. He had just failed the test for a firefighter's position. He got into his van and opened a beer. The disappointment of failing the test was bad enough, but it was also a whole career down the drain.

He had been going to the fire station for two weeks to practice for the physical agility test. One particular task, raising a seventy-pound weight fourteen feet on a pulley, was difficult, but he had failed it only once in all his practice runs. For the actual test, the rope was different. The gritty practice rope was replaced by a new, slick rope that slipped easily through his hands.

Bindner managed to get the weight within five feet of the top, but no farther. It wasn't just a job. It was a career, and it was hanging there. He couldn't do it. He was devastated.

It was the first day of Thanksgiving vacation for the kids who attended the Hillview Crest School in Hayward, twenty miles south of Oakland.

Even the light rain couldn't dampen the enthusiasm of nine-year-old Michaela Garecht, a fourth grader at Hillcrest, or her friend Lisa. They began their day with a scooter ride to the Rainbow Market. The grocery store was on Mission Boulevard, two blocks away from Michaela's house. It was shortly after 10:00 A.M. when they came out of the store with their snacks.

Someone had moved Michaela's red scooter. She spotted it back in the parking lot next to a car. When she went to get it, a man jumped out of the car, grabbed her, dragged the screaming and struggling child back inside with him, and drove away.

Lisa watched in shocked, helpless horror, then ran back inside the market.

It was a witnessed abduction, and the law enforcement response was rapid and heavy. Police broadcasts described a man in his early twenties, between 5'8" and 6', 180 pounds, clean-shaven, with shoulder-length, dirty blond hair and an acne-scarred complexion.

They also had a description of his car—large and cream-colored with a battered front bumper.

Hayward police saturated the area, notified neighboring communities and the California Highway Patrol, and monitored the roads in and out of town. It was as if a phantom had slipped in, taken the child, and vanished. Officers stopped cars, questioned people. Sirens screamed in all directions. Again in the Bay Area, in a matter of seconds, a child vanished.

Case number: 88-112127.

Lisa helped police put together a composite drawing of the man who took her friend. She was doing her best, but she had been traumatized by what she saw.

The accuracy of the composite was questionable, but it was all they had. Investigators began going over the photographs of registered sex offenders to see if any matched the composite drawing.

In the first sixteen hours after the abduction, volunteers printed and distributed 42,000 flyers. Michaela's picture was on them, and so was the composite of the pockmarked man. Stranger abduction. Witnessed.

Local businesspeople established a reward fund that would grow to more than $150,000. San Francisco football great Joe Montana issued a public appeal in the case.

That first evening, Kim Swartz went from the Amber Foundation to the Garecht home. It had been five and a half months since she had experienced the same horror.

The house was chaotic. Just as Kim had transformed Amber's bedroom into a command post, the Garechts did the same with their living room. The phone rang more than thirty times an hour. The anticipation that went with each call was something Kim knew all too well.

The phone continued to ring, and people kept coming to the door. Kim was talking with Sharon and Rod Garecht, but she looked up as the door opened. Tim Bindner stood in the doorway.

Bindner says he drove back to Oakland shortly after failing his test. He hadn't seen anything unusual while he was in Hayward and didn't know anything about Michaela's abduction until he saw the early evening news on TV. He told his wife he was going back to Hayward to poke around.

He talked briefly with Michaela's father about places the child might go to play or just to hang out. He asked Sharon Garecht where she wanted him to search.

He got out his map. He wanted to start searching

for her that night. Garin Park is a vast wilderness area of mountains and canyons east of the city. Bindner said, "I'm gonna go up in this park and just look around and see if there's anything up there."

Later, Bindner said that his feeling for the case was that the guy with the straggly hair went out that morning knowing it was the day he was going to do it. He was going to get him one. It was a plan, a fantasy. So the man hung out at the market. When he saw Michaela and her friend, he knew he wanted the blond one. He watched her park the scooter and started getting excited. The excitement diminished whatever fear he might have felt doing it in front of witnesses. Michaela came over to get her scooter—walked into his trapline—and he snatched her.

When Bindner left the Garechts' home, he drove the short distance to Garin Park. He stopped at a house there to let a neighbor know he had parked his van on the residential street and was going up into the wilderness area to look for the missing child.

He walked in with a probe and a flashlight, and called Michaela's name. As he started his search for the child, the Hayward police were looking for him.

Bindner was comfortable in the woods at night. Ever since he was a kid he had roamed through forests, climbed mountains, hiked long distances. He had majored in forestry in college. That night, not long after he entered the park, he heard a helicopter overhead. He wondered if they were looking for the child or looking for him, so he walked up to the ranger's residence.

"The police are looking for you," the ranger told him.

"Well, I'm done searching," Bindner said. "I'm gonna walk back down and I'll meet them on the way out."

When Bindner met Ken Gross of the Hayward police department, he didn't like the cop's attitude. It was as if the guy were telling him he had better things to do with his time than chase around after some lunatic in the middle of the woods. Bindner felt almost like a nonentity.

"I'm only looking for Michaela," Bindner said. "I want to participate in this search."

"I don't want you doing any searching," Gross said.

"Well, what if I get involved in distributing flyers?"

"That's the volunteer center," Gross said. "I don't have any control over that. The people doing the flyers are handling that."

The Hayward cop ran warrant checks and looked through the contents of Bindner's wallet. Finally, Gross called in the East Bay Regional Park District Rangers, and they issued Bindner a ticket for trespassing in the park after dark.

"Now get in your goddamn van and go back to Oakland," Gross told him.

The next day, Sunday, Bindner returned to Hayward and stopped at the volunteer center. He picked up two hundred flyers and went door to door distributing them and talking to people.

He kept coming back to Hayward to do roadside searches. He spent weekends searching the outlying roads—the same thing he had done with Amber. He checked the culverts. He checked the bridges. The cops left him alone. Maybe they didn't know he was out there, or maybe they didn't care.

Bindner said he could form a mental picture of a man seizing the child and throwing her into his car. He formed another mental image while searching through an abandoned drive-in in Hayward. The screen and the concession booth were still standing, but the speakers were gone, and grass had grown up through the asphalt, reclaiming the ground. There were encampments—ratty sleeping bags, cardboard boxes, blankets—of homeless people all over the place. Garbage was strewn all around. Bindner could picture a man with the blond nine-year-old girl. The man was looking around, trying to choose the place where he was going to commit his crime. The child was alive, struggling.

> *Anybody could be down there doing their thing and as long as they didn't bother anybody else, they probably wouldn't be bothered. When I was walking through there I was thinking, "This could be the place," and I spent several hours there.*

But Bindner found nothing in the old drive-in.

When Ken Gross sent the Oakland man packing, he didn't know that Bindner had been in Hayward that morning—just a few miles from the Rainbow Market—or that he had been there on other occasions in recent weeks to practice for his test. Nor did Gross know that in June 1988 Tim Bindner had predicted to an FBI agent that the next victim would be nine or ten years old.

The FBI had picked up on the possibility of a connection between the Bugay and Swartz cases. Special Agent Barry Mawn had told the media it was possible that Angela's killer had waited five years to strike again.

Now Bindner fired off a letter to the Bureau. Maybe the killer was rubbing their noses in it, he wrote. There were four and a half years between Angela and Amber, but Michaela Garecht's abduction was five years to the day since Angela Bugay disappeared, and it was the first time since 1983 that November 19 fell on a Saturday.

THREE

INVESTIGATION—
THE COP

12

Nikki Campbell had been missing for three days.

As Barry Hom reviewed Fairfield's case for the group of area investigators, Harold Sagan couldn't help thinking how similar it was to the other Bay Area cases. What did they have on their hands—an epidemic of child abductions?

Amber Swartz and Nikki Campbell were both taken on Friday afternoons. Angela Bugay and Michaela Garecht on Saturdays, both November 19, five years apart. The time of day was roughly the same for Angela, Amber, and Nikki. The neighborhoods were similar in all the cases. Each victim had blond hair, blue eyes. In the Swartz case, searchers had found children's socks near the family's home, even though they had already examined the area without results. The same thing had happened in Fairfield's own case. When they moved their mobile crime lab from in front of the Campbells' house, an officer found a pair of child-size blue socks.

Investigators at the meeting kept coming back to Bindner. FBI Special Agent O'Toole talked about meetings she'd had with Bindner in 1988 and 1989. She briefed the group on Bindner's background, his involvement in the cases, his personality, his intelligence. O'Toole also mentioned that during one interview with Bindner in 1989 he had admitted that he possessed the characteristics of someone who could kill a child, but said that he had not killed anyone.

Harold Sagan knew that O'Toole had investigated Bindner, but the Fairfield detective hadn't known the details that he was hearing now.

In his interviews with other FBI agents, Bindner had also admitted to unusual sexual practices. But he had no criminal history—except for his brushes with law enforcement whenever he involved himself in the missing child searches. The Contra Costa County district attorney had dropped charges against Bindner for annoying children in San Pablo.

During the weeks following Amber's disappearance in 1988, Bindner was under twenty-four-hour surveillance. He often visited Angela's grave. Sometimes he sprawled on top of it, or he would sit there drinking beer, talking to the grave. The agents placed electronic surveillance devices at the cemetery plot and in Bindner's vehicle.

He also left coins at the grave—Indian head pennies, just like the ones he had sent to Sheila Cosgrove.

O'Toole voiced a word of caution. There are many people infatuated with child abductions and child homicides who remain in a fantasy situation and never act out those fantasies, she said.

Harold Sagan didn't buy it. O'Toole was the behavioral expert, but this Bindner guy was too bizarre and had been in too many of the right places at the right times. This was beyond coincidence.

Rich McEachin, the Antioch detective assigned to the Angela Bugay case, told the group about the letter that Bindner had sent to their chief. McEachin empha-sized that Bindner was not a suspect in this investiga-tion. Yet, continuing to involve himself in the case, Bindner had written that law enforcement people needed to be more thorough if they were dealing with a serial child killer. He referred to two southern Cali-fornia cases—Victoria Vick had disappeared in Palm-dale on January 24, 1983; and Laura Bradbury had disappeared from a campground at Joshua Tree Na-tional Monument on October 18, 1984.

Pinole's Detective Phil Pollard told the group that bloodhounds had indicated strongly on Bindner's van after Amber's disappearance. But because Bindner had been inside the house on Savage Avenue, the cop questioned the evidentiary value of the dogs' behavior.

Sagan was hearing most of this for the first time and wondering why no one had ever gotten a handle on the guy. The Fairfield detective was stunned when Pollard reported that the dogs had also indicated the presence of Amber's scent at Angela Bugay's grave in Oakmont Cemetery, fifteen miles from Pinole. Bindner had even suggested the possibility of a link between the two cases, and the dogs seemed to be confirming that theory.

Ron Homer told the gathering about an interview he had with Bindner in June 1988. The veteran FBI polygrapher had administered three tests. The first two were inconclusive (that is, not interpretable as ei-ther deceptive or truthful), but the third clearly indi-cated deception.

Sagan was shocked by how much attention had been focused on Bindner over the years throughout the Bay Area. He and Barry Hom agreed that they should use a different approach with the Oakland man this time around. In the other cases, police had used obvious surveillance, or simply hauled Bindner in for interviews. "That will be what he's expecting," Sagan said. "We're not going to play the game the way he's used to having it played. If he calls, we don't call back.

We use covert surveillance. We don't interview him until we're ready."

The game plan was to do the background and investigative work as fast as possible so Bindner could be ruled in or out.

O'Toole remembered something else. Early in December she had received a Christmas card from Tim Bindner. On it there was a picture of a little Russian girl holding up four fingers, indicating her age. The child bore a remarkable resemblance to four-year-old Nikki Campbell.

———————

After the meeting, Sagan drove the forty miles to Oakland and found Fifty-third Street for the first of what would be many times. He drove by Bindner's house—a modest, Victorian-era, wood-frame building—just to get a look at it. Then he headed for the East Bay Municipal District (EBMUD), the sewage treatment facility where Bindner worked.

He checked Bindner's work schedule. Thursday and Friday were his days off. He had reported for work at 10:45 P.M. on the twenty-seventh. That gave the eccentric former cemetery worker opportunity. And, if what the other investigators had suggested about the man was true, he had motive.

Sagan waited in the EBMUD parking lot long enough to watch Bindner arrive for work. The detective snapped some surveillance photographs, then drove back up onto I-80 and headed toward Fairfield.

He was sitting at his desk at 4:35 P.M., when a dispatcher walked in with a call-in sheet from the Nikki Campbell hot line. A caller wanted to help find the missing child.

Tim Bindner.

"He doesn't exist," Sagan said, returning the sheet. "As far as we're concerned, right now, he doesn't exist."

Sagan didn't want Bindner coming into Fairfield.

He didn't want the contamination that had affected the other cases. "Keep the guy away until we're ready to talk to him on our terms," he thought.

Harold Sagan was confronted with the disappearance of a child in his city, and he was just now starting to uncover the eight-year history of abductions and sexual homicides in the Bay Area. He anticipated receiving the full cooperation of the other jurisdictions involved and thought that ruling Bindner in or out would be a simple task.

The veteran cop couldn't have been more wrong on both counts.

13

Born in Germany on August 13, 1948, Harold Sagan was a military brat. His father was career air force, stationed in a rural area of southern Germany—Sagan lived with his mother on his grandmother's farm, a couple of kilometers from the nearest village. He began his education by skiing to a one-room schoolhouse, complete with potbellied stove. The girls sat on one side of the room, the boys on the other. Everyone spoke German.

There were artillery batteries—remnants of World War II—in his grandmother's fields. Sometimes the young Sagan would wander out there, and the soldiers would give him chocolate bars.

He remembers hearing stories of the years when Hitler was in power. One story was about a young man on a neighboring farm. He was a tall, muscular, fairhaired boy. German soldiers came by one day looking for recruits. The boy had doubts, but not about Hitler or the Nazis. He was just unsure of himself, didn't think he could live up to the high standards of the

Third Reich, and didn't believe he would make a very good soldier. The soldiers marched him to the side of a barn and shot him.

Sagan's grandfather was an outspoken, independent man who had railed against the Nazi atrocities. Sagan's grandmother had had to stifle the old man. She didn't want any gang of storm troopers marching him off to a barn.

When Sagan finished first grade, the air force transferred his father to New York City. The family packed everything they owned and traveled by train to a port city on the Baltic Sea. They crossed the Atlantic on the SS *United States*.

Sagan didn't speak a word of English, so he had to repeat first grade in the parochial school where his parents placed him. He doesn't remember anything resembling tolerance or compassion coming from the nuns, who rapped his knuckles because he couldn't speak the language. Sagan's education in being different had begun. Throughout his life, he would feel that he was somehow outside things. It wasn't something he chose. It was just there, a feeling that would grow to haunt him.

The family's stay in New York was brief. They soon returned to Munich. Later there were stints in Texas and Minnesota—sites that required his father's skills in radar. Sagan moved from school to school, always the new kid, the outsider. He started high school in Marin County, California, in the middle 1960s. The family lived in Novato while his father worked at a radar site on nearby Mount Tamalpais. To Sagan, Marin County seemed exclusive, a place for the rich. His status as a military dependent set him apart. Although he always had the support of his family, when he stepped out the door in the morning he was on his own.

The name-calling began right away and continued for more than three years. Students and teachers alike called the young man "kraut" and "Nazi." He struggled with the slurs and the ridicule until the second week of his senior year. Then he erupted, and fought with another student. The principal dusted off the other kid and sent him back to class, but he dragged Sagan into his office and started in on him. The high school senior dropped the principal with one punch.

"I walked out," Sagan remembers. "I drove straight down to San Raphael and joined the army. I was at the Oakland induction center the next morning."

By the following night Sagan was at Fort Lewis, Washington, for basic training. His father wasn't happy with his actions, but he understood. Sagan's mother feared that her son would end up in Vietnam.

The army sent Sagan from Fort Lewis to Fort Gordon, Georgia, for schooling in advanced radio and telephone communications. He completed the school, then languished in Georgia when the military lost his orders. Out of boredom, he volunteered for jump school. He went first to Fort Benning, then to Fort Campbell, Kentucky, home of the 101st Airborne Division—the Screaming Eagles of World War II. By November, the nineteen-year-old was on his way to Vietnam in a long-range reconnaissance patrol unit (LRRP).

He spent a year in the jungles of Southeast Asia, returning home with the rank of sergeant—and two Purple Hearts, the Bronze Star, and the Vietnam Service Medal.

Sagan settled in San Francisco after serving in the war. He often traveled across the bay to Berkeley, where the antiwar demonstrations continued. But the young veteran had no interest in the speeches, the teach-ins, the hordes of young people who descended on the campus. On his own he had developed a love of learning. He was awed just walking among the buildings where mathematicians and physicists had performed the calculations that contributed to the development of nuclear power.

After completing junior college, his first civilian job was as a computer programmer for an international conglomerate. He was working on an IBM mainframe, but the job bored him. One day a classified ad caught his eye—applicants were wanted for positions with the Fairfield police department. He jumped at the chance, and he got a job. After a quick stint at the police academy and a single day of on-the-job training, Sagan went to work.

One Sunday morning during his second week as a cop, there was a call from dispatch to respond to Armijo High School. No one else on duty wanted the call. They figured it was a juvenile matter.

Then the dispatcher called again. "It's regarding an unnatural sex act," she said.

Suddenly there was a parade of patrol cars headed for the high school. It was Sagan's call, and he had to handle it. What he found was a man chasing a chicken. The young cop didn't see anything particularly twisted about this until the man explained that his reason for chasing the chicken was sexual. Nothing in Sagan's training had prepared him for this. He wasn't even sure if the law covered it.

"Have you ever done anything like this before?" he asked.

"Well, yeah," the man said. "But with a horse."

Sagan hadn't observed anything but a man chasing a chicken. There was no basis on which to make an arrest. He drove the guy home, and they met his wife at the door of their trailer.

"What's he done now?" she demanded.

Sagan hesitated, but finally told the woman.

"Not again," she said.

The rookie cop drove away shaking his head. He had been in a jungle war thousands of miles from home, but there was so much in his own backyard that he hadn't seen and couldn't even imagine.

His career in law enforcement satisfied his need for action and gave him a sense that he was contributing something to the community. It also offered him the opportunity to learn. He studied training and management, and attended crime analysis school. He moved into investigations as a member of a four-person crime-reduction unit. Rather than working

reactively from one burglary to the next, the unit focused on the suspected burglar and developed all the
intelligence they could.

He was working with Chuck Timm then. Both men
soon realized that wearing a suit and tie and working
eight to five was insane. The bad guys didn't come out
of their holes until six or seven at night, didn't wear
suits and ties, and didn't want anything to do with people who did. Sagan and Timm started wearing jeans
and coming in at five or six in the evening.

Both men feel the partnership was a good one.
They worked together for eighteen months and cleared
cases. Whatever had to be done, they did it. If they
could get help, they accepted it. Otherwise, they operated on their own. The two men complemented one
another well. Timm was always ready to charge ahead
at full throttle. Sagan was the thinker, the one who
wanted to consider all the options before acting.

Eventually, Timm wanted to go back into uniform,
and Sagan was growing impatient with administrative
politics.

Sagan spent three years working the streets before
moving back to investigations in 1989. There he handled homicides, sexual assaults, and most of the department's cases involving crimes against children.
Unlike other cops, who burn out on that job after a few
years, Sagan never grew tired of it.

The detective learned everything he could about
the varieties of physical and sexual abuse people committed against children. He educated himself, studied
pedophilia and other sexual aberrations. He got to the
point where he could even predict a child molester's
responses to questions during an interrogation.

Sagan wants to be as knowledgeable as possible,
but he also feels that no one ever can be knowledgeable enough. There's always something else out there
that you don't know.

He had seen head injuries in children that had
been diagnosed as injuries suffered in a fall—but
Sagan wondered how many were actually caused by

child abuse. He read clinical studies of head trauma and bought a medical dictionary to translate the terminology. He spent $300 on books and read each of them cover to cover.

Harold Sagan is always a tenacious investigator, a by-the-book cop who works to make a case that will guarantee conviction. Whenever someone victimizes a child, Sagan becomes even more determined. He had been in this specialized investigative role for two and a half years when he heard the radio call that turned his stomach over.

Nikki Campbell was gone.

The law enforcement officials who gathered in the Fairfield department's conference room that December Monday morning, three days after Nikki vanished, also were looking for some trace of young girls who had disappeared and were presumed to have been abducted and murdered. All of them had at least some interest in Timothy James Bindner.

It was time for the detective to take a closer look at the man from Oakland.

14

It was before dawn when Harold Sagan drove the forty miles to Oakland. He stopped on Fifty-third Street and walked back to where Bindner had parked his lime-green Toyota station wagon. Inside and out, the car was immaculate. The Oakland man had a reputation for being something of a slob, but the condition of the car did nothing to attest to that. This time of year, few people tried to keep their vehicles clean. You washed them and they got rained on.

Bindner's old wagon gleamed.

Later that morning, Chuck Timm appointed Sagan lead investigator in the Nikki Campbell disappearance. Barry Hom had been working a major drug case that was coming to a head. He didn't have the time to handle both cases. Besides, Sagan was the expert on crimes against children, and he had been gathering intelligence on Timothy Bindner ever since Bindner had written those strange letters to little Sheila Cosgrove.

It was a hunch.

Sagan knew that in the summer of 1988 the search and rescue team's bloodhounds had detected Amber Swartz's scent in Oakmont Cemetery near Angela Bugay's grave. He wanted to run the dogs there with Nikki Campbell's scent.

Tim Bindner had raised the question of a connection between Angela and Amber. Now the detective was preempting Bindner. It there *was* a connection, the cop would discover it. If not, they would put the matter to rest.

At eight o'clock that night, the dogs and their handlers, along with FBI agents and Fairfield investigators, congregated north of the Meditation section of the Oakmont Cemetery. Dale Myer gave his dog, Friday, the scent article—Nikki's Christmas dress. The big dog was agitated and took longer with the article than was typical for him. He picked up the scent immediately.

Friday ran into the center of the Meditation area, then back and forth, parallel to the five-year-old's grave. It was the most frantic behavior Myer had ever observed in the animal. Friday ran, scratched at the earth, retraced his path, and whined. Nikki Campbell's scent was definitely there.

Sagan looked around at some freshly dug graves. He saw a slag pile over at the north side of the hill. He asked Mary Ellen O'Toole about pulling back the sod on a new grave, removing some dirt, placing a body there, covering it, and replacing the sod. Nobody would be any the wiser. Would a killer do that?

The special agent was noncommittal; it was possible.

Suddenly Friday bolted across the cemetery toward

a mausoleum one hundred yards to the south. He continued his frantic behavior on the rear pavilion—whining, running back and forth. He jumped up against a railing that overlooked a maintenance shed at the foot of the hill.

Linda Hubbard, one of the dog handlers, was standing next to Sagan. She began to cry.

"What's wrong?" Sagan asked her.

"It's the same thing they did with Amber," she said.

Linda and her dog, Duke, had run the search for Amber at the Oakmont Cemetery in the summer of 1988. Dale Myer knew that Duke had detected Amber's scent, but he had no idea what kind of trail the dog had run. "Friday's running the same trail," Linda said.

Sagan could hear the dog down at the mausoleum. He looked through the blackness illuminated in haphazard fashion by flashlights. He heard the voices of the officers in the distance. The tall, gray-haired cop looked back at Linda's tear-stained face.

"My God, what are we dealing with," he muttered.

Everyone on the hill was getting spooked. Sagan's flashlight batteries died. His spare lasted ten minutes, then it too went out. There wasn't any moonlight. The noises from the mausoleum sounded like something from a Mary Shelley nightmare.

When Friday came out of the mausoleum, he circled it, then started down a service road toward the maintenance shed. Sagan walked to the north end of the mausoleum, where he noticed an odor he knew well from his years on the force and from his tour in Vietnam. Death.

He told Barry Hom, and the two men examined the wall. The smell was coming from one of the vaults. Below it, there was a basket filled with small teddy bears. Sagan ran his palm over the cool marble surface of the vault and wondered if it contained Nikki Campbell's decomposing body.

He was the lead investigator now. The whole operation was on his shoulders. He was thinking,

"Everyone is looking to me for direction. What do I do? What do I tell them?"

He didn't have a clue. He couldn't formulate a plan. One thought kept banging around in his mind, distorting his thoughts, confusing and disorienting him: Nikki's scent is here. Either someone brought her here or someone who had held her—someone who'd had close contact with her—was up here.

The group gathered in the absolute blackness, the smell of death hovering around them. "We'll come back in the morning and open it up," Sagan said.

On Thursday, at 7:00 A.M., Sagan and Hom met with the cemetery's assistant manager to open the vault. They didn't need a warrant or the family's consent. It was a health and safety problem.

When they removed the square marble slab, dust and cobwebs were evident. No one had disturbed the vault. The casket was just improperly sealed.

After months without any letters from Bindner, one arrived addressed to Sheila Cosgrove. It bore an Oakland postmark and was dated January 3. Liz Cosgrove turned it over to the Fairfield police.

"It was with shock and sadness," Bindner wrote, "that I learned that little Amanda Campbell is missing and that she lives close to you. I have searched for other missing kids. Amber Swartz and Michaela Garecht. If I have a chance, I will try to find Amanda also."

15

JANUARY 7, 1992

Harold Sagan was sitting at his desk when the call came in. It was Detective Joe Allio. The last Sagan knew, Allio had taken off in his car. He had been looking at a city map, asking himself, "If I took the kid, where would I go with her?" Then he was gone.

Allio usually pushed himself—played with an idea, then tested it out. A six-year veteran of the department, Allio was thorough, a meticulous cop. He was the best man in the department when it came to search warrants on a residence. He knew where and how to look for evidence and how to return every closet or dresser drawer to its original condition and appearance.

Get the kid to a safe spot, Allio thought. Grab the kid and move fast—a couple, three miles at most—to a place where nobody's going to interrupt him. Once there, he can do whatever it is he has in mind. He doesn't have to worry about getting caught. Any search activity would be taking place in the child's own neighborhood.

Allio drove in ever-widening concentric circles around the city. A devout Christian, the cop prayed as he drove.

Where would an abductor go? Mankas Corner was a straight shot out Waterman to Mankas Boulevard—three miles—a matter of minutes. Allio ended up out there and continued past the country store onto Gordon Valley Road. It is a rural area of farms, peach orchards, and, especially as you approach the Napa County line, vineyards. The fields and the trees were barren with the withered look of winter.

Now Allio was on the phone. "Bindner's out here," he said.

He saw a man walking ahead of him on the side of the road—a slightly built man wearing a blue baseball cap, a dark-colored sweatshirt, and jeans. The young detective had seen the surveillance photographs and knew he was looking at Timothy Bindner. He was out of radio range, so he stopped at a house and called Sagan.

Sagan interrupted Chuck Timm. "Joe Allio's out on Gordon Valley Road. Tim Bindner's wandering around out there."

The two cops agreed that what they wanted was a loose surveillance. Timm briefed Lieutenant Tigert and Barry Hom as they headed down the hall toward the sally port. Sagan caught up with them after putting in a call to the California Highway Patrol.

"CHP has a helicopter on its way," Sagan told Timm as he got into the car. "They'll stay at about three thousand feet, let us know where he is."

The detectives used alternate radio frequencies. The media people were monitoring scanners and would know that anything that pulled the investigative team out that fast had to relate to the Nikki Campbell case. Once they were in position to observe Bindner, Sagan watched as he stopped his car, spent a minute or two at a location, then got back in his car and

moved on. He stopped again, stood by the side of the
road, crossed the road, retraced his steps, and drove
on—all at a leisurely pace.

Sagan did not view Bindner's behavior as that of
someone seriously searching for a missing child. "He's
out here playing," Sagan said to Timm. "If he isn't out
here to see if he can get a tail and have fun with the
cops, then he's on some fantasy trip. This guy's got to
be operating in several different worlds at once."

Bindner drove north into Napa County, then reversed direction and covered the same ground without
stopping. On the climb out of the valley, back toward
the city, he didn't stop at all, didn't pause and reflect.
He got in his car and headed nonstop toward Nikki
Campbell's neighborhood.

"No brake lights," Sagan said. "This guy knows the
area. He isn't looking for street signs, isn't slowing
down. He knows where he's going. No hesitation. He's
been here before."

Sagan figured Bindner could have been there
many times before. From May—when Bindner had
started writing the letters to Sheila Cosgrove—until
January, he could have made as many trips to Fairfield
as he wanted.

When Bindner turned the corner onto Salisbury,
Timm slapped his "Kojak" light on the roof of the
unmarked car and waved Bindner over to the side of
the road.

Sagan approached from the back of the lime-
green Toyota. "Put your hands where I can see them,"
he said.

Bindner put his hands out through the open
window.

Sagan walked up to the driver's side of the station
wagon and looked down at the man who had haunted
his investigation from its earliest moments. "You've
been avoiding me, buddy."

Bindner didn't say anything. He slowly turned his
head and looked back at the cop.

"Nice to finally meet you," Sagan said. "I called

you a couple of times. Wanted to talk to you about Sheila Cosgrove."

"I don't really want to talk about that," Bindner said.

"What were you doing out there?" Sagan asked.

"I'm looking for Nikki Campbell."

Sagan noticed a news photographer from the *Fairfield Daily Republic* approach. He suggested that Bindner drive a few blocks out Norwalk so they could continue talking with more privacy. Bindner complied, then got out of his car.

Sagan told Bindner that he was not under arrest. "I want to talk to you about what you were doing in Gordon Valley, and any information you might have about Nikki Campbell."

"I was out there looking for a missing child," Bindner said. "I've searched for other missing kids, especially Amber Swartz."

He showed Sagan the search log he was keeping and the Fairfield street map he was using. Bindner explained the log—that he recorded his odometer readings along with reference points, such as bridge numbers, and a probability rating. "I'd be glad to send you a copy of it," Bindner said.

Sagan looked at Bindner's muddy boots and dirty clothing. Through the man's body odor, the cop smelled alcohol on Bindner's breath. But Bindner didn't seem to be impaired—his speech wasn't slurred, and he seemed able to coordinate his body movements. Sagan glanced in the back of the station wagon and saw a shovel, as well as a black, five-gallon bucket and a collection of weathered beer and soda cans.

"I don't think a child would be buried right in her own neighborhood," Bindner said. "A three-mile radius is more likely. Mankas Corner and Gordon Valley are about three miles out."

That was exactly what Joe Allio had been thinking earlier that morning. Both men—Allio and Bindner—were assuming that the child was dead.

"I came in here to get some flyers to take back to Oakland," Bindner said.

Sagan couldn't hold Bindner. The man hadn't done anything wrong. "You can get those at the police department," Sagan said, and he told Bindner how to find 1000 Webster Street.

> *The day was over, man. I was ready to go home. All I wanted to do was pick up some flyers.*
>
> *Harry came up to the side of the car, flashed his badge, told me he was a police officer, told me to keep my hands in plain view so I stuck my hands out the window.*
>
> *He said he wanted me to come down to the police station to talk to him. I said, "I don't really feel comfortable with that." But see, the way they got me to come down to the police station is the same reason I was in the neighborhood. I wanted to get some flyers to pass out.*
>
> *So I went down to the police department, and that's where they ambushed me for the interview. I'm escorted into a police department by about fifteen cops. You're not under arrest, right? You haven't been charged with a crime. But there's about fifteen cops there, and they're all walking around you, surrounding you.*
>
> *What I should've realized at that particular time, before I went through the door of the police department, is, I can make a U-turn here. I can get back in my car and I can drive home. But when you want to cooperate, you want to help—when your heart's full of love and you're just trying to be nice—you don't feel that way. And they take advantage of you. So I walked into the police department, and I spent about four and a half hours there.*

Fairfield officers followed Bindner back to the station, and this time he drove like someone following directions and working from a map—someone unfamiliar with the city. He looked at street signs, made a wrong turn, but eventually ended up at the rear entrance to the department.

A uniformed officer waved him into the police parking lot. With an accompanying group of officers, Bindner entered the building through the sally port. Sagan was right behind him. The detective wanted to question Bindner, and Bindner agreed to talk.

They walked into Lieutenant Tigert's administrative office at 4:30 P.M. Sergeant Timm explained to Binder that he was free to leave at any time.

Sagan and Bindner sat in easy chairs in the office. "You're not obligated to answer any of my questions," Sagan said, "but I'm interested in what you might have to say about the kind of people who abduct kids. How do you think a serial killer abducts a child?"

"He knows the area," Bindner said. "He scouts around, has an escape route planned, and a preselected area where he intends to take his victim. Maybe he parks off the road in some place where he won't be conspicuous, sexually molests the child, and most likely strangles her. It's all over in an hour or two. That minimizes his chance of getting caught."

Sagan watched the man. He seemed so detached, so unemotional, calm and laid back, but with a quiet cockiness. "How would he get a small child into his vehicle?" Sagan asked.

"He doesn't drive right up to her," Bindner said. "Kids are somewhat suspicious. They're taught not to get into vehicles with strangers. But the abductor may have seen the child, parked a short distance away, and walked up to her. Maybe he complimented her on her bicycle. Got her talking about herself or her family. Maybe he told her he had lost his kitten or his puppy and asked her to help him search. Maybe he even had a picture of his pet."

It is a basic child lure, one that can be found in any of the literature on preventing child abductions. The man approaches the child. He seems like a decent guy. He's lost his kitten or his puppy. He needs help. The animal needs help—especially on such a damp, chilly evening. The child is gullible, trusting, and wanting to help.

"It makes a difference how the guy is dressed," Bindner said. "The way I'm dressed wouldn't convey authority or command respect the way a shirt and tie would."

"What if she started struggling or screaming?" Sagan asked.

"Maybe the guy would threaten to hit her. That would quiet her. Or he could put duct tape over her mouth."

"Where might a guy like this take his victim?"

"It would be a place he picked out ahead of time," Bindner said again. "A place like where I was searching. Just zip up the freeway looking for open country, and go there. He assaults her somewhere off the road—maybe in his vehicle. Then he buries her in a ravine, maybe only a foot deep, but some distance off the road. He might mark the area. I'd probably use three rocks in a row, or in a triangle. Or maybe he'd bury her near a bridge, so he could find the place again."

Bindner had marked bridge numbers on the sheets of his search log.

"In the Angela Bugay case," Bindner said, "she was found about twenty feet off the road, but a piece of her clothing was sticking out of the dirt. That's what led to her discovery. Whoever took Angela had to know the neighborhood and the apartment complex. When I went out there to look around, I got lost."

What was transpiring between the two men was casual and tense at the same time. Sagan would later describe it as two dogs of equal size and strength circling one another, each looking for some advantage, neither finding it. It was a game, and it was real.

Sitting there in his Oakland Housing Authority baseball cap, brown pants, black tennis shoes, purple sweatshirt, and 1988 Oakland A's World Series T-shirt, Tim Bindner said he knew he fit the profile of a serial killer. It was the same thing he had told Mary Ellen

O'Toole. He had read the literature on child abduction, serial killers, and homicide investigations. He had also obtained materials from the Kevin Collins Foundation on how to protect your children from being abducted.

The two men talked about the possible linkage among the cases. Angela and Amber had similarities, and Nikki seemed to share some of those. "It's certainly a possibility," Bindner said. "It crossed my mind before I even came up here."

"Why do you think there's such a time lapse between the Bugay homicide, the Swartz abduction, and Nikki?" Sagan asked.

"Maybe the guy has a conscience," Bindner suggested. "Maybe he's remorseful. Maybe he's afraid of being caught."

Bindner thought that the Michaela Garecht abduction had been a different perpetrator. "That guy took unnecessary chances. He took her from outside a store. There were witnesses. People saw his face and were able to describe his vehicle. The guy who did Angela, Amber, and Nikki wouldn't take chances like that."

In the three cases Bindner considered as possibly linked, the kids were close in age and they looked somewhat alike. They had disappeared from neighborhoods that offered quick access to highways, and no one had been supervising them.

"The person who grabbed Michaela was bold, but he was a disorganized type of offender," Bindner said, alluding to one of the FBI categories for serial killers. "Whoever took the other three kids was much more careful. I'm inclined to think that the same person took all three. But with Michaela, it seems impulsive. With the others, it seems planned."

Bindner told Sagan about his having been investigated in the Amber case because he went to see the family, offered to help, and walked the roadsides with a shovel looking for a grave site.

The man's cockiness—he was speaking on a subject he knew well, and he had a rapt audience—

seemed punctuated with nervousness. At times he avoided looking at Sagan and gazed at the backs of his hands, hesitating before he answered a question.

"It could also have been a Satanic thing," Bindner said. "I worked as a groundskeeper in a cemetery once. I found upside-down crosses and the heads of roosters at graves."

As the two men talked inside, Joe Allio called Steve Andrews at Contra Costa Search and Rescue and requested bloodhound assistance. The Fairfield detectives wanted the parking lot, with Bindner's car in it, checked for Nikki Campbell's scent.

"Why a four- or five-year-old?" Sagan asked.

"It's more likely that kids that age would be out playing in the street," Bindner said. "And they're easier to get."

"What about the timing?"

"Late afternoon is the best time of day. It's after school, and there are more kids that age outside playing. It's getting dark then, too, which makes it less likely he'll be seen. Most of the time the kid's just in the wrong place at the wrong time. By the time parents realize the child is missing, they don't know the kid was snatched, and they don't want to believe that. They go searching in the neighborhood. They don't know where the kid could've gone."

Bindner returned to his speculation about the abductor. It was sexual, he told Sagan, an urge, an impulse the guy can't control. "A guy like this doesn't commit a crime like this once," Bindner said. "It's part of him. He's triggered by his attraction to children, his sexual lusts. A person like this would have to be void of any feelings. Some guys enjoy the sexual fantasies, and some get a thrill out of killing children."

He speculated that it might have upset the man who took Angela when searchers found her body. "If it's the same guy who took Amber, maybe he went farther out. By that reasoning, too, the place I was searching for Nikki makes sense."

Bindner told Sagan that all of his interest in the

cases had originated with Angela Bugay, with the impact that case had had on him. He often visited her grave, and had even been there a few times after the cemetery closed. He said he liked to go to cemeteries at night, especially St. Mary's in Oakland. "It doesn't bother me like it does other people. I used to work in a cemetery, and I've been interested in them for about ten years."

Sagan asked him when he'd first heard about Nikki. Bindner thought it was on Sunday, December 29, when he read the *Oakland Tribune*, and when he saw it on TV.

"Have you been in Fairfield before today?" Sagan asked, thinking of Bindner's ease in driving from Mankas Corner to Nikki Campbell's neighborhood.

"This is my first time here," Bindner said. "I've never been in Fairfield before."

Sagan also wanted to know about the letters to Sheila Cosgrove. "I meet lots of kids all the time," Bindner said. "I'm friendly with kids. I get their names and addresses and write to them. I don't see anything wrong with that."

"Some people get upset," Sagan said. "They get angry like the Cosgroves did."

Bindner said he hadn't realized the extent of people's anger at him simply because he was so friendly with children. "I wrote the letters to Sheila," he said. "I met her at an Oakland A's game and saw her name and address on a camera case. I was reading Lewis Carroll's *Through the Looking Glass* when I was writing to her. I saw the mirror writing and figured I could use it when I was writing to my pen pals. So I wrote the letters to Sheila that way."

> *He went out for a while and came back with the book. I believe it was* Through the Looking Glass. *He wanted to know something about one of the letters I'd written to Sheila, something about the indications on the back of the envelope or something. And he wanted to know about the book. I don't remember what it was.*

It may have pertained to the mirror letters, letters writ-
ten backwards. You had to hold them up to a mirror.
'Cause I had written one of those to the girl. But I'm
not sure what he asked me about it. He did bring it in
and ask me a couple of questions about it. I think he
was trying to fish for whatever the significance of it
was. I remember saying something about, it didn't
really have a significance. It wasn't important to any-
thing. It was just a book I happened to be reading at
the time. Which was true. . . .

He showed me one of the letters and showed me a
notation I'd made on the outside of the envelope. He
asked me what I meant, and I told him I didn't remem-
ber. I'd have to see the letter. I'd have to read the letter
to tell you what it meant. Which wasn't true, but I told
him that anyway, 'cause I didn't want to tell him what
the notations meant.

It was close to 8:00 P.M. when Dale Myer and Friday went to work in the parking lot. Again the scent article was Nikki Campbell's Christmas dress. Friday
moved along the line of more than twenty parked cars,
circled and examined Bindner's Toyota, then went
downwind to the farthest point in the lot, near the wall
and the Dumpster. The dog turned back upwind into
the light breeze, pulling Myer to Bindner's car. This
time he was all over it, sniffing along the bottom of the
passenger door, then finally rearing up against the
back of the car and running his nose along the window
gasket. According to Myer it was an unequivocal hit.
Nikki Campbell's scent was in the lime-green station
wagon.

Chuck Timm called Sagan out of his meeting with
Bindner and told him Nikki's scent was in Bindner's
station wagon.

When Sagan returned to Tigert's office, he told
Bindner about the bloodhound's behavior. The Oakland man's face reddened. He had been sitting back in
his chair. Now he leaned forward. He looked frightened. "I was picking up cans out there while I was

searching for her," he said. "That's probably how her scent could have gotten in my car."

He came back and said the dogs smelled this girl's scent on your—I mean, he was excited. He thought he had just solved the world's biggest crime. I could see it in his face. The man thought he had it all together. Before that I thought, this is just another one of those interrogations. I've gone through this before with the FBI with Amber. I can get through it. But when he came out of the parking lot and back into the police station, he was almost gleeful, like, "I got you now."

He said, "I've got some bad news for you. We brought in some dogs and they smelled Nikki Campbell's scent on your car." . . .

The dogs were kind of a new one on me. I was feeling scared that this is getting crazy. At that point I'd been through it all before. At the time he mentioned the dogs sniffing the girl's scent, I didn't know what that meant. I thought that was actual evidence. I began to wonder at that point, "Am I going home tonight, or am I going to be arrested?" So I was starting to feel afraid. Fear and anger.

Here I am being harassed again, and now they're saying this dog smelled this girl's scent. I was afraid I was going to be arrested based on that allegation of his, but I was mad at him too. I kind of lost my cool a little bit. I was mad, and I was upset. I said something about, "I hope they didn't smell her on one of the cans I picked up out in the valley," or something like that. 'Cause I had been picking up recyclables while I was out there. Cans—I think some bottles, too. I did the same thing with Amber.

That was the only possible thing in my mind, the only way these dogs could've detected the girl's scent in my car is if they got it off one of those cans and she had handled it. That's the only way that child's scent could be in my car.

"We have other evidence that points in your direction," Sagan told him. "I know the facts of the case.

I'm putting this together, and all I have to do is get twelve people to agree with me."

"I would never hurt a child," Bindner said. "I didn't abduct or hurt Nikki Campbell. I was only looking for her. I love children."

The detective never said "You did it." His tone remained conversational. There wasn't any heated confrontation, but there was an unmistakable tension between the two men.

Sagan asked Bindner if he would take a polygraph in the Nikki case. Bindner refused.

"I know you took a polygraph in the Amber case," Sagan said. "And I know it indicated deception. You failed it."

––––––––––––

When Tim Bindner thought about it later, it was another example of cops looking for something that wasn't there. He wanted to help, and that's why he was there. He had searched on Gordon Valley Road and through Mankas Corner. He'd hiked a streambed where someone had cut away berry vines and poison oak. He'd found a soccer ball and a volleyball and tossed them into his car. He'd prowled around on Suisun Valley Road. He had been trying to help find a missing child. That was it, and that was all.

> The night Nikki Campbell disappeared, I was working the grave shift after my day off. I had Thursday off. I believe I did work Christmas.
>
> I don't really know how I heard about it. I remember that me and Sandra got into an immediate argument. I said, "I'm gonna go look for that girl." She said, "No, you're not going up there."
>
> I think it came down to the point where I said to myself, if I'm gonna save this child's life, I have to do this today. And that was January 7. . . .
>
> With Nikki, it was like I was afraid to go up there. I

was afraid. They were gonna bludgeon me, man. I knew they were. My wife knew and I knew they were gonna bludgeon me some way. . . .

I told my wife. I said, "Hey, I'm going up to Fairfield. I'm gonna do a one-day search. All I'm gonna do is go out and along the roads, see if I can find anything. I will be back. I will probably not find anything." . . .

It was kind of a dreadful feeling. Oh, no. Here's another one. It might be the same guy. I had that feeling immediately with Nikki just like I did with Amber— that it might be the same guy that took Angela. A sinking feeling. It might be the same guy, and he's got another one. . . .

I wanted in. I wanted to be part of it, part of the search, part of the effort. With Nikki, I wanted to try to find a way into that effort to find her. . . .

Harold Sagan stopped me that day because he thought I killed Nikki Campbell. Because I was writing letters to that little girl.

I knew that's what the connection was. I had been avoiding him. I didn't want to talk to him. I had no reason to talk to the man.

The whole thing is Twilight Zone. *I can't believe it. Look at that Christmas card.*

Fairfield officers photographed and fingerprinted Bindner and impounded his car. Again, the eccentric man from Oakland became the prime suspect in a child's disappearance.

If I had abducted Amanda Campbell—first of all, I have a conscience. I have a sense of guilt for things I do wrong. If I had abducted Amanda Campbell, I would've went crying to the police as soon as I was confronted. I would've told them exactly what I did. I'd be doing life without parole, or I'd be in a death penalty trial right now. That's number one. If I had done it, I would've told them about it. Same thing with Amber.

Number two. They do not have any evidence whatsoever that implicates me in any of these crimes that they've been investigating me for since Amber disappeared in 1988. None whatsoever. They have speculations. They have theories. They have ideas. They should keep the speculations and the theories and the ideas to themselves. Put 'em in the files. Work on 'em. See if you could come up with something. See if you could produce some evidence.

They're not ever gonna produce any evidence against me because I did not take any of these children. That's where Harry Sagan made his mistake.

Much later, when looking back on the early days of the investigation, Harold Sagan would acknowledge that he and his team *had* made mistakes. Sagan incorporated those mistakes into a curriculum and protocol he designed to educate officers from other departments in managing child abduction cases.

And there were bits and pieces of information from those first few months that Sagan concedes are debatable. But there was no debating the circumstantial case that was building around Tim Bindner.

16

The morning's *Daily Republic* carried a photograph of Sagan talking to Bindner after the stop on Salisbury Drive. Barry Hom stood in the background. Another photograph showed Bindner's station wagon in the police department parking lot, complete with license plate.

POLICE QUESTION MYSTERY MAN. The article detailed the surveillance—the CHP helicopter, Mankas Corner and Gordon Valley Road—but didn't name the man police had questioned for hours. Although the local news reporters knew who Bindner was, Sagan persuaded them not to identify him. But Ian Thompson's news story did mark the beginning of the Oakland man's notoriety in the East Bay child cases. Who was he? What was he doing in Fairfield?

Harold Sagan wondered the same thing. What on earth was this guy doing? They had circumstantial evidence pointing in his direction. Law enforcement agencies all over the Bay Area had an interest in him. Bindner knew this. He knew Fairfield had worked a case on his letters to Sheila Cosgrove. He hadn't returned Sagan's calls, but he had written to Sheila again after Nikki's disappearance. He'd even called the hot line set up to take tips after Nikki's disappearance.

Finally, he drove into town and made a show of looking for the kid. How many times had he done that since December 27 without attracting any attention? When FBI agents and Fairfield officers went through the neighborhood the previous Friday, January 3, they showed residents an automobile photo lineup—four vehicles, one of them Bindner's Corolla wagon. They had gotten some hits, but Sagan questioned their reliability. One was from an eleven-year-old who thought she might have seen the car a couple of weeks before, near her school. It was greenish or yellowish—had one white male sitting in it. Maybe it was the car, maybe it wasn't.

Bindner had sat in an office in the police department and talked about abduction and murder, organized and disorganized offenders. He sounded like a graduate of the FBI Academy, but he kept pointing the finger at himself.

Had he designed it this way to make himself look like *less* of a suspect? Bindner wasn't stupid. Whatever else he might be, the man was smart. He knew that he would attract attention. Sagan wondered if the whole performance were a charade, an elaborate taunt.

———————

On January 8, Barry Hom obtained a warrant allowing the search of Bindner's car. Sagan expected the search to be an exercise in futility. He had seen the vehicle on New Year's morning, when it was spotless.

During the search, on January 9, the investigators found no trace evidence they could link to Nikki Campbell. They removed three unopened McDonald's

straws, some napkins, a wrapper from a straw, two
barrettes (one blue, one pink), a twelve-ounce can of
Old Milwaukee beer, a sixteen-ounce can of Magnum
malt liquor, two pamphlets about an organization for
gravestone studies, Bindner's metal probe, his map of
Fairfield, and the folder labeled "Search Chronology
and Assessment."

Sagan examined the folder containing the search
log and the map of the city. Bindner's chronology included columns for time, miles, notes and findings,
probability, and visibility. The first thing the detective
noticed was that Bindner hadn't recorded anything in
the time column. On a similar set of sheets the investigators had removed from his car—regarding a 1990
search he had conducted after a young woman disappeared while jogging south of Oakland—the meticulous Bindner had filled in the times to the minute.

Also, the mileage was off. On the 1990 documents,
Bindner had included the last three digits of his odometer reading, a decimal point, and a fourth number representing tenths of a mile. The January 7 search log
had three digits. The distance from the intersection of
Larchmont and Oliver to Mankas Corner was either 11
miles, or, if Bindner had inadvertently omitted the
decimal, 1.1 miles. The actual distance was about 2
miles.

According to Bindner's notes, the distance from
Mankas Corner to the bridge over Ledgewood Creek
was either 14 miles or 1.4 miles. The creek was less
than one thousand feet from the corner.

Sagan dismissed the search log as another of
Bindner's props, but the detective had to wonder why
the man would engage in such a convoluted ruse. He
couldn't make any sense out of it.

———————

After completing their work at the Fairfield police department the night before, Dale Myer loaded Friday into

his Jeep and drove out through Mankas Corner and up
onto Gordon Valley Road. Fairfield detectives wanted to
know where, off-road, Bindner might have wandered
before they had him under surveillance. Myer scented
the bloodhound with Bindner's Oakland A's T-shirt, and
the dog picked up the suspect's freshest scent, the "car
trail" back toward town. Friday ran Myer a mile and a
half down the road before the handler called it quits.

On the afternoon of the eighth, police were back
out in the rural area searching for any signs of Bindner's movements. Officer Christine Golez worked Suisun Valley Road back from I-80 toward Mankas
Corner. When she reached the Suisun Valley Elementary School, she walked along the south side of the
building. As she approached the back of the school,
she passed two small storage buildings. By a tree at the
foot of a hill she saw three large rocks stacked in a
pile. When Sagan looked at the rocks, he realized it
was exactly what Bindner had told him about marking
a location with three rocks.

Investigators photographed the marker and completed a cursory search of the area but dismissed the
rocks as another of Bindner's possible taunts. If they
had any significance at all, Sagan reasoned, it was as a
reference point for some other location. But where?
Thousands of acres of fields, orchards, vineyards, hills,
and forest surrounded the school.

The next afternoon, Harold Sagan received a letter
from Tim Bindner postmarked January 8, the day after
their meeting.

Dear Mr. Sagan
    My anguish is not in that you would lie to
me about dogs "hitting" on my car, or people
identifying it from a book of photos, because I
know that lying to suspects is an "accepted" technique (I also know it causes innocent people to
confess—I firmly believe Bradley Page did not
kill Bibi Lee—and innocent people to spend

years in jail—Shawn Melton spent nearly 2 years behind bars during the long process that—finally—resulted in dropped charges.)

Nor is my anguish and anger in that you stole my car, a nice little cheap reliable hummer, to support your lie about the dogs (my wife says you rubbed Amanda's clothing on the car first, then actually let the dogs "sniff" it out. I think you just lied about the whole thing and had no qualms about taking the car illegally.)

No, my anguish is this, that I must now go to Angela's grave and cry for her again and tell her that I can no longer keep the solemn promise I made to her—to do anything in my power to find out who killed her, see that he is punished, and that he cannot prowl for more.

My anguish is that I must now agree with my wife, that suspicion begets vindictive, punitive actions and that it can easily tear our family and our marriage apart. Her familiar refrain, "You should have learned the last time" (Amber, which caused me to lose my job and much of my faith in human dignity)—now rings true.

I still believe that my approach is valid and that it can—and should—be used in efforts to find missing children. How many people get out and really pound the brush like I do? Too few, I know that!

So I'll cry again in anguish for Angela and tell her that it's over, that my efforts for her are finished, that I did my best as I promised I would, but that I must maintain a wife and a life and a family. And that, the next time a kid disappears, I'll have to sit home, looking at the maps, twitching, wanting to be out there searching, but knowing that I can't.

And this is a genuine, painful anguish, because I love them all. Do you?

                                                    Tim

There were biblical citations at the end of the letter—Proverbs and 1 John. People who live by violence consume themselves, and those who live in darkness will face the day of judgment.

Sagan read the letter a second time. He studied it. The Bible he had brought into his office during the Cosgrove investigation was becoming a standard reference.

Bindner seemed to have a way of interpreting the world that was slightly off-center. He seemed to have created a construct in his mind by which the cops—in this case, Harold Sagan—in their pursuit and interrogation of a suspect, became responsible for the cases never being solved. The cops had removed Bindner from Mankas Corner, causing him to violate the pledge he had made to Angela Bugay.

Sagan didn't know much about the Pinole case, but he did know that the Social Security Administration had fired Bindner for violating the agency's policies and procedures. They caught him because of the attention he attracted in that case, but Bindner had given the situation a martyrlike spin. According to Bindner, the SSA had fired him because he went searching for a missing child.

Bindner was a game player who moved swiftly and well. Sagan wondered if he was getting in over his head.

That night, *America's Most Wanted* ran a segment on the Nikki Campbell case. Calls continued to pour in to the Fairfield Department of Public Safety.

———————

At 8:30 A.M. on January 11, Sagan and his team took Bindner's T-shirt with them and met Dale Myer and the other search and rescue team's dog handlers at Oakmont Cemetery. They had determined that Nikki Campbell's scent was in the cemetery. Now Sagan wanted to know about Bindner's scent.

They met in the main parking lot, directly below the mausoleum, not far from the maintenance shed. When Jesse Green arrived, representing Oakmont's management, he walked through the lot and picked up an empty Jolt soda can next to the back door of the administration building. "This wasn't here last night when I closed," he said. "I was the last one to leave."

Littering perturbed him. Oakmont takes great pride in its pristine appearance.

The group started up the road and found another Jolt can near the children's section. Again, the director picked it up.

When Myer scented Friday with Bindner's World Series T-shirt, the big dog went immediately to the curb where the Jolt can had been. Then he walked around the outside edge of the children's section before taking off down the main road to the maintenance yard. He appeared to have picked up Bindner's scent. There was another Jolt can in the middle of the road. This one was half full.

Friday made a loop through the cemetery and came back to the children's section, then down to the mausoleum. He found another Jolt can. The dog was running a strong trail, linking the soda cans as he went. According to the dog's behavior, Bindner's scent was in the cemetery and it was on the cans. Myer wondered if the man had spent the night walking around drinking sodas, then leaving the cans prominently displayed, thinking to himself, "I'm going to place these out here in case they try something."

He couldn't have known they were coming out to Oakmont that morning, but the message seemed clear: "Here's to your bloodhound, buddy."

In analyzing the dog's movements, the handlers agreed that whoever had carried the Jolt cans came into the cemetery through the main gate, walked up the hill behind the mausoleum, then walked around the cemetery and ended up at the administration building.

That Bindner's scent was in the cemetery wasn't

worth much. It was no secret that he spent a great deal
of time in cemeteries, especially Oakmont.

There was another aspect to all they were discov-
ering that was beginning to bother Harold Sagan.
Rather than avoiding an investigation, letting the cops
flounder around looking for evidence, this suspect
jumped right into the middle of it. It was the kind of
move that can corrupt and misdirect an investigation.
The Fairfield detective thought that was probably what
had happened in the Amber Swartz case in 1988. The
guy ran around that valley for months, with a tail on
him most of the time. Was he playing games with
them, leading them away from the child's body? He
talked to them. Superficially, at least, it looked as if he
was cooperating in the investigation. "Could this behavior be part of his high," Sagan thought, "a continua-
tion of the excitement of the murder itself, the rush
that would occupy him until he took another child?"

Of course they would check for his scent at Oakmont. Bindner would know that. But his timing was
eerie.

When Sagan got back to his office, there was another letter from Tim Bindner waiting for him.

Dear Mr. Sagan,
      I believe it's the right of the public to cri-
tique the performance of their employees, (since
we pay their salaries), and I've found yours to be
rather abysmal (your performance, that is! I
don't know your salary).
      While *I* take these matters to be of the utmost
seriousness, since the lives of precious children
are at stake, *you* referred to your investigation as
a "game" and yourself as a "varsity player." In our
interview you engaged in the use of unsolicited
and unprovoked profanity, including the use of
the word "fuck" more than once. (Police officers
should be trained never to use profanity, because
of the violence it can provoke, and the disrespect
it shows. Should we not treat *all* persons with

Fairfield detective Harold Sagan.

The revised composite of the main suspect in the Michaela Garecht witnessed abduction.

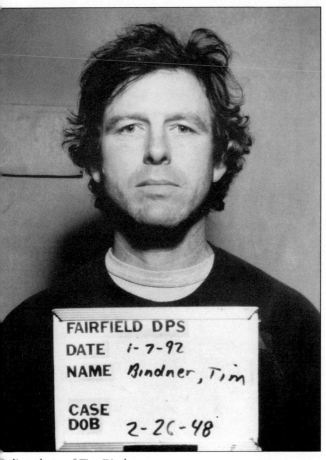

Police photo of Tim Bindner.

Fairfield Police parking lot, where Friday the bloodhound detected the scent of Nikki Campbell on Tim Bindner's Corolla wagon, photographed here by a surveillance team.

Detective Sergeant Chuck Timm, who appointed Harold Sagan as lead investigator in the Nikki Campbell abduction.

Fairfield detective Barry Hom.

PLEASE POST

MISSING

REWARD OFFERED

AMANDA NICOLE EILEEN CAMPBELL
NICKNAME "NIKKI"

DESCRIPTION

White, Female 4 years old, Now 5 years old   D.O.B. 5/7/87
Height: 3 ft. 6 in.   Hair: Blonde
Weight: 55 lbs.   Eyes: Blue

Two Distinct Dimples

Amanda was last seen at 4:30 pm on December 27, 1991. She was wearing
a pink jacket, sleeves too short for her, purple short sleeve top, purple
pants, and white tennis shoes. She develops rash around her mouth. Her
bicycle was found on Norwalk Place near Salisbury Drive, Fairfield, CA.

911 or Fairfield, CA Dept. of Public Safety
HOTLINE 1-707-428-7364

FAIRFIELD, CA POLICE DEPT. CASE NO. 91-18474

AMBER Foundation for Missing Children   P.O. Box 565   Pinole, California 94564-0565

TOLL FREE: 1-800-541-0777   FAX 1-(510) 758-0319

NATIONAL CENTER: 1-800-843-5678 Case No. NCIC M-536133336

The missing-person flyer distributed after Nikki Campbell was
abducted.

View of Nikki Campbell's and Sheila Cosgrove's neighborhood from the Kolob Hills. Friday the bloodhound tracked Tim Bindner's scent all over these hills. Police believed Bindner could have been watching the house of Sheila Cosgrove, to whom he was writing letters, when Nikki Campbell disappeared.

The intersection where Nikki Campbell was abducted.

Tim Bindner's "LOV YOU" van.

Tim Bindner sitting on Angela Bugay's grave.

respect, no matter who they are, or what they've done? You also said you "know" that I "snatched" Nikki, even though there is not a shred of evidence to that effect, and never will be. You also accused me of thinking that you are stupid, while treating me as if I am (when I made the simplistic observation that a well-dressed man might more easily take a child because he'd command more respect as an authority figure, you insulted me with the ludicrous statement to your partner, "Gee, I've never thought of that. Have you?")

Since your performance exacerbates my own anguish, and since it is consistent with the performances of scores of other officers and investigators I have encountered, I have made the decision never again to make any statement or conduct any interview with any law enforcement person. With one exception.

I intend to cooperate fully with any investigation. I have in the past, and I have in this case. However, from now on any questioning or "investigative interviewing" of me must be conducted by special agent Mary Ellen O'Toole of the FBI. She's the only one who has never used profanity, never treated me with open disrespect or acted as if I'm stupid, never referred to her investigation as a "game," and never said that she "knows" I did something.

If she contacts me, I'll talk. But this should not at all increase her workload, because I've done nothing wrong and never will.

Sincerely,
Timothy J Bindner

P.S. Please find it within your heart (?) to reassure the family of Sheila that there will be no further contact—I promise. My contact with her was a little "give-away" fantasy, done whimsically and meant only to convey a sense of happy mystery. It is consistent with my past behaviors—

(Reference—National Enquirer, March 11, 1986, page 2)

Sagan went looking for Barry Hom and Mel Ferro. He didn't remember using any profanity. If anything, it had been a stilted interview, almost too polite and formal. The other detectives confirmed that Sagan had been civil. They didn't remember any profanity either.

Bindner was bright, had a sharp sense of humor, and seemed to be continuing a cat-and-mouse game with law enforcement that was hitting Sagan blind. Had he done this with O'Toole? What about Pollard in Pinole, and Ken Gross down in Hayward? Sagan knew that Bindner had written to the Antioch police department.

It was a challenge, Sagan thought. Although Bindner protested his innocence, he also emphasized the absence of evidence of his guilt. Unless the detective could prove that he had done something, he had done nothing.

Sagan wrote back to Bindner, and he began reading. He dug up every book he could get his hands on that dealt with the characteristics of psychopaths, how the minds of murderers work, why pedophiles fixate on children, and the nature of the narcissistic personality. He started with what Bindner referred to as "Ressler's book"—*Sexual Homicide: Patterns and Motives*, by Robert K. Ressler, Ann W. Burgess, and John E. Douglas.

Published in 1988, *Sexual Homicide* is the authoritative basic text on criminal profiling. Ressler and Douglas both were FBI legends, pioneers in the art of deducing offender characteristics from what they could glean at a crime scene. The distinction between organized and disorganized offenders originated with them and was as common to viewers of tabloid TV as it was to students of investigation.

While telling Sagan about the book, Bindner admitted that he fit the characteristics of the organized offender—with the exception of having a car that was in good running condition. When Sagan read the book, he had to agree. He didn't know about Bindner's car, but the rest of it certainly sounded like Tim Bindner. Intelligent. High birth order (Bindner was the second oldest of five). Lived with partner. Use of alcohol.

The list also included "controlled mood during crime." Sagan couldn't know about that one, but if Bindner's demeanor during their meeting was any indication, the guy remained cool under pressure. The characteristics were generic, but they fit.

There was still too much Sagan didn't know about Timothy Bindner. Basic investigative techniques—talking with people who knew the man, contacting other agencies that had dealt with him—would fill in some of the blanks. But there was more, something unique but intangible, about the diminutive, wiry man from Oakland.

Sagan had wanted to dictate the terms of his first encounter with Bindner, but Bindner had wrested any advantage out of the cop's hands. The idea of a quick resolution—rule him in or rule him out—had evaporated. Sagan knew the case was going to be long and complicated, but he was in it for the duration.

In January 1992, he had no idea just how long that would be.

FOUR

INVESTIGATION—
THE SUSPECT

17

Tim Bindner dug his fingers into the cracks of a granite ledge forty feet above the ground. He was slipping. He was sure that he was going to fall and plummet to his death on the rocks below.

He lost one hand grip. Then a foot slipped away.

He was just a kid—a teenager fooling around, climbing the rocks and ledges in the San Bernardino Mountains, just as he had dozens of times before. This time he had been inching his way up Pink Falls, called that because of the crags of pink granite that thousands of years of heavy rains had carved out of the canyons.

He shifted his weight, slipped his fingers into another handhold, then found a narrow crevice and secured his foot. He rested, confident now that he would be able to escape across the rock face. He survived, but it wouldn't be his last brush with death.

Timothy James Bindner was born on February 26, 1948, in Hammond, Indiana. His father was a career army man, a lieutenant colonel with twenty years of service who spent much of his time in the Signal Corps, where he was one of the pioneers in radio communications. The family lived in Alaska in the late '50s while Bindner's father worked on the Distant Early Warning (DEW) line.

Tim Bindner still remembers the vast wilderness that was Alaska—the herds of elk and caribou, the endless mountains, the miles of tundra. He also remembers boxing lessons at the military base.

He was eight or nine, and his father wanted him and his brother to learn how to box. Bindner tolerated one lesson. Another kid stung him on the nose with jabs a couple of times, and Bindner told his father, "I'm not coming back. I don't want any part of this."

Bindner says the experience marked the beginning of his distaste for violence of any kind.

Bindner, his three brothers, and his sister did most of their growing up in San Bernardino, California, east of Los Angeles. The family home sits near the San Andreas fault. He remembers a few earthquakes when he was a kid, but no big ones.

Bindner's mother was an army nurse during World War II. She worked on DC-3 flights ferrying wounded soldiers from the European theater back to the United States. She served for six years.

In San Bernardino, she managed the home and the five children. In the early years, her husband was often away—the Korean War, then a stint in Puerto Rico. Later, he preferred to work on his radios out in the garage. She provided the structure and the discipline for the kids.

When he talks about his childhood, Bindner often portrays himself as a victim. When he was in the sixth grade, a couple of kids used to chase him home from school and threaten to beat him up. It went on for months. One day they caught up with him, chased him into a yard, and one of the toughs said that he was going to fight Bindner.

The battle lasted all of thirty seconds. Bindner hit the other boy, gave him a bloody nose, and the kid ran home.

Bindner says the violence confused and frightened him. He didn't understand it in others, and he didn't like it in himself. The kid seemed to want to fight mainly because Bindner *didn't* want to.

One time his sister, Shelly, hit him on the head with a hammer. They were outside playing, and she walloped him. He doesn't remember why. They were playing on a swing set. His mother was in the house talking on the phone. The two kids got into an argument about something, and Shelly popped him on the head with the hammer. It wasn't a serious injury. It didn't crack his skull, but he was bleeding a lot.

When he walked into the house, the blood all over his head and face dripped down onto the floor. He told his mother what had happened.

She talked into the phone. "I gotta go. My son's bleeding all over the floor."

She cleaned him and examined the wound, then called Shelly in to find out why she had hit her brother.

What stands out in Bindner's mind is that even as he walked into the house crying and bleeding, he didn't feel any anger toward his sister. He never has.

> *I grew up in a household where anger was supposed to be controlled. You know, the attitude was, if you say something in anger, you'll regret it later. . . .*
>
> *So I may be, you know, angry. I may be mad, but at the same time be trying very hard to control and remain outwardly calm and think, you know, cautiously and carefully. . . .*
>
> *Our parents just did . . . you didn't yell. You weren't supposed to. I mean, it did happen, but they were constantly telling us things like, "Knock it off. You can do better than that." Or, "That's not going to solve anything." You know, getting mad and showing it was never a solution.*

In 1962, at the age of fourteen, Bindner says he swore a vow of nonviolence. He was in junior high school, and remembers it as a time when kids squabble and try to outtough each other. He got into an argument with another kid at the school and picked a fight with him. It was the only time he had ever picked a fight with anyone. They exchanged a couple of punches, and the other boy's nose started to bleed.

The kid's sister, an eighth grader, was there watching. She told Bindner, "Someday you're going to be sorry for this."

He already felt terrible about what he had done. When he got home that night, he swore to himself that he was never going to do anything like that again. "I don't need to hurt people," he thought. "This is not going to be my life."

Bindner was an A and B student at Pacific High School. He was a long-distance runner on the track team and an avid hiker who liked to roam the wilds of the nearby San Bernardino Forest. In 1965, he was the drummer in a rock band called the Vandals. When band members' parents objected to the name, they changed it to the Penetrators. No one caught on to the double meaning. They played a couple of gigs, dances at the YMCA, then drifted apart.

One boyhood friend he remained close with and often thought about over the years was Eddie. Bindner worried about the guy. He could get into some strange, even sadistic, behavior—like the time he killed a frog with a blowtorch. Eddie also liked to take live lizards, tie strings around their necks, and hang them from the trees in his backyard.

Eddie did these things in front of Bindner and didn't seem at all embarrassed. The torture and destructive behavior appalled Bindner. As much fun as the two boys had together, Eddie sometimes seemed totally off-base.

"Man, this guy's terrible," Bindner thought. "But he's also my playmate, my friend."

The two boys often hiked together, usually in the

San Bernardino Mountains. They spent entire days winding their way up through the woods, blazing their own trails.

"Where do you want to go?" Bindner would ask.

"Let's climb that mountain over there," Eddie would say.

"But there's no trail up that mountain."

"I don't care. Let's find a way up it."

So they'd give it a shot. If they didn't make it to the top, it didn't matter much. It was all part of the good times they had.

In some ways, hanging out with Eddie was like hanging out with a crazy man, and Bindner didn't want to deal with that craziness. The things Eddie did were more than strange. Bindner saw them as violent, evil. Eddie not only let himself get out of control, he did it in front of other people. He seemed to have no control over his impulses. He laughed about it, as if what he was doing were a joke.

In later years, when Tim Bindner thought about the types of people who might abduct and murder children, he wondered what life had been like for them as kids, and he thought about Eddie. As far as he knew, Eddie hadn't killed anyone, but Bindner wondered what happened to the fantasies, the ideas.

If you enjoy killing, you enjoy killing. How much of a transition would it be to go from torturing small animals to killing people? Bindner believes the fantasies involved in behavior like Eddie's can become recurrent and obsessive. Kids who can't control themselves become impulsive, aggressive adults.

Eddie had safe spots back in the mountains. Hiding places. He knew the woods. He knew that when they got to the top of the hill, it was time to take their shirts off and remove the ticks. In some ways, Bindner thought the guy was a genius. He also thought, "If he knew the woods, and he knew the places, and he even knew when you had to pick the ticks off your body, he also could've known where to put bodies."

There was an incident—seventeen-year-old Eddie

in a motel room with a fourteen-year-old girl, but she complained only to her boyfriend, and no one brought charges against Eddie. The girl was a little flirt, anyway, Bindner thought—but it *did* sound like an assault.

Bindner graduated from Pacific High School in 1966. That fall, he began taking classes at Cal-Riverside, fifteen miles from his home. But the forestry curriculum at the school didn't satisfy Bindner, so he transferred to the University of Idaho in 1967. After five minutes in Moscow, Idaho, he knew that he wouldn't be completing his degree there. The place was depressing.

He worked the summer of 1967 at Glacier National Park in Montana. He remembers a dry lightning storm that hit the area that summer and the fires it ignited in the mountains. He sat all of one night and watched the flames rage up the side of a mountain.

One of the bosses told him, "Sit here on the road, man. We don't know where we're going or how we're gonna fight this thing. Sit on the road there and watch the fire."

So he did. He sat and stared, transfixed by the power and the beauty of the blaze. He commented on the majesty of the firestorm to another worker sitting next to him.

"You're sick, man," the guy said.

"No, I'm not sick. Look at it. It's beautiful."

He wasn't crazy. He knew what fear was. He knew what his own limits were. He didn't enjoy the destruction of a fire that swept through the hills back home devouring the buildings and the people in its path. He would help to fight fires, but he also loved to watch them burn. Sometimes, he thought, destruction really could be beautiful. It's part of nature, like an earthquake. In its purest essence, an earthquake is beautiful because it's something that's been happening for millions of years. It's the earth doing what it's here to do. He doesn't see anything ugly about that—or tragic, or catastrophic—except that we don't know how to deal with it. Just to be alive means there are risks.

Tim Bindner didn't know it then, but there was a fire in his future, and an earthquake.

On September 7, 1968, he married his high school girlfriend, Terry, then began his junior year at Berkeley. His nickname there was "Peter Plant," because he always carried a botany book around with him. Other students often saw him picking and pressing flowers and the leaves of plants. He studied biology, botany, and forestry, and graduated with a 3.62 cumulative grade-point average.

When he thought the army would draft him during the Vietnam War, he applied for conscientious objector status. He had taken a solemn vow of nonviolence in 1962, he told his draft board. They denied his request, so he arranged to flee to Canada. Then he got lucky. In the first draft lottery, Bindner's number was 365. He knew he was safe.

Tim and Terry moved often in those early years. Oregon. Alaska. In September 1972, they moved to Old Orchard Beach, Maine, where Bindner took a job with the Portland Water Company. He moonlighted at a local McDonald's and used that money to finance flying lessons at the Biddeford Airport.

In May 1973, Bindner and some other workers were framing up forms to pour concrete for some vaults to house pipes. Bindner was at the bottom of a ten-foot hole. They hadn't shored up the sides of the hole, and it had been raining. Everything was wet, soggy, muddy.

There were men working on either side of him. A chunk of dirt hit one of them on his hard hat.

"What the hell's going on?" the man said.

Then the whole wall started to move. Just as the two other workers dove in opposite directions away from Bindner, the wall let go—slamming Bindner against the framing. The cave-in buried him under three feet of mud.

Bindner was in pain—bad pain—and he wanted it to be over. He was sure that he was going to die. Hundreds of pounds of dirt and mud were crushing him.

He wanted to lose consciousness. The air was getting stale and he was starting to fade when he heard shovels hitting the dirt above him.

Volunteers from the Windham fire department, across the road, had joined the workers. They had Bindner's upper body free in three or four minutes. He was sore, but he didn't have any broken bones.

He was alive. He felt lucky. He felt grateful. He still does. Again Tim Bindner had a brush with death and walked away.

For all the years of his marriage to Terry, Bindner had fantasies about other women. He fell in love with them. There was Megan, the waitress in Maine. She was coming on to him. She was all over him. He couldn't resist her.

It was a short-term thing. They worked together at the restaurant, fell for each other, and went a little crazy with it. He doesn't know what attracted him to Megan. All he knew was that he would get up in the morning and, for the first time in his life, he was eager to go to work. On his days off, he still wanted to be at the restaurant so that he could see her. He couldn't help it—even though he also still loved Terry.

In 1973 the couple returned to southern California. The cold and snow of Maine winter and the muddy spring were more than Bindner could tolerate. In 1975, he landed a job working for the Social Security Administration. The opportunity required a move to Richmond, in San Francisco's East Bay area.

Besides work, his life consisted of reading, hiking, and collecting coins. He searched libraries for books of chess moves and read them from cover to cover. He was an avid baseball fan. Those who knew the 5'6", 150-pound Bindner seldom saw him without his Oakland A's baseball cap.

Tim and Terry's marriage drifted into 1979. Then the two divorced. He didn't want children and had had a vasectomy in 1976, so there hadn't been much holding them together. A high school friend wondered how the two ever got together. She was quiet and reserved; he was always on the go.

By 1978 Bindner had met Lola, a woman he worked with at Social Security. She was a single mother of two. Shortly after his split with Terry, Bindner and Lola moved in together. The relationship was a volatile one. They were both drinking a lot—too much, Bindner says.

Lola had a bad temper and could get physical, especially when she had been drinking. The relationship lasted almost five years, but things came to a head one day when Bindner was walking to the local BART station. As he passed a bar, Lola came out. She was drunk and wanted him to join her inside. When he refused, she swung a pool cue at his head. He deflected it, but it still slammed into his shoulder, leaving a bad bruise. Bindner considered that incident the end of things.

On August 27, 1983, Bindner was returning from an Oakland A's game. He had put away some beer and was feeling buzzed. He saw an attractive woman and two kids standing at the bus stop at Sixty-third and San Pablo. He stopped to see if she wanted a ride.

Bindner used to do that kind of thing back then— stop and offer a stranger a ride. Usually they didn't accept the offer, but sometimes they did, and he would make a new friend. He considered himself a product of the hippie generation, when that sort of thing was not only ordinary but expected. The woman's acceptance of the offer amazed him.

Sandra Wilson had been waiting for the 72P going south. She and her two kids were going to visit her sister. He dropped her off there, then stayed to talk for a while. He came back later that night and they talked some more.

Bindner had started out at Social Security as a benefit authorizer in 1975, making adjustments in people's

128   JOHN PHILPIN

claims. Somebody dies. Somebody gets born. Benefits change.

In 1979, after his superiors promoted him to claims authorizer, he processed initial applications for benefits. He had to check birth certificates, proofs of marriage, and proofs of divorce to determine an applicant's eligibility.

He also spent time dealing with inquiries—distraught people who would call because they hadn't received their checks. Maybe they lived in McLean, Virginia, and their checks were going to McLean, Texas. Someone had to take the time to straighten things out, and Bindner enjoyed doing it. He was helping people.

He was doing other things as well. It was one of his "fantasy things." He culled the names and addresses of young girls from the confidential computer files and kept lists of their ages and birthdays. On each girl's fourteenth birthday, he sent her $50 of his own money—almost $2,000 in all. He called them his "Colorado kids" since most of them lived in the Rocky Mountain state.

Bindner's fantasy ended in 1985, when his supervisors caught and fired him. The cards and gifts had frightened some of the girls, and they notified the police or postal authorities. There was nothing threatening in the cards, and he had broken no laws. But the Social Security Administration believed that he had violated policy.

I made a trip in '85 after I got fired from Social Security. It was supposed to be a hiking trip. I was trying to just chill out. I was emotionally burnt. My career is over, right? But I had a little bit of money because they had to pay me my retirement money and all this bullshit. So the trip started out to be a hiking trip, but it ended up being mostly a cemetery trip. I fixed gravestones in Utah. I fixed gravestones in Idaho. I fixed gravestones in Montana.

Hop on the Greyhound bus, go to the next town, get a map, find out where the cemetery's at. It was great. I loved it. I did nineteen of 'em at a cemetery in Boise. It was beautiful. That place needed work. I think I found every gravestone in that cemetery that needed to be fixed, fixed it in one day, and then left. Just got in there and got out.

Bindner spent two weeks on the road—traveling by bus, hitchhiking. He spent some time in Glacier Park, but the cold and the rain drove him out. He ended up in Great Falls in need of a bath.

Sure enough, there's a cemetery within walking distance of the motel, a couple of miles away. So I went up there the next morning. Spent the whole morning checking out the gravestones, looking at the pictures, talking to the kids. Found a couple that needed to be fixed and fixed 'em up. There was a little girl—Katerina Santoni, I think her name was—a seven-year-old girl who had a little ceramic picture on her grave. It had come loose, so I popped it off and glued it back on.

The firing from Social Security had devastated Bindner. He felt that he hadn't done anything wrong—and with the trip he was trying to grab on to something, to get some new direction for himself.

I don't react in anger. I react in love or compassion or in something I am interested in or want to do. But it's always got to have a positive focus to it.

He fought his dismissal, and officials reinstated him sixteen months later. He was still working for Social Security on June 4, 1988, the day after Amber Swartz disappeared in Pinole, when he and Sandra Wilson boarded an Amador bus and went to Reno to get married. The wedding trip almost didn't happen, and the experience led Bindner to coin a new word—*idiodyssey*—a combination of *idiocy* and *odyssey*. The couple had started out in their car, which began almost immediately to make thumping noises. A used tire Bindner had bought was rubbing against the car's frame. Finally, forty miles north of Oakland on I-80, the tire blew out.

Bindner changed the flat, then drove back to Big O Tires, where he had bought the used one. It had a thirty-day guarantee, so the store replaced it.

Tim and Sandra returned home and had something to eat before starting out again. This time they got about a half mile up the road before steam started spewing out from under the hood of the car. Again they drove home, and Bindner parked the car. He found a break in the water hose.

"Maybe somebody doesn't want us to get married," Bindner said to his bride-to-be.

They decided to take the bus. The experience was enough for Bindner to swear off riding buses forever. It was like being in a sardine can. Halfway to Reno, Bindner was experiencing intense anxiety—a claustrophobic panic so strong that he almost told the driver to stop and let him off.

The couple arrived in Reno at midnight. Dazed by the five-hour trip, they wandered the streets looking for the American Motel. Eventually, Bindner found the place and they got some sleep. In the morning they were married in a chapel that offered rates for weddings and funerals. They did a little gambling, then returned to Oakland on Sunday.

Monday afternoon, Tim Bindner knocked on Kim Swartz's door.

18

Tim Bindner remembers his first interview with an FBI agent as a screening. He expected the agents to seek him out again, pass him along to a more senior and experienced agent, and they did. That night he met Special Agent Mary Ellen O'Toole.

He had heard the rumor that O'Toole was the model for Clarice Starling, the FBI profiler played by Jodie Foster in *The Silence of the Lambs*. He knew that O'Toole had trained at the Bureau's Behavioral Science Unit in Quantico, Virginia.

Bindner walked into the interview room and noticed a jump rope lying on the table. It wasn't a kid's jump rope. It looked like an adult's leather exercise rope. Nobody said anything about it. He figured it might have been Amber's and somebody found it. Later he read in the papers that they hadn't found it. The agents must have placed it there to see if he or anyone else being interviewed would react. It was a ploy, one of their psychological tricks.

Bindner's first thought about O'Toole was that she was cute, but she didn't impress him all that much. "I was more impressed with the movie," he said later.

O'Toole went into more detail than the first agent, and wanted to theorize about how the crime could have happened. Bindner freely expressed his opinions, his speculations about what might have happened to Amber and where she might have been taken. He considered it a valuable exercise, one that he had engaged in himself since Angela Bugay's abduction and murder.

He knew that O'Toole was investigating him, but the FBI was looking at many people. It didn't seem real to him that he could become a suspect, the focus of an in-depth investigation. By the end of that night with O'Toole, he knew. Interviews with others were taking fifteen to twenty minutes, but the assembly line stopped with Bindner. He was in there for hours.

He was tired, but not particularly worried. He had shown interest in the case, so the cops were showing interest in him.

The next day, he resumed his searching.

———————

Bindner was in the Pinole police station talking with FBI agents on June 11 when Dale Myer and the dog handlers arrived from the sheriff's department. Myer worked as a runner again, and they started the bloodhound with a piece of Amber's clothing a block away from where Bindner had parked his van in front of St. Joseph's Church.

The dog moved along Tennent Avenue to the church, then up the steps to the door. He sniffed around the door, then turned and ran down the steps to the blue van, where he jumped up and clawed at the window.

Myer thinks the dog was tracking two of Amber's scent trails. St. Joseph's was the child's church, and she had been there with her family the week before.

Bloodhounds work to find the freshest scent trail, and if they are tracking in the missing person's neighborhood, it's common for the animals to cross an earlier trail. They have to check it out, but then they go back to the stronger trail. This time the stronger trail was the Dodge van, and the dog was frantic.

————————

Mary Ellen O'Toole asked Bindner to go with her out into Pinole Valley, to do some searching, to show her some of the spots that he had already checked, and to speculate about what might have happened to Amber. Bindner figured it was another FBI technique, something right out of the procedure manual.

Bindner liked O'Toole. He thought of her interviewing technique as both sympathetic and realistic. She cared about Amber, and she wanted to know what happened to her. "I felt she sincerely wanted to know if I did it," Bindner said later, "and she sincerely wanted to know, if I didn't do it, what happened to the girl."

He never forgot that it was part of her approach, but he liked it. She trusted him enough to go out in the valley with him alone. If he had killed a child—if he had killed anyone—what was to prevent him from killing her?

They drove out through the valley, stopping at one or two places. Bindner saw a spot that looked like a prime location to him, one that he hadn't searched yet. "Let's stop and look around," he said.

For ten minutes the agent and the suspect hiked around a creek bed. Bindner wandered back into the woods. There was a trace trail going down the hill. He followed the trail and looked around down there but didn't find anything.

As they drove on, Bindner shared his thoughts about the abduction. If the guy had headed for the freeway, there wasn't anything he, Bindner, could do. That's why he was concentrating his efforts in the valley.

The whole thing would have happened fast, Bindner

told the agent. Whoever grabbed Amber knew that he had some lead time—that parents would run aimlessly around the neighborhood looking for the kid before they called the police. He could get into the valley, do his thing, and get out of there.

Bindner knew of a ravine he wanted to check just beyond Oakmont Cemetery. The agent and the suspect both explored it for about half an hour, again without success.

Bindner never asked O'Toole about his suspect status. It was a game. The FBI wanted to solve a case. It was as if they were saying "Help us," and he complied. Whatever layers of unreality they were putting on it, he considered it all very real. He believes that Mary Ellen O'Toole knew he recognized the game for what it was, but neither said anything. She was soft, as if she were a friend just there to talk to him. If Bindner had done it, he says—if he had taken the child—he would have laid his head down in her lap and confessed. "Then she would have dragged me off to the gas chamber," he said with a laugh when talking about their encounter later. "The woman can make you feel guilty even if you haven't done anything. She's smarter than the average serial killer."

O'Toole stood with Bindner at Angela Bugay's grave in Oakmont Cemetery. It was late, approaching dusk. El Diablo—the devil's mountain—was a shadow in the distance, its isolated twin peaks towering three thousand feet above the Bay Area.

It's strange how certain details stick in your mind. Tears seemed to well up in O'Toole's eyes but never flowed down her cheeks. Bindner watched her eyes, waited for the tears to come, but they never did. He had never seen anything like that before. That was when he decided on a nickname for O'Toole—"Onion Juice."

There was a story about a door-to-door salesman who brought his kids with him when he approached a house. He dabbed the juice of an onion at the corners of his eyes and told prospective customers that he had to sell one more vacuum cleaner that day or he and his kids wouldn't have a place to spend the night. Tears seemed to well up in his eyes, and he made the sale.

She kept me there, made sure I was there after dark. We watched the sunset. It was a beautiful sunset. She kept talking to me, and it was after dark. Other FBI agents were in plain sight up on a hill with their dogs, searching.

After we finished all this talking, she said something about, "I know you have a lot of feelings for Angela. Would you like to be alone with her for a few minutes?" I said, "Yeah, I would." And then she retreated about fifty or seventy-five yards, out of earshot. Of course, at the time I didn't know that they'd already bugged the grave so they could hear everything I said. They gave me a court order later saying that the grave had been bugged. That's how I found out it was. I think she thought I was gonna see all this activity going on and realize—and feel they were closing in on me, and admit something at Angela's grave, either to her or to God or whatever. I don't fault them for trying to make people feel guilty. A lot of times you do get criminals with consciences that you do get to come through and confess.

Bindner didn't see anything wrong with the Bureau's techniques. They wanted to know what he knew, find out what he was about. He knew that psychological tricks were part of the overall investigation and that he had to be careful. It could be a setup. Although he didn't object, he would have preferred something more open. They say what they have and what they want to know. Everything is on the table. What do you think I did? Why do you think I did it? But he knew that it didn't work that way. The FBI doesn't put their evidence on the table. They thumb through their procedure manuals and use their investigative techniques and their psychological tricks.

O'Toole asked him if he would be willing to take a polygraph. He was wary of it, said he would think about it. It was a way of clearing him, she said.

They wanted him to break down. They wanted him to confess. They thought he took Amber, killed her, and they wanted him to tell them all about it. The whole scene was heavy. Scary. Unreal.

19

When Tim Bindner looks back to the summer of 1988, he thinks of himself as naive about police investigation. He was getting an education. He was willing to speculate about how someone could have grabbed Amber. It would be a matter of seconds. All a person had to do was put his hand over her mouth and drag her into a car. There would be nothing but silence. He could remove the child from the area, sexually assault her, kill her, and be on his way in an hour or less.

When he first heard about Angela Bugay, he wondered if her murder might be one of a series, and wrote to the Antioch police department to suggest they look into that possibility. Now he suggested to Mary Ellen O'Toole and the other agents that they consider a possible connection between Amber and Angela.

Both kids vanished in the late afternoon, grabbed right in front of their homes. They were about the same size, and they resembled one another. Both neighborhoods offered quick access to main roads leading out.

The agents asked Bindner to speculate about what their abductor might be like. It was the same technique that interviewers had used with Ted Bundy. Get him to speculate. Get him talking in the third person. Those investigators knew Bundy was talking about himself.

Bindner didn't think it was a big deal. The cops were speculating, too, and talking in the third person. Did that mean *they* were killers?

Bindner said that the man who killed Angela Bugay probably experienced urges, evil impulses over which he had no control. When he acted on those impulses, there was no sense of guilt or remorse.

The killer might visit the child's parents, join in the search for the child—do the very things that Bindner himself was doing.

Angela's killer would have followed the case in the newspaper. Bindner did this.

He would go back to the place where he buried the child, then visit her grave in Oakmont Cemetery. Bindner went to these places, too.

If the same guy took Amber, Bindner speculated, he would return to the place where he buried her. He would be angry that searchers had found Angela— angry that they had disturbed the grave he made for her. He would have been more careful with Amber. He would have taken her farther away and buried her deeper in the ground. No one would find her.

And he would do it again. A guy like this gets excited when he sees a kid alone and vulnerable. He wants to have her, and he can't control himself.

Bindner talked about how to manage a child—just tell the kid what you do and don't want her to do. The man who took Amber wouldn't have had to restrain her or tie her up. She was a timid child. She would have been afraid—shivering and shaking.

Angela was five. Amber was seven. Maybe the next one would be nine or ten, he said.

Bindner finally agreed to take the polygraph. He

was concerned about what the test measured and how accurate it was, but it was starting to feel like something he had to get out of the way.

He arrived for the test on June 15 at 6:00 P.M. He had spent part of the day searching and was tired. The polygraph was part of the investigative process, a way of eliminating himself as a suspect.

> It was a bizarre night, and I don't remember what happened when. I know I was freaked out. I know I was scared, and I know I was guilty. I know a lot of other things happened that I'm not supposed to talk about. . . .
> My other feeling at the same time was, I didn't do anything. I didn't hurt anybody. So let's cooperate. Let's go through it. If you've never been through this kind of situation before, you're scared. And I was a little bit scared. I never talked to FBI before. I never talked to investigators before. I never dealt with any of this stuff before.

At the same time, his house and his workstation at Social Security were being searched with his consent. He figured investigators would be looking for trace evidence that the kid had been in his car or something, but he didn't have anything to hide. So he told them to go ahead.

He didn't realize that he would never again see anything they seized. He didn't knew they would take his books, files, all of his diaries.

The polygraph measures heart rate, blood pressure, and galvanic skin response (GSR), the electrical conductivity of the skin. The subject wears monitors across his chest and on his fingers, as well as a blood pressure cuff. The examiner takes a baseline measurement. A machine automatically records on a graph any deviations from that baseline, and the examiner notes the fluctuations as the subject answers the questions.

Bindner's understanding of the machine is that it reveals stress. If a person is telling the truth but under stress, the polygraph will react and reflect that stress.

Because of his intimate involvement in the search for Amber, he didn't consider it a viable way to prove himself innocent. He knew the family. He was emotionally involved. Of course the machine would show stress.

The polygraph examiner was Special Agent Ron Homer, an FBI veteran who had administered thousands of polygraph examinations throughout his twenty-five-year career. He is a skilled professional who understands the nuances of the machine and who knows the techniques of interrogation.

Bindner told him, "I can probably fake a GSR for you right now. I can freak out right now and you're gonna get a reaction."

Homer didn't say anything.

Bindner described a state of mind, a place he enters where he can feel a tingling in his fingers. He holds himself still and feels the sensation coming up from inside all the way out into his fingers. He calls it a neural sensation, and he can make it happen.

He told Homer, "I think I can fake that stuff, man. So what good is that machine?"

Again, Ron Homer didn't respond. He had questions for Bindner about any possible behavior the Oakland man might have engaged in that could contaminate the testing.

Bindner told Homer that he had never met Amber Swartz, and that before June 6, he had never been on Savage Avenue in Pinole. He did have some ideas for the agent regarding what might have happened to the child. Homer encouraged him to go over his thoughts about the abduction.

The guy would be drinking and driving, Bindner said. Savage Avenue offered easy access to the valley. He saw Amber in front of the house. She was jumping rope, and she was beautiful.

She was beautiful.

The guy probably parked his vehicle, Bindner continued, and looked over the neighborhood to see if it was safe for him to take her. Then he would have approached Amber, placed his hand over her mouth, and dragged her back to his van or his car. He might have hit her to keep her quiet, to keep her under control. He would be getting increasingly aroused because he knew that he was going to molest her, but he didn't intend to kill her. That wasn't part of his plan.

He could have killed her while he was having sex with her. He strangled her. He couldn't control himself.

Maybe he had a shovel with him. He had come prepared—in case he did kill her and had to bury the body.

Later he would feel remorse, and deal with this by going to see Amber's family, offering to help the police, and searching for the child.

"He would probably do the same things I'm doing," Bindner said.

The first polygraph trial was inconclusive.

"We've got a problem here, Tim," Ron Homer said.

Bindner wondered what might be contaminating the test. He had told the agent about tracking Susan Bugay's address via the Social Security computers. He knew that might look suspicious. He had written to her on June 2, the day before Amber disappeared. But that was a coincidence.

"The letter came back," he said. "I threw it away. I knew I was a suspect, and I figured if the letter was found it would be misunderstood."

He said he put the letter in a brown paper bag and threw it over a bank on Carquinez Scenic Drive, about a mile from the Alhambra Cemetery.

On the second trial Bindner's responses were again inconclusive.

Bindner thinks that the agent then asked him about sexual fantasies involving children.

> Those types of questions are going to make you uptight, and I was already uptight. It was just getting worse and worse as it went on. I was just getting more uptight.

Bindner told the agent that he might be capable of molesting a child. He said that he had to be wary and repress that kind of thought. He wasn't sure if he would always be able to control those urges, he said, but so far he had never hurt a child.

Agent Homer's third polygraph trial left no room for equivocation. It indicated deception on four questions.

The strongest response Bindner remembers having was when Homer asked him if he had hit Amber. He says it was a physical reaction, not guilt. His stomach twitched. When he heard the question, he could feel somebody hitting the child. He was responding to the idea of a man striking Amber Swartz, and it affected him personally.

Bindner doesn't recall all of what he said or did that night.

> They burned my mind. They snapped it off. I was gone. I was exhausted. It was the middle of the night. I was under extreme stress. They made me feel guilty. And I just lost it. I don't remember a whole lot of the questions they asked.

Bindner does recall turning to the man at some point early in the morning and saying, "I did not take that girl. Whatever else I've told you, I did not take that girl."

The polygraph expert was equally firm. There was no question about the test results. Bindner was being deceptive.

They were trying to box him in. They almost had him believing that he could have taken Amber—that he had gotten drunk, blacked out, went up to Pinole and took her.

However vague about his alibi for that Friday afternoon he may have been in 1988, he was clear when he was interviewed about it again in 1994.

> I know goddamn well where I was when Amber was taken. I was in the cemetery. Yes, I was drinking beer. I drank two or three beers. Yes, I walked around. I fixed a couple of broken gravestones. I know exactly what I

*was doing, where I was, who saw me. I know where I
went when I left the cemetery. I took the freeway and
drove south to my house. You can't tell me I blacked
out and took a kid if I know where I was. That's my explanation of the Amber abduction. I was in the cemetery fixing gravestones when that child was killed.*

Bindner feels they were doing the same thing to
him that night that Oakland detectives did to Bradley
Page in 1984. Page was a Berkeley student charged
with the murder of his girlfriend, Roberta "Bibi" Lee.
Police interrogated Page for sixteen hours, telling him
they had evidence—fingerprints, a witness—that proved
he had killed Lee. Page gave police a confession filled
with what he thought had happened, what he pictured,
assumed, envisioned. Then he recanted. At his first
trial, a jury found him not guilty of first- and second-
degree murder, but hung on the question of man-
slaughter. A second trial resulted in his conviction.

Page participated in the search for Lee, whose
body was found in Redwood Regional Park, in the
Oakland foothills—where she, Page, and a friend had
been jogging.

According to Bindner, the main difference between the two cases was that with Bradley Page they
had a body. With him, they had nothing.

*I've known since the guy was convicted that Bradley
Page didn't kill Bibi Lee. I know he didn't. I can't say
100 percent, but 99.9. That's the way I feel about it. I
just know the kind of ordeal he went through and the
kind of guy he was. I just believe that he got brow-
beaten into what he said. They told him they had physical evidence that they found at the scene. They lied to
him. It's crazy. If you trust law enforcement, you're not
gonna think they're lying to you. What strikes me about
that is just the way this so-called confession came out.
It was like he was trying to help them, trying to cooperate with them, and the more pressure they put him un-*

*der, the more he tried to cooperate. He didn't want an
adversarial situation. He wanted to cooperate and help
them. . . .*

*My thought always, throughout the whole thing,
was "I'm innocent, so let's cooperate. They're not
gonna find anything against me in this investigation,
so let 'em clear me as quick as they can, and let's go on
about our business." You know, I had a lot of faith in
those guys. Probably too much.*

*I think if they had done to me what they did to him,
they probably would've got me to say I did it. I mean, if
they had said, "We found her fingerprints. We found this
physical evidence. We know you were there. You might
as well tell us."*

Bindner felt trapped. It was as if they were trying
to make him think that he had blacked out. The scenario they created was that he had left work, went up
to the cemetery and got drunk, then headed for Pinole.
Did you hit Amber?

Bindner was frightened. They were trying to wring
a confession out of him. In the early morning hours he
felt something snap inside his head. It was real, a
physical sensation, a neural flash, a jolt. After that, he
felt crazy—or, at the very least, as if he were going
crazy. Something changed, and it terrified him. He was
spinning out of control. They were going to get him.

It was as if he couldn't move. He sat perfectly still,
trying to regain control, but it wasn't working.

Had he been on Savage Avenue? Did he take Amber? Was he holding anything back?
Did you hit Amber?

If they had convinced him that day that they truly
had evidence—if they had offered a plausible scenario—Bindner thinks he might have given in. He
wouldn't have been saying "I did it" but "If you've got
that, it must be true."

Just like Bradley Page.

Bindner figures he would have given it up if they
had said something to him like "We found Amber's

body. It's up at St. Joseph's Cemetery down by the creek. We found your fingerprints on some rocks down there. They were tossed aside from where her body's at. She was hit on the head by a rock."

Bindner maintained his innocence. He insisted he hadn't taken Amber Swartz. If he confessed to taking her, that wasn't going to help anybody, because he couldn't tell them where to find her.

> *The trouble with a lot of that is that—particularly after I had that neural sensation, that snapping busi-ness—is that I don't really remember what I said, or whether I was prompted to say it, or whether I was just going on, and what . . . where he came in and I faded out. Some of the details are there, and some of them aren't. It's kind of hard to remember it. I remember go-ing through the third set of questions too, but I don't remember really anymore what any of them were—except that one.*

Did you hit Amber?

Special Agent Ron Homer had Bindner on the box for eleven hours. The Oakland man's responses on the polygraph were clearly deceptive. His alibi was vague. He had insinuated himself into the investigation, then pointed out that this was something the abductor might do. He acknowledged having sexual feelings about children. He pointed the finger at himself every time he speculated about the kind of person who abducts children.

Tim Bindner had become a suspect in Amber Swartz's disappearance.

20

It had been seven months since Amber Swartz disappeared, and six weeks since a man grabbed Michaela Garecht at the Rainbow Market in Hayward.

At 7:00 P.M. on the sixth, San Pablo Patrol Sergeant Mark Foisie made the turn onto Church Lane. He saw a light blue Dodge van with the license plate LOV YOU straddling the sidewalk. The engine was running and the parking lights were on. The white male driver was talking to a group of kids through the open passenger-side window.

Foisie pulled in behind the van and switched on his emergency lights.

Tim Bindner drove his van forward into the parking lot of V.P.'s Restaurant, stopped, got out, and walked over to the patrol car. He identified himself and gave Foisie his driver's license.

"Why were you parked on the sidewalk?" Foisie asked him.

"I was talking to the kids," Bindner said.

"You know them?"

"I don't know them. I was just making friends."

Foisie walked over to the van and looked in through the window. He saw an open forty-ounce bottle of Meister Brau beer on the floor, with a small amount of liquid remaining in it. He also smelled beer on Bindner's breath.

The cop pat-searched Bindner, then asked him to remove an object from his left front pocket. It was a large piece of stone. "It's a broken angel's wing from a young girl's marble headstone," Bindner said. "I didn't know her, but I would have liked to."

Foisie radioed for backup, then crawled inside the van to look for any other open containers of alcohol.

He saw boxes filled with old cans at the back of the van, but it was the shrinelike quality of the vehicle's interior that struck him. The off-white walls were covered with primitive drawings in crayon and ink, biblical quotes, children's names—Amber Swartz, Michaela Garecht. These two, Foisie knew, were children who had been abducted. The guy had plastered missing person posters all over the van. There were also about two dozen photographs of young girls—all the girls about seven to thirteen years of age—taped to the visor and roof, interspersed with playing cards. There were more pictures lying on the front seat, along with a book from the Richmond Public Library—*Infanticide*.

When Foisie's backup arrived, the two officers checked Bindner for DUI. Bindner wasn't drunk, but he had been drinking.

The sergeant went over to talk to two of the girls. The man had frightened them, they said, and they wanted the cop to take him to jail so he couldn't come after them.

Lynn Rodriguez and Diane Alvarez, two twelve-year-olds, said they were in Adobe Liquors, a neighborhood liquor and variety store, when Bindner got

there. Lynn had dropped a quarter on the floor, and
Diane started looking for it. They didn't know Tim
Bindner and had never seen him around the neighbor-
hood. They told him they didn't talk to strangers.

"I'm not a stranger," he said. "I'm your friend.
We're already talking."

He asked the girls where they lived. Lynn didn't
want him to know where she lived, so she told him
North Richmond. She also told him she needed a
quarter for the bus. He offered her the money, but she
declined.

Then Bindner offered her a ride. "It would be
more dangerous to ride the bus than to ride with me,"
he said.

The girls left the store and walked around the corner to Church Lane to join their friends. Bindner followed them, offered them beer, said he had bags of
guts in his van—as if that were something that the
girls would find interesting.

Foisie handcuffed Bindner and placed him under
arrest for annoying and disturbing children—a violation of Section 647.6 of the California Penal Code. He
transported Bindner to the San Pablo police department. Police towed the van.

Foisie called Phil Pollard in Pinole and Ken Gross
in Hayward to tell them what he had found in Bindner's van. He also notified Mary Ellen O'Toole. All
three investigators knew of Bindner. He did have an
unusual interest in the missing child cases, but there
was no evidence—physical or otherwise—to link him
to any of them. The photographs and posters in the
van were nothing new.

At 8:00 P.M., a San Pablo detective named Thrower
interviewed Bindner. Mary Ellen O'Toole was present
in the room. Thrower read Bindner his Miranda
rights, which the Oakland man waived. He was willing
to talk about the incident.

Bindner told the story the way he remembered it—
that he first saw the kids inside Adobe Liquors when
they asked him for a quarter. He gave them the money,

bought some beer, and left. He said he started driving north on Church Lane when one of the girls flagged him down. Bindner thought she was being flirtatious, so he was, too. He does that with kids sometimes, he said.

Bindner acknowledged making the statement about having beer—he had a twelve-pack in the van—but he insisted that he had not given any to the kids and wasn't serious about that remark. It was only banter. He didn't know whether the kids had taken him seriously. "They may have," he said.

He also agreed that he could have said something like "I might have some bags of guts in here."

If he did, it was more banter. "If I scared them, it was inadvertent," he said.

Bindner told the detective that one of the girls had said she was planning to take the bus to Point Richmond, and he had offered her a ride. He said the girls struck him as naive, and he would have rather given them a ride than let them take the bus because Point Richmond is a tough neighborhood.

"Did you tell the kids they were cute and pretty?" Thrower asked.

"Yes," Bindner said. "I think all little girls are cute."

He told the cop he often cautioned kids about the potential danger of talking to strangers. Even though he, himself, was a stranger to these girls, he thought they would be safer with him than on the bus.

"Do you see any contradiction in that?" Thrower asked.

Bindner didn't answer.

When asked about the missing child posters, Bindner said that his only involvement in those cases was that he was doing everything he could to help find the kids.

O'Toole wanted to know what he had done, what the whole thing was about. What had he said to the little girls?

He told her that he had talked to them about the

missing kids. Amber's and Michaela's posters were on the outside of the van. "I gave them some of the flyers."

"What did you say to them?"

There was that little girl standing in the back of the group, craning her neck to see over the others. It looked as if she were frustrated, feeling left out. "I told the boy that was standing next to the window to tell Shorty back there that I think she's kind of cute. I didn't actually say it to the girl. I said it to the boy."

The kids were feeling safe, he insisted, because they were all in a group. They were curious about him, the van, the posters. He was telling them to be careful. As he gave them some flyers, he said, "I hope I don't see your picture on one of these one day. You better be careful out here, goofing around on the street like this."

O'Toole looked at him. "Tim, you know they're just little girls."

She was telling him that he shouldn't have been talking to the kids at all, that he was doing something bad. It struck him as odd that she would say that. He was treating the kids as equals.

When the police were booking him, officers found handwritten notes in his wallet. One was a prayer for strength to keep searching. One had "Kayla"— Michaela Garecht's nickname—printed across the top and consisted of some quotations from the Bible. Another read:

> I love you, Amber. You are my first, and I
> tried so hard for you. Tried + cried and still ache
> in my heart. They will always try to pull me back,
> but I never will. They don't know about us.
> They've never heard of us.

On January 11, 1989, Detective Thrower issued a special information bulletin on Bindner.

> Above subject was arrested on 1-6-89 for annoying children (89-258). A complaint was issued by the DA for this offense. It was also learned that he has been a

suspect in the AMBER SWARTZ and MICHAELA
GARECHT disappearances. At this time there is no
evidence to link him to these disappearances. His van
is very distinguishable as it has posters of missing
children attached to the exterior and interior. He also
likes to frequent cemeteries, especially the grave sites
of deceased children.

Bindner spent the rest of the night and all the next
day in jail before making bail. Eventually the D.A.
dropped the charges, saying he couldn't prove that
Bindner had had any intent to do anything to the girls.
There was nothing threatening, nothing sexual.

Bindner looks back on the incident with bitter-
ness. "I was charged with two counts of child molesting in San Pablo," he says, "and I was never accused of
touching anyone. All I did was talk to the kids."

Less than seven months had passed since Amber
disappeared. Most area law enforcement agencies
were aware of Bindner's searches in the Pinole Valley.
Bindner figured they just followed him around trying
to pin it on him.

Less than two months had gone by since Michaela
Garecht was abducted, and Bindner was also searching
in Hayward. He was peripherally involved in both cases.

Then they grabbed him in San Pablo, thinking he
was trying to entice the two girls into his van. Bindner
says his arrest was another example of the cops paying
too much attention to him, and the public's hysterical
reaction to kids being snatched in the Bay Area and
nobody knowing where they were ending up.

The cops labeled him a molester—the statute under which they arrested him covered that offense—and
the automatic assumption is that anyone wearing that
label is a monster. They placed him in a category, gave
him a label. The next step was for them to put him in a
cage for a lot longer than twenty-four hours.

On January 30, 1989, two weeks after Tim Bindner's arrest in San Pablo, thirteen-year-old Ilene Misheloff was walking home from the Wells Intermediate School in Dublin, thirty miles east of Oakland. It was 3:00 P.M. as she approached the four-lane Amador Valley Boulevard near the Shamrock Shopping Center.

She was taking the shortcut that all the kids in her neighborhood used: through a wide alley behind the shopping center, behind the Sawmill (a furniture store) and Gallagher's Pub, then across the boulevard and through John Mape Park, along the dry creek bed.

Ilene was an ice skater, well-known in town for her talent in the rink. She had a private lesson scheduled at Dublin Iceland that afternoon and was always in good spirits when she knew that she would soon be skating.

Ilene didn't make it home that day. She became the third child in eight months to vanish.

Volunteers searched creek beds, drainage canals, and the hills west of Dublin. They distributed flyers and tied yellow ribbons to phone poles, trees, and fence posts all over the city. They walked the route Ilene always took on her way home from school. There was no trace of her.

Dale Myer and the dog handlers from the Contra Costa County Search and Rescue Team tracked Ilene from the Wells School to the alley behind the shopping mall. Because that's where the scent trail ended, Myer suspected a "vehicle exit" from that location.

Later, searchers found Ilene's backpack in a creek bed beyond the shopping center. Dublin police rejected Myer's conclusion that someone had abducted the teenager behind Gallagher's. Instead, they focused on a possible confrontation in the creek bed. Myer shrugged it off and kept his opinion to himself: the backpack was like that pair of socks in the Amber Swartz case—it wasn't there the first time they searched the area, but the second time through, there it was. And this time they knew it was the missing child's.

On February 11, 1989, Tim Bindner drove to Dublin to search for Ilene Misheloff.

> *When I went to look for Ilene, I was already think-ing that the cops are gonna be following me. So I drove my van out there. I had my map with me, and I was gonna do this road. It wasn't a road. It was really a stream course. But on the AAA map it looked like a road, and it looked like a rural road going up to the west of Ilene's house. So I said to myself, I'll just poke along that road for a while, but I'm not gonna let any-body know I'm here. I was afraid that they were gonna harass me.*
>
> *So I parked my van about a half mile away from Ilene's house. They don't ever print your address, but they print your street in the papers, so I knew what street she lived on. And it had a description of where she had walked home from school and where she had cut through the park, across a creek into the park to get home. So I wanted to trace that route and just get an idea what somebody might have done. So I did that. . . .*
>
> *There's a road that's perpendicular to the canyon, so I just went up that road, assuming if somebody had taken her up that canyon, that maybe nobody had bothered to look there yet. Which is probably a stupid assumption, 'cause it was several days later that I went up there.*
>
> *I didn't find anything. But when I came down out of the canyon there was an FBI agent waiting for me. Flashed his badge, said, "I'm with the FBI." I said, "Well, what can I do for you?" He had a guy with him. He said this guy said he found a shoe up in the canyon. "We wanted to take him back up there to see if he could show us where he found the shoe." There was a young guy there, about a nineteen- or twenty-year-old white male. They went walking on up the canyon like they were gonna go up and look for this shoe.*
>
> *That was another one of those things that rings a bell in your head and you go, "This is not real. This is*

not real." Okay, go look for your shoe, guys. Let me get the hell out of here and not come back. So I didn't come back. So I didn't look anymore for Ilene. That was it, man. They scared me off.

FBI agents went to the Oakland Housing Authority where Tim Bindner worked and verified that he had checked in on January 30, the day of Ilene's disappearance. Bindner was a groundskeeper, moving from one housing project to another in the course of his workday. While the agents could be certain that the Oakland man had logged in and out of work, they didn't know where he had been between those two times.

It didn't seem to matter. There was little law enforcement interest in Tim Bindner as a suspect in Ilene's disappearance. Dublin investigators focused their attention on a local suspect.

Like so many of the Bay Area child abductions, the investigation went nowhere.

———————

After his aborted search for Ilene Mischeloff, Bindner picked up some flyers at the volunteer center, then drove back by way of Oakmont Cemetery. Someone had preceded him there, placing a yellow ribbon on Angela Bugay's grave.

21

Sixty thousand fans jammed Candlestick Park in San Francisco for game three of the first Bay Area World Series between the Oakland A's and the San Francisco Giants. The A's had swept the first two games at the Coliseum and were looking unbeatable.

Moments before the first pitch, the light poles began to sway, the concrete support pillars vibrated and began to wobble. The earth shook and rolled in waves. Slabs of concrete broke free and fell into the stands.

Earthquake.

Tim Bindner had been at the Oakland Coliseum when Jose Canseco, Mark McGwire, Terry Steinbach, Dave Stewart, Ricky Henderson, and company thumped their rivals from across the bay, 5–0 and 5–1. He was just getting home from work on the seventeenth when the phone poles on Fifth-third Street started their arrhythmic wavering. There was a rumbling noise as sidewalks separated from the streets. Standing in front of his house, Bindner could see smoke rising in the distance. It was a big one.

It was a strong tremor, and it knocked down a few chimneys in the neighborhood, but I didn't think it could knock down a freeway. And we go walking down there, and I get down within two blocks of the freeway, and I see a little section of the top deck still up, and both sides of it are broken off. That was when it hit me. Hey, some bad stuff has happened here, folks. They need my help. I gotta go down there and see what I can do.

I didn't get there until after an hour. By that time there had been rescuers that got everybody off the top deck already. And only the brave ones were crawling between decks to see if they could get anybody out of the smashed cars that were down in between the decks.

I went in there. I worked on a guy in a smashed car that had two dead people in the front of it. But he was in the back, and he was moaning and he was still alive. I managed to get the door to the car open. We got him out and I did just a check of his major bones to see if anything was broken. We were trying to figure out how to get him off the freeway. There was a couple other people there. And we couldn't figure out how to get him down. There was a ladder, but it was just a little thin ladder. So eventually I went back up on the top deck. Fortunately there was a fireman up there with a backboard. We got down there. They eventually signaled to a fire truck that was nearby, and they came by and got him out from between the abutments. It hadn't smashed all the way together. There was still a couple of feet distance there, so we got him down that way. And he lived. He made it. He had a collapsed lung and a concussion, couple of other things wrong with him I can't remember right now.

The two in the front seat were dead. I gave CPR to the driver for about ten minutes, 'cause when I got to him he was still warm. I couldn't find a pulse or anything so I just went into my CPR training. No pulse. No breathing. Go for it. That was quite an experience.

Over sixty people died in the quake. Property damage soared into the millions. Six years later the process of rebuilding was still going on.

The California Highway Patrol presented Bindner with an award, a framed certificate for his efforts on the Cyprus Street overpass. Bindner considers his work during the Loma Prieta earthquake to be one of the crowning achievements of his life. He says it was the same motivation that sent him out to look for the missing children—trying to help people.

It was also the same when wildfires ripped through the Oakland and Berkeley Hills in 1990. Bindner drove out there, not knowing what he would find. The fire was blowing, and it was coming down out of the hills. He knew he had to get under it. He ran through the smoke and blowing debris to the bottom of the hills and found a college prep school—a $3 million complex of buildings, all with exterior cedar shingles. It was like an expensive pile of kindling.

> One goddamn spark and the whole school goes up. So I said to myself, "Here we are. Let's go. Let's do it. Let's fight it." No damn fire hose. No exterior hoses. All I could find was a damn garden hose. I did find a squirt nozzle, so I had a chance to fight the fire.
>
> It was a vacuum fire coming down the hill. I fought that sonofabitch—basically just put water on it, threw some dirt a few times. That was the only place I could find where that fire could be fought.
>
> Every two minutes you'd hear this big explosion, and we would look at each other and say, "What was that?" Gas tank. Water heater. We just made sure we stayed far enough away from this shit so it didn't hit us.

Thousands of people were burned out that day, but the school remained intact. It was another of Bindner's successful rescue missions. God had placed him in North Oakland for a purpose.

FIVE

CAT AND MOUSE— THE MAKING OF A CELEBRITY SUSPECT

22

Harold Sagan was almost three weeks into his investigation of Nikki Campbell's disappearance when he sat down with Tim Bindner's ex-wife, Terry. She had remarried and was living in another part of the state.

Sagan's first impression of the woman was that she was a grown-up flower child—a little vague, a little spacey, but pleasant.

She and Tim had met on a blind date in high school in San Bernardino when she was sixteen. They dated for three years, then married on September 7, 1968.

"When did you last hear from Tim?" Sagan asked her.

"Christmas—just before Christmas. He sent a card."

The card was generic—some ice skaters on a pond. He wondered how her life was going and said that he had helped save a school in a fire. The last thing he wrote was "Can I see you again before I die?"

Terry said she heard from Tim now and then, usually when something was troubling him. She remembered the FBI agents coming to talk to her in 1988, and then she got a letter from Tim saying that the agents had questioned him about Amber Swartz's disappearance.

She said that she and Tim separated in 1978. There were many reasons: "He was seeing other women. He was strange. It was like he had other things on his mind besides our marriage."

The women he got involved with had two things in common: kids and problems. He tried to solve their problems for them, and would come home and tell Terry about their financial, emotional, and physical difficulties. There was one particular woman—Lola— he worked with her at Social Security. When he got involved with her, the marriage ended.

Lola had young children and her own set of problems, and Tim said that he wanted to take care of everybody—Lola and her kids *and* Terry.

Terry wanted no part of it and gave him an ultimatum. "He left the house like he was going for a walk. I didn't see him for years after that," she said.

He left his wife as if ten years of marriage weren't a big deal. He called a few times. There were the Christmas cards. But that was it.

Sagan asked the woman what she meant when she said he was "strange."

He was antisocial, she said. "He had only a few friends. He seemed to get along better with women. He didn't take care of himself."

He was sloppy—hygiene and appearance. "The clothes he wore made him look like a bum."

Terry remembered seeing him at his brother's place in Pittsburg years after the divorce. Tim showed up—his hair a mess, wearing an unkempt beard, dirty clothing, and shoes that didn't match.

Tim just never seemed to grow up. "If he went with me to visit my family, he'd go outside the house and climb a tree and spend hours up there while we were in the house visiting."

He was like the character named Yossarian in *Catch-22*, looking down at the strange rituals other people engage in. He was detached. Never showed any emotion. A loner.

Tim enjoyed writing poetry, read a lot, and had a fantastic memory. He could memorize complete books of chess moves. Terry didn't remember Tim's having any interest in cemeteries back then. He loved to hike. The year he had a summer job at a national park in Idaho, he hiked more than three hundred miles. He also had an extensive coin collection, and had sold part of it for the down payment on their first house in Richmond.

"He holds his emotions in," Terry said. "He doesn't let other people know what he's feeling. He never let *me* know."

Nor did he talk to her about his family life when he was growing up. She suspected that his father wasn't around much and that he didn't get along with his mother. According to Terry, she was a controlling woman—always telling others what to do with their lives—and she often lost her temper. Tim's mother paid for his education while he was at Cal-Riverside and the University of Idaho, but when he married Terry and enrolled at Berkeley, she refused to pay.

Tim was bitter—about himself, about life. "He acted like he was angry at the world. I never understood that. Nobody ever caused him any harm or gave him any reason to be so bitter."

If his attitude had been different, he could have made something of himself. He blamed society, acted as if society was out to get him. "He just didn't have any goals in life."

It was a waste. He was so intelligent. He had such great potential.

"He was always angry," Terry said. "But he never expressed that anger."

On January 14, 1992, Sunnyside Farms in Cordelia
shipped 500,000 cartons of milk with Nikki Campbell's
picture on them. Friends volunteered to print and mail
flyers. They planned fund-raising events, designed
highway billboards, and seized every opportunity to
keep the story alive in the media. A local business-
person, Craig Wheelright, offered a reward of $10,000
to anyone who found Nikki Campbell.

On January 15, at 9:30 P.M., Sagan's team again met
Dale Myer and the dog handlers from Contra Costa
County. This time they were in the area of the undeveloped Kolob Hills—the vantage point from which, according to Sagan's theory, Tim Bindner could have
been looking for Sheila Cosgrove. He could have spotted Nikki walking alone in the fading light of December 27.

Fog rolled through the hills. It was like a night on
the English moors—the weather, the mood, the
hounds. The temperature dropped into the forties, just
as it had the night when Nikki disappeared.

The team went to Gillespie Court, on the east side
of the hills. Myer scented Friday with Bindner's T-shirt,
and the dog wandered around sniffing but not locking
onto any scent.

The group moved to the end of Rustle Court, walking in a northerly direction toward one of the hills.
When Friday reached the top of the hill, he bolted. He
had Bindner's scent, and he was moving fast beside a
chain-link fence around a water tank.

The dog stopped and lingered near a concrete culvert. He stalled there at a scent pool. The dog had to
work the pool until he found the freshest trail out of it.
Then Friday bolted again, straight down the face of the
north side of the hill. Myer struggled to stay upright.

When they reached Waterman Boulevard, they crossed and headed west. At the intersection of Vista Grande, Friday stopped. He began whining and wandering around in the yards there. The scent trail ended.

Myer's report indicated only that the suspect's scent had been found, but Friday had intersected a trail on top of the Kolob Hills and followed it to the east, away from Nephi Drive. The dog's behavior suggested that Tim Bindner could have parked his car on Vista Grande, crossed Waterman, and hiked up the back of the bluff, where he would have passed the water tank and continued to the westernmost edge of the hills. Once there, he would have been facing Sheila Cosgrove's house, on Nephi Drive.

The officers couldn't see the house through the dense fog, but they knew it was there, right at the foot of the hill.

By January 17 Sagan's investigation had generated more than five hundred leads. Some were the usual—sightings of the child as near as Benicia, as far away as Texas. Some were bizarre—like the psychic who had a vision of terrorists snatching Nikki by using a laser to put her in their car. Some were tips on people the police should be looking at, and a few of these were about Tim Bindner.

The first call came in on January 3, even before Sagan's initial encounter with Bindner. It came through the Nikki hot line and was from a co-worker of Bindner's. The man was reluctant to talk but said that he didn't like Bindner because he was a strange guy who once had brought a copy of a pornographic magazine into the break room at work. It contained pictures of nude men and little boys. The talk around the plant was that the cops were investigating the guy for something. "You people should take a look at him," the caller said.

A call from another of Bindner's co-workers came in on January 10. This man said he knew that the FBI was looking at Bindner for something involving children, and that Bindner had showed up at work one time with a copy of NAMBLA (North American Man Boy Love Association) magazine. He knew Bindner volunteered at Children's Hospital, and that concerned him. "He hangs around cemeteries a lot," the man said, "and he puts up posters of missing children in his locker and on the bulletin board. He said he'd rather work in a crematorium than work here."

Sagan asked the man what Bindner's demeanor had been since December 27, the day of Nikki's disappearance.

"He's more subdued," the man said, "almost reserved."

The Fairfield investigative team had other suspects to look at.

One suspect lived near Mankas Corner and was being looked at in the disappearance of another child. He had never been cooperative with the police before, but he insisted he had nothing to do with whatever happened to Nikki Campbell, and he wanted to clear himself.

A second confided in a volunteer from the Amber Foundation that he knew where Nikki Campbell was. He said that he was a psychic who used a needle and thread held over a map as a pointer to locate missing persons. Nikki was tied to a tree at the Robert Louis Stevenson State Park in Napa, he said. She wasn't, but the investigators had to look at him.

A third suspect had an alibi for the night of the abduction, but Detective Mel Ferro noted how nervous the man was when talking about Nikki's disappearance. They would have to check out his alibi.

The team was working fast. Within a week they cleared all three men. Tim Bindner remained a suspect.

Sagan, Allio, Hom, and the others moved in on Fifty-third Street in Oakland and interviewed Bindner's neighbors. They were willing to talk.

Bindner is strange, one said. He always wants to be around kids.

He used to work at Social Security, but they fired him for sending money to kids.

He's like a kid himself.

The FBI came and took him away one time.

Bindner had sent one neighbor's fourteen-year-old daughter a letter that seemed to her father to have sexual overtones. The man went to a lawyer, but there wasn't anything he could do about it. That year, for the first time in four years, the family received a Christmas card from Bindner—the little Russian girl holding up four fingers. It was the same card Bindner had sent to Mary Ellen O'Toole.

Harold Sagan received another letter from Bindner. It was getting to be routine.

> *Once* a symbol of love, hope, compassion and resolve. Its deterioration, physically, consistent with its deterioration in possibilities of the heart, to a present of despair, anguish, frustration and, finally, the death of a dream. *Now* are brought together in utmost sadness Amber, Angela, and Amanda.
>
> I'll always love them. Will you?
>
> (Lest you think I am playing a "game," as you have told me *you are,* let me assure you I am *not.* This page presents the *only* proper catharsis for me.)

Bindner had taped some dirt to the page, cited some biblical quotes, then added a postscript: "This is *not* 'evidence.' It is 'anti-evidence.' (Just like 'anti-matter' is not 'matter')."

Sagan knew that matter and antimatter neutralize one another. Again, Bindner was saying that the issue was moot.

There was another postscript in which he demeaned the polygraph used on him in Pinole and the dogs used on him in Fairfield. He also said he wasn't going to write anymore.

Much later, Bindner was uneasy talking about that particular letter to Sagan.

> *I sent him a piece of paper with some dirt from Angela's grave on it. It was a note that said basically—I don't remember the exact words, but something like, "These children are now together in sadness for you." Something like that. I was saying, "If you're gonna take me away from this, it's in your lap now." But I also said in the note, "This is not evidence. This is anti-evidence. Just like matter is [not] anti-matter." And what I was trying to do was get him to look in the mirror and see that it's not what it looks like. So, in a way, it could have been construed as a taunt, or a slap in the face, but it wasn't. . . .*
>
> *He's taking away from me this I've had with me for ten years. I can't do this anymore. So here's some dirt from her grave. Here's the children. Now you do it. It's yours now. That was my way, basically, of turning it over to him.*

On January 30, more than five hundred people attended a fund-raiser for Nikki Campbell at the Chuck E. Cheese Pizza Time Theater. Sports celebrities signed autographs and auctioned sports memorabilia.

These were the things you had to do to maintain the fragile belief that you weren't helpless.

Bindner did communicate with Sagan again. He sent the cop one of Gary Larson's "Far Side" cartoons. Two police officers are standing in a doorway. An apparent murder victim is hanging upside down, dressed in armor and decorated with Christmas lights—with flippers on his feet, a fishbowl on his head, and a frog in his mouth. The caption reads: "Same as the others, O'Neill. The flippers, the fishbowl, the frogs, the lights, the armor. . . . Just one question: Is this the work of our guy, or a copycat?"

Beneath that Bindner printed, "Just as well I didn't find Amanda's body, eh, Harry?"

Bindner had written a number on the door to the apartment—the same incorrect number of the Cosgrove house on Nephi Drive that he had used when he was writing to Sheila. The two cops in the cartoon had name tags: Timm (Sagan's sergeant) and Sagan.

———————

On February 14, Kim Swartz and the Amber Foundation sponsored a highly publicized gathering that included nine mothers bound by the horror of having had a child abducted by a stranger.

All day they stuffed flyers into envelopes—more than twenty thousand in all. The atmosphere was almost festive. Children who were old enough to work did so. The littlest ones played or slept.

Then the mothers faced the cameras.

Sharon Garecht said, "My main hope at this point is that my daughter is alive and that she is in a situation where one day she will find the strength to get away."

Kevin Collins's mother was there. He would be eighteen—he had been ten when he disappeared from a San Francisco street.

Ilene Misheloff would be seventeen the next month.

Patricia Wetterling was there from Minnesota. Her thirteen-year-old son Jacob had been coming back from a video rental store with two friends when a man wearing a mask and wielding a gun confronted them. He took Jacob away.

Kim Swartz said that it was therapeutic for all of

them to get together. Each of them knew the feelings. "We've all gotten really desperate," she said. "We're tired. I'm sure there's not one of us here who wouldn't do anything to have her child back."

The newest member of the group was Anne Campbell. Six weeks had passed since Nikki had vanished. The other mothers supported and comforted her as she said, "I wake up every morning knowing today's gonna be the day they find her. If not today, I know for sure it's gonna be tomorrow. And that's all we can hope for."

These women, the old and the new members of a unique sorority, were well aware that after the camera crews were gone, the public would forget their children. But they couldn't let that happen.

"We love our children," Kim said, "and we can't go on without knowing what has happened to them."

As they gathered that day and stuffed envelopes, outside there were police in unmarked cars, watching. They recorded license plates. They took photographs. Harold Sagan was one of them.

There was always the chance that someone would show up who didn't belong there. It's why cops attend the funerals of murder victims.

———

Tim Bindner was having his own problems with surveillance. He knew police were following him. He would come out of work, ready to begin his jog home, and spot the dark sedan with the lone, white, suited male watching him. After he had jogged a few blocks, the first tail would drop off and another one would slide into place. They were interchangeable, and they were obvious about what they were doing. Bindner called it "hostile surveillance."

He went through it in 1988, over the Amber case. Now, here they were—at it again.

He was in his yard on February 17 when two men

pulled up in a van. They seemed nervous, came into the yard and asked him if he had seen a small black box with wires dangling out of it.

"No," Bindner said. "Let me check with my wife."

Sandra had seen it. She had picked it up in the yard and thrown it into the trash.

After Bindner told the two men—FBI agents—what his wife had said, they retrieved the box and left.

Bindner figured the box was a transponder, a radio signal-emitting device that, when attached to a suspect's car, enables cops to follow the vehicle without having to see it.

"Our tax dollars at work," Bindner thought. These people were spectacularly inept.

———————

A week later, Sagan received another letter from Bindner. The Oakland man wrote that he had spoken with FBI Special Agent Larry Taylor ("He knows this case and has studied me").

> If you want a man to open his heart to you, even confess his sins to you, don't you have to reach out and touch his heart? I believe so; Larry + Mary Ellen seem to, also. You never tried to touch anything except my anger, which I held in then, but feel toward you now; for haven't you denied my dream? These children are my heart; It is not hard to tell when somebody doesn't really care.
>
> But I'm *not* unusual, I'll take help wherever I can get it. Even from the FBI, (or you.) Be nice, "Bud."

> Tim

Sagan read the letter as an invitation. Bindner wanted to be "studied," to have law enforcement professionals pay attention to him. If Sagan could get close to Bindner, convince him that he cared about him, maybe Bindner would "confess his sins."

Sagan wrote to Bindner, thinking of their correspondence as two adversaries sitting across a chess board from one another. Bindner had made some moves; now it was Sagan's turn.

Bindner, the man who read book after book on chess strategy, responded immediately. "Harry. Chess? Sure. Let's play a game by mail."

23

When Kim Swartz and the Amber Foundation sponsored the gathering of parents of abducted children,
an army of cops descended on the neighborhood.
Sagan was there, and Kim made a point of speaking to
him. She liked the fact that he didn't talk down to her,
didn't try to placate her. If he could answer her questions, he did. He seemed caring and was open to any
ideas Kim might have about the missing children
cases. It was a refreshing change.

Kim recalled that, late on December 27, 1991, as
police and neighbors fanned out through Nikki Campbell's Salisbury Drive neighborhood, staff and volunteers at the Amber Foundation in Pinole heard that
there was a child missing in Fairfield. A child's disappearance was an all-too-common occurrence for
them, although most of the time the child turned up or
had been taken by one parent involved in a squabble
over visitation or custody. This time, as was often the

case, the foundation knew few of the details of the disappearance.

That night, Kim Swartz saw the late TV news report about four-year-old Nikki Campbell. It hit her hard.

The feeling that there might be a connection between Nikki Campbell's disappearance and Amber's was insidious. Kim couldn't get away from it. The two girls were wearing the same colors. Both were fair-skinned, blue-eyed, and blond. Nikki was younger, but she was big for her age. They even lived in similar neighborhoods.

On Saturday morning, the day after Nikki's disappearance, a foundation staff member called the Fairfield police and talked to a detective who was working the case. She told him about Amber's disappearance. The detective took the information and thanked her.

Kim had received a note from Tim Bindner the day after Amber's birthday. He sent a card or a note every year. This time he said that he had spent part of the day in Amber Park—the two-acre lot where Amber used to hunt for bugs and rocks—and down along the creek behind Kim's house. He'd met some kids whose parents had dropped them off there. One of them told him that the police suspected a man in a blue van of taking Amber.

> Sometimes i try to show people that i am in control and know exactly what i should do. Then sometimes i feel so helpless. The North slope hills were lovely today!

Kim wondered what he was talking about. Developers had maimed the only north slope hills around the neighborhood. They were blooming with split-level California architecture.

After receiving that note, she didn't hear from him for months. It bothered her whenever he went silent. As uncomfortable as he could make her feel when he was around, she still wanted to maintain a connection with him.

It was difficult for her to recognize and accept her own feelings about Bindner. Sometimes when he went silent, Kim even felt a sense of loss. It was like a void in her life because she had become so conditioned to talking to him. She missed the conversations. The silence made her feel as if she were losing Amber all over again.

Kim Swartz believed that Tim Bindner had psychologically seduced her—that he had fostered a dependency in her, dangled possibility in front of her. One of these days he was going to slip, she thought. He was going to say something that he shouldn't, and she needed to maintain the connection until that happened.

Before Christmas in 1991, he had sent a card. "I want you to know," he wrote, "that your strength in time of anguish has helped me and given *me* strength. You are a very special woman and I think of you often, with love."

Bindner also told Kim that he had some daffodil bulbs left from a cemetery project and he wanted to know if he could plant them in Amber Park. He said that he wanted to see Kim again soon.

On Sunday, December 29, Kim drove to Fairfield to visit with Anne Campbell. Later that week, Kim called the Fairfield police. It wasn't enough that a detective had taken the information from the foundation worker. Usually she had to push cops to get them to pay attention, so she asked to speak with the lead detective, Harold Sagan.

Sagan impressed her. He seemed to know all the basic information already, including everything about Amber, Tim Bindner, and Bindner's letters to Sheila Cosgrove. This was a cop who got up to speed in a hurry.

She had been through one detective after another on the Pinole police department. No one had kept the case for very long, but they all shared a disturbing habit: They took days or even weeks to return her calls. The latest one, Galloway, referred to her as "babe" or "dear" whenever he did call. Kim considered that inappropriate and offensive. She wanted professionalism, not sexist familiarity.

Sometimes the cops told her that if Tim Bindner was a suspect, he was just one of many. Other times, they insisted that he wasn't a suspect. Pinole cops seemed to take their leads from the FBI, jumping only when the Feds said to jump.

Kim Swartz had lost all respect for the FBI. Two years after Amber's disappearance, she had made an appointment to see Special Agents Mary Ellen O'Toole and Duke Diedrich. She wanted to know what was going on with the case; she needed to get involved in the investigation. "I know I can help you out," she said.

The agents were expecting her, but they had a different agenda. They kept her there for six hours, interrogated her, wouldn't let her go to the bathroom, wouldn't allow her to eat, kept firing questions at her, then put her back on the polygraph.

Again, Ron Homer told her that she was clear. "I've been doing this for years," he said. "If you're lying, I'll quit my job."

"Thank you," she said. "It's nice to hear somebody believes me."

When she left O'Toole and Diedrich, Kim thought, "If they're still investigating *me* after all this time, they haven't done a damn thing."

———————

As Kim and Sagan talked at the gathering on February 14, she told the Fairfield detective about her problems with the police and the FBI. He listened. He seemed to understand.

Sagan explained that if Pinole's public position was that Tim Bindner was not a suspect in Amber's disappearance, he had to respect that. Privately, it was a different matter. He knew Bindner's status, and so did Kim. Besides, Bindner was the primary suspect in the Nikki Campbell case.

Although he knew that the Antioch police had a solid suspect in the Angela Bugay murder, Sagan also knew that Angela Bugay linked the Pinole and Fairfield cases: both Amber's scent and Nikki's scent had been found at Angela's grave on the hill in Oakmont Cemetery. The scents of these two little girls, who had never met and who came from different cities, had been tracked to the grave of yet another little girl. There was only one connection among the three children—Tim Bindner, the frequent visitor to Angela's grave. Bloodhounds had indicated that Amber's and Nikki's scents were in Binder's vehicles. The man had shown up to search in both cities.

"You think Tim Bindner will show up here?" Kim asked Sagan that day when the parents of abducted children were gathered at the school in Pinole.

"It's the kind of thing he might do," the detective said.

The area was crawling with police. Sagan assured Kim that they would stay out of the way.

She shared with Sagan some of her questions about Bindner. She wanted to know why he kept hanging around, why he wrote those letter to her, why he was so obsessed with the cases.

Sagan wanted to know the same things—and more. He said they would talk again, but Kim didn't hear from him for a long while. She didn't take the silence personally; she knew the cop had his own case to worry about.

In May, when Bindner stopped by her house, she called Sagan and told him about the conversation. "He just stopped by around five-thirty. I didn't know he was coming. He said he'd been at a cemetery in Benicia fixing headstones, and then went to Oakmont to visit Angela's grave."

She and Bindner had talked for about fifteen minutes. "I told him that it was still hard for me, even after four years, to think I couldn't go outside the door and find Amber jumping rope. I said that was what I thought she was doing the day she disappeared. Tim

said, 'She *was* jumping rope.' A chill went right through
my body. He was just so sure that's what she was
doing."

Sagan asked her about Bindner's visits. Did he
stop by often? What did he want?

"He's stopped by from time to time—offers to help
in any way he can. He expresses love for me and anguish over Amber disappearing. This time he asked
how he could help, and I told him by searching for
Amber. He said he'd do that, but that the only thing he
expected to find at this late date was bones."

She told Sagan that Bindner had some ideas about
places to search, but he was also reluctant because the
cops always stopped him.

"He said he doesn't know who he can trust anymore, because coincidences keep happening."

"What kind of coincidences?" Sagan asked.

"He didn't say, but they're the kinds of things that
make him look bad."

She was beginning to feel that this was one cop
she could trust, one who had a genuine interest in
solving the cases. "I think he took my daughter," she
said simply. "That's why I tolerate having him around
here. I keep waiting for him to make a slip."

24

Harold Sagan received a note from Tim Bindner, along with a play sheet for a game of chess.

> Harry—
> Chess? Sure. Let's play a game by mail. I prefer "old style" chess notation (rather than "A to H").
> Also, since in your letter you said you've made the "recent move," I'll take white and go first.
> If you want to play just send back your move on the play sheet.
>
> Tim
>
> P.S. I do not wish to participate in any of your other silly "games."

Sagan responded on the twelfth. He reiterated an offer he had made earlier—that he would work with Bindner to find Amanda—but said that if Tim wanted to play chess, they would play chess.

Bindner wrote back:

Dear Harry,
    Regarding your note, I wish I *could* work to find Amanda, or Amber, or Michaela, or Ilene, or Gina—and I *have* done my best for them. However, I had no involvement in the disappearances of any of these children—so the only way I can— and have tried to—help, is by going out and searching. You told me, "I know you snatched that kid." Sorry, guy, no way. Although man often kills the things he loves, (even as our pioneers killed their wilderness), I am not capable of hurting a child. I don't suppose you'll ever "know" that, though.

Sagan recognized the name Gina—Gina Ellison was a young woman who had disappeared while jogging. Bindner's search notes in that case were in the folder with the notes he'd kept while wandering around Mankas Corner.

In his letter, Bindner confirmed the notation they would use and outlined the rules for the chess game. Referring to chess books or other players was permissible.

Sagan's reaction was immediate. "Shit," he told Chuck Timm, "I don't know how to play chess. I don't even know what you call the pieces."

Bindner had set the rules. Sagan could refer to other players, so he called an organization in Sacramento that had done research and computer work for law enforcement agencies in the northern part of the state. He explained his dilemma, and they put him in touch with a student at Berkeley who was one of the top ten chess players in the United States.

Sagan met with the young man on the university

campus. The kid seemed pleased to be assisting the police, but he knew none of the details of the case. He brought his credentials with him—his national ranking, magazine articles about himself. He wasn't bragging. He wanted to assure Sagan that he was genuine. The cop felt more than assured.

Bindner was eager to play.

> It was almost symbolic to me. Like, that's the only game we're ever gonna have that's gonna make any sense is this chess game. That was my feeling when we began the game. This is the only thing that's really real here. Let's have something be real. Investigation isn't real. Suspicions about me aren't real. And I've told Mr. Sagan numerous times that he's going in the wrong direction. If he's ever gonna solve his case he has to look elsewhere and follow up on other leads. So the only thing that was really real between me and him was the chess game.

The Lewis Carroll classic *Through the Looking Glass* opens with a bored Alice playing with chess pieces and trying to educate her kitten about the game. The kitten won't cooperate. So, as a punishment, Alice holds the animal up to a mirror to see her own pouting reflection. From this gesture comes the fantasy of the Looking-Glass House, where everything is the reverse of the rest of the world—including the words in books, which "go the wrong way."

When she passes through "the bright silvery mist" of the mirror and into the Looking-Glass World, Alice discovers that the chess pieces are alive.

In his note to Sagan of April 13, Bindner included a puzzle from another Carroll book, *Alice in Wonderland*. He wrote: "Sheila was not my Alice. I wanted to introduce her to Alice, and to Charles, but felt that I would probably fail, as I did. Then Amanda disappeared, and I fell down a rabbit hole."

Sagan assumed that "Charles" referred to Carroll's

real name, Charles Lutwidge Dodgson. He also wondered about all the "A" names: Alice, Angela, Amber, and Amanda, Nikki's real first name.

As Alice moves through the Looking-Glass World, she sees that brooks and hedges crisscross the countryside. The effect is to divide the land into squares—a chess board the size of the world, and life is a game of chess.

Bindner's letter of the thirteenth continued:

I sincerely hope you solve the Amanda Campbell (Nikki) case and find her, for the sake of all our children, because I simply cannot believe that all 4 of these little girl kidnaps (actually 5, counting Angela) are unrelated. This person, or these people, have to be stopped, a resolve I obtained on 2/16/1984.

February 16, 1984, was the day of the drunken dream on the bus coming back from the ball game. Angela needed help. Bindner had to help her, but he couldn't get to her.

Alice's worlds are dream worlds, layer upon layer of fantasy. As with any dream, there is a core of reality: Alice had been trying to teach her kitten the game of chess. The Red Queen teaches Alice chess according to rules that make as much sense to Alice as her own ramblings probably made to the kitten.

When Alice meets Humpty Dumpty, perched precariously on a wall, he asks her how old she is. She tells him she's seven years, six months old. He would have "left off at seven," he tells her. Critics have interpreted this passage and much of the book as Carroll's own injunction against aging. There is no real escape from growing up, Humpty Dumpty suggests, without "proper assistance." The only way to remain a child is to die.

Sagan kept the correspondence going. He wanted to maintain communication with his suspect, and the

Oakland man continued to be willing to talk. But what was he saying?

What was he *thinking*? How did Tim Bindner's head work? Was he a killer of children, an avid player of mind games, or a terribly unlucky victim of coincidence and circumstance? Sagan had worked to clear other suspects, but Bindner was frustrating. Sagan couldn't clear him, and Bindner wasn't helping.

Yeah, I played games with him and I taunted him in certain ways. The word "taunt" is kind of a tainted word because it implies guilt. "Poked fun at" would be more appropriate, I guess. I poked fun at him a couple times, and then tried to appeal to his own sense of humor. But throughout the exchanges that we had, the message that I was trying to get through to the guy was, "Hey, you know, whatever you may think of me— however bad a person you may think I am—I did not kill this little child, and you better look elsewhere." He better follow up on other leads. And I told him that to his face. I told him that over the phone. I told him that in my letters. And I'll tell him today. "Man, if you're gonna solve this case, you better look elsewhere. You better start digging a little deeper than you been digging, 'cause it ain't me."

See, that's been my focus on the Nikki Campbell case. In the beginning, I spent one day looking for that little baby. I didn't find a damn thing that had any value. If I had, I would've reported it. That's it and that's all. That's my total involvement in the case. That's the only connection I have to the case. . . .

Take a look at the actual facts. Take a look at what you got. You don't have any evidence. You don't have anything concrete. And I've told press people this on numerous occasions. There's nothing there. He's not gonna build a case. There's not gonna be an arrest. I mean, I guess my favorite line to declare my innocence would be: I have not committed any of the crimes with which I will never be charged.

Sagan wasn't receiving help elsewhere, either. Word was moving through law enforcement agencies in the Bay Area that Sagan was plowing ahead, going after Bindner in a highly aggressive way. That was how the Fairfield police operated, and Sagan made it clear that he wasn't backing off. Detectives in the other departments with missing child cases were slow to return his calls—if they returned them at all. Some of it was understandable. They had cases to protect from discovery motions should Sagan arrest Bindner and bring him to trial. What if a jury acquitted Bindner and the trial exposed their evidence?

The FBI was worse. They had a wealth of intelligence on this guy, but they weren't sending any of it Sagan's way. He could see no excuse for that.

Sagan's idea was simple enough: Rule the guy in or rule him out; make a case or stop wasting time on him.

Once again, Sagan was alone—as he had been when he was the only kid in his New York City parochial school who didn't speak English, or the only military dependent in an affluent Marin County high school, or his unit's point man in Vietnam. It seemed he was always out there on his own.

On May 7, Bindner wrote:

> Law enforcement's latest "move"—the Bill Falk "gambit"—is tiresomely redundant, an insult to my intelligence, transparent as cellophane. Nevertheless I think I'll take 7-10 days to evaluate my proper response, for I must continue to be emotionally and religiously assertive of the love which Jesus said should be unending. Maybe they know that. Maybe they're just doing it because they know they'll get some kind of a response.

When Sagan answered the note with his next move in the chess game, he asked Bindner to explain the Bill Falk gambit. The truth was that Sagan already knew about it.

———————

Two years earlier, on January 24, 1990, the Oakland police had assigned undercover cop Bill Grijalva to attend a conference—the Asian Advisory Committee on Crime—at the Hilton Hotel. The workshops were about child pornography and child sexual exploitation. Steve Mauser, a youth service officer, told Grijalva that a man named Timothy Bindner had signed up to attend the conference.

Mauser said the FBI had looked at Bindner in the kidnap and murder of Angela Bugay in 1983. When Grijalva checked with FBI Special Agent Duke Diedrich, Diedrich confirmed that Bindner had been a suspect in that case, as well as in the kidnapping of Amber Swartz in Pinole. "We aren't concentrating on him right now," Diedrich said, "but he hasn't been ruled out."

It was 7:05 P.M., and Grijalva had just registered at the conference, when Bindner approached him and introduced himself. "What agency are you with?" Bindner asked the bearded cop.

"Big Brothers of America," Grijalva said. "My name's William Falk."

Bindner seemed surprised that William Falk wasn't with a police agency. "I just have an interest in this subject and I signed up for it when I read about it in the newspaper," Bindner said. "I'm particularly interested in hearing what Teddy Unterreiner has to say."

Theodore Unterreiner was a Bay Area pedophile who specialized in molesting Asian children. Once the cops were wise to him, he fled to Canada. Authorities there caught and extradited him. Now law enforcement used Unterreiner to talk to interested groups about his sexual attraction to children and about the successful lures he had used.

Bindner told the Oakland cop that he first became

interested in child exploitation following the murder of Angela Bugay in 1983. He conducted his own investigation in the Amber Swartz case and had spent hundreds of hours searching for the child. "Because of what I was doing in that case, I ended up becoming a suspect," he said. "The FBI followed me, the Pinole police. The FBI even accused me of burying little girls' clothing. All I did was try to help out, and I end up being a suspect."

Bindner told the cop, "I think I know where Amber is buried, but I can't look in that spot."

"I'd help you look," Grijalva offered. "I mean, it would put an end to her parents' suffering."

Bindner agreed. Grijalva noted that Bindner kept the conversation on the subject of the murder of children. If the cop steered the conversation elsewhere, Bindner brought it back. He seemed to know about every kidnapping and murder involving children in the Bay Area. He knew the children's names, the parents' names, the names of any suspects, and the details of the crimes.

"What do you do besides being a Big Brother?" Bindner asked.

"I have my own import and export business," the cop said.

Bindner said he had been looking for another job.

"I'm just getting off the ground," Grijalva said. "Maybe in six to eight months I'll be looking for employees. I don't have anything right now."

The two men exchanged phone numbers.

"If you're still interested in looking for Amber," Bindner said, "there's really only two ways the guy could've gone after he kidnapped her. Well, there may be more than one person, but he or they would either go down Savage Avenue, which leads to the valley, or up Savage, which takes you out to the freeway. I've searched the whole valley, but I've got a spot in mind where Amber might be buried. I've also got a spot in mind in Hayward where Michaela Garecht might be buried."

"Oh, did you work that case, too?"

"I put in about three days looking for Michaela."

"What about the kid in Dublin?" Grijalva asked.

"I only looked for Ilene Misheloff for one day."

"Where do you think the Swartz kid might be?"

Bindner described a building opposite the golf course on Highway 4. "It's a perfect place for someone to take her behind, do things to her, kill her, and bury her. There's a lot of area back there. What we'd have to look for would be indications of a shallow grave."

They agreed to go have a look on Saturday, January 27. Bindner also recommended Ressler's book to the cop.

Grijalva gave him a ride home. On the way, Bindner told the cop that his wife was applying for a child-care license so she could do child care out of their home.

On the second day of the conference, Bindner again sought out the cop. "Somebody was murdered across the street from us last night. It was about an hour before you dropped me off. My wife and kids are terrified."

At the end of the day, Bindner begged off on going on the search for Amber. "My family's still pretty upset about the shooting, and I should spend the weekend with them. I'll call you."

Grijalva checked with Homicide and confirmed that there had been a shooting on Fifty-third Street at Genoa the night before.

———————

On May 21, 1992, Bindner wrote to Sagan with his latest move in the game.

> The Bill Falk gambit is the Behavioral Science Unit of the FBI's latest attempt to get me to "lead them" to Amber's body. One of their *theories* is that I killed her, and buried her, but want to ease her familie's [sic] pain, and thereby my own guilt, by letting them have her remains and

"closure." So Bill calls me and says he met me 2 years ago [i.e., their meeting at the conference sponsored by the Asian Advisory Committee on Crime, January 24, 1990]—well, I *don't* remember him—but within 2 minutes he's talking about places I mentioned should be searched in case Amber's remains are there. The gambit is obvious. No good can possibly come of it, so I decline. It's a stale gambit, anyway. An Oakland cop tried it 1 1/2 years ago.

Sagan knew that Bindner was smart, but did he have a lousy memory? Was it all the alcohol he routinely consumed, or was there some other reason why segments of his experience seemed to be unavailable to him?

Why do detectives always seem to believe we are lying? Most of the people you investigate and interview are innocent, so most of them are telling the truth. Yet I receive that blank stare that says, "Yeah, sure, make up another one"— and sometimes it's even put into words. Why did you tell me "I know you snatched that girl"? By now, you should be convinced that I *didn't*.

Other than that, new contacts, and more hurting people, I've found who I'm going to try to help and comfort. The love of Jesus flows, always.

Sincerely, your investigatee,

Tim

25

At three in the morning, the car moved slowly through the sleeping city of Pinole. All was quiet until, finally, the woman spoke.

"One of the kids, I think, was taken from here. I'm not sure."

Harold Sagan looked at the woman in the backseat. He and Chuck Timm had met her and her lawyer after the attorney had called to say that he had a client who was talking about bodies buried in Napa, Solano, and Contra Costa Counties.

The woman directed them first into Contra Costa County, to Pinole. They were at the end of Savage Avenue when she spoke. Any doubts Sagan might have had about the woman began to evaporate. She had brought them to within yards of where Amber Swartz had vanished four years earlier.

The woman told them where to drive next—up to

Highway 4, make a turn on McEwen Road, drive for a while.

Then she told them to stop.

"Late at night the body got dumped over the edge here," she said.

Sagan notified the Pinole police, and an intensive search of the area followed.

Used mostly by locals, McEwen Road is two and a half miles long and two lanes wide, connecting Port Costa, above Carquinez Scenic Drive, and Highway 4. It wasn't possible to divert traffic, so the media quickly caught wind of what was going on.

Sagan was up there, but he observed protocol. It was Pinole's case. He watched as the Pinole cops, the Contra Costa Sheriff's Department, and the FBI dug holes and probed the area for some trace of evidence.

Tim Bindner saw the press release describing the search in the woods along McEwen Road. He tried to call Kim, but she wasn't around. He left a message. One of the volunteers at the Amber Foundation returned his call.

Bindner was angry, wound up, and sounded as if he had been drinking. The San Pablo cops had rousted him on June 3, the fourth anniversary of Amber's disappearance. They had detained him for a half hour while they did a warrant check and looked through his car. "They looked like they were tweaking to arrest me but couldn't figure out a way to do it," he said.

Police followed him all the next day as well.

"How did you know they were there?" the woman asked.

"I know when I'm being followed," Bindner said. "I know when people are investigating me, and I know how to approach them. And I know how to keep my hands in the right places so I don't get shot. This is serious. I have learned they were after me. It was hostile surveillance. It wasn't covert surveillance. Thursday last week—you never know why—but that's the day they were doing the big search up on McEwen Road. So does this have something to do with me? Do they think I put Amber's body up there, or some evidence of the crime up there? I don't know."

He told her he had searched up there on August 16, 1988. "Somebody might have seen me up there, walking around with a shovel."

Just as they had seen him at so many other places out in the valley—with a shovel, a probe, and a bag for cans.

Bindner was talking nonstop to the volunteer—now about Fairfield. "I waited a week and a half because I knew they were going to follow me up there. I knew somebody was going to be on me because they've been on me ever since Amber disappeared. Still, I went to conduct a six-hour search of the same type I did for Amber in the Pinole Valley, and I ended up becoming a media celebrity, a suspect, and the whole bit. They didn't arrest me, but they took my car. Told me to get my butt out of town and don't ever come back. If it was the first time you could say 'That was Fairfield—a bunch of hick cops.' But it's not the first time. It's not the second time. It's not the third time. I've been going through this every time I go out looking for somebody. It's a bit sickening. It is frustrating."

He asked about Kim and how she was handling the McEwen Road situation. "Does Kim think that maybe I took her daughter?" Bindner asked.

"I don't think so. She's never told me that. I think she doesn't know what happened, and at this point she wants any help she can get."

"Over the years now I've felt like I should probably keep my distance a little bit, just because of the fact that the authorities still consider me a possible suspect."

"Knowing Kim as you do," she said, "do you honestly think if she thought you had anything to do with it she could talk to you? Think about it. Kim is good, but she's not that good. I honestly don't think she could do it."

"Yeah," he said. "You're right. You're right."

————————

They were wrong.

Kim Swartz was angry. For four years Pinole police had shunted her from one detective to another, didn't return her phone calls, and came up with no leads. It didn't matter who the detective was—Pollard, Price, Galloway—Kim ended up feeling like a second-class citizen.

This time, the Pinole police hadn't told her anything about the search on McEwen Road. She saw the press release in the *West County Times*. It was the last straw.

The cops were chasing phantoms all over the East Bay, but they weren't paying any attention to Tim Bindner. He was a suspect, they said privately, but all they did was hassle him when he came around. That wasn't investigation, and it certainly wasn't going to get any information out of him. When she stopped at the Pinole department that day, she overheard some uniformed cops laughing about the latest roust of Bindner by San Pablo in St. Joseph's Cemetery.

She had two notes from Bindner and a message on her answering machine. So she called him.

"They had me shaking," Bindner told her. "I thought I was going to be arrested."

Then he laughed.

"I'm just so tired of this," Kim said.

Bindner asked her about McEwen Road.

Kim told him that she had seen the press release but knew nothing more. "I opened up the paper and there it was," she said.

"Like I told you," Bindner said, "I did go up there three years and nine months ago, but I only spent a couple hours, and basically what I did was roadsides, culverts, trace trails—basic roadside search like I did out in Pinole Valley. It was just another road to search. It wasn't any lead or anything like that, and I didn't find anything out there."

"How can a kid just disappear like this? I'm just—I guess I'm just tired."

"Well, they do," Bindner said. "The real question is how could anybody do something like this?"

"And what's happening to them?"

"I think a lot more work has to be done in that direction," he said. "I think a lot of it's being ignored. I think there are some things that I've dealt with in the last year, that I've seen, where there's been attempts to prevent people from investigating these kinds of things, or even acknowledging that these kinds of things exist. There's a lot of stuff that ain't right."

"Taking my little girl from me is definitely not right."

"And nobody's doing anything about it. Or too few people are doing something about it."

Kim was critical of the whole McEwen Road fiasco. Why hadn't the cops kept her informed?

"They haven't told me anything," she said.

"Well, don't judge them," Bindner said. "Don't judge. It could be a well-meaning person that really wanted to solve the case. You just don't know."

"I'm having a hard time knowing who I can and can't trust, who I can and can't believe. At this point it's just real hard. And it's real draining."

As fast as the roughness in Bindner's voice appeared, it vanished. Now there was an almost hypnotic, seductive quality to it. "Well, I'll tell you something. You can trust me. You can believe me. And you can believe that if there's any possible way—"

Kim cut him off. "I mean, what's our next move? What would be your next move? Because I tell you what, I don't believe the FBI in the least."

"I know what anthill they're crawling out of," Bindner said. "I know how they investigate. I've read books on it. I've done their scenarios. I read the Ressler book. I know where they're coming from. I know how they investigate. And I know that it has no further applicability to Amber. It doesn't."

There was no crime scene, no evidence, not a hint of what had happened to Amber. Neither the FBI nor the Pinole police had any place to start. Technically, Amber's fate was an unexplained disappearance.

"You know, they're chasing at threads," Bindner said. "If they want to chase threads, let 'em chase threads. And they're trying to build boxes around people."

Kim had heard that before from him. She also was aware of a claustrophobic problem the man seemed to have. He didn't like being inside—at least not in places that were strange to him. He got restless and had to move around. Whenever she knew he was coming by the house, Kim opened windows, raised the garage door—made the place seem open and airy so he wouldn't feel boxed in.

"I think they're a little bit embarrassed, too, Kim," he said. "They're zero for whatever, you know?"

"They should be embarrassed," she said. "I'm beginning to feel that Pinole can't do anything without FBI approval. And they don't know what they're doing anyway."

"I never put as much time and effort into any extracurricular activity as I have in trying to find Amber. And I really don't know what to do next. I'm afraid I'm going to get swooped on if I just drive up to Pinole. Did you get my letter?"

Bindner's letter had described the roust at St. Joseph's Cemetery in San Pablo on June 3. He was up there looking for broken grave markers to fix when the cops arrived. They detained him for forty minutes while they questioned, frisked, and photographed him. One cop finally went over and looked at some of the repairs that he had done, and seemed to believe the Oakland man.

"I'm just running out of strength here," Kim said.

"Let me ask you the same question. Where do we go from here?"

"I have no idea," she said, and couldn't hold back her tears. "I don't know what to do anymore. All I know is I miss my daughter. I just wish I knew something—anything. I'm going to miss her regardless. My life's probably never going to be the same again."

Sometimes it felt to Kim that Bindner was the only person she could talk to, even if what he said irritated her or sounded odd. She couldn't get anything out of anybody else; at least she could have a dialogue with him.

"Well, let me get this straight now," he said, returning to the subject of the McEwen Road search. "An attorney called."

"Right."

"And said there was some evidence of some buried things."

Kim reviewed the few details she remembered from the press release.

"I don't really want to call attention to myself," Bindner said, "but I'm just thinking about the possibility that maybe they're dealing with some leads about me. There have been some going around."

"You think they did all of this for that?"

"It's possible," he said. "I've seen so much weirdness in this case that it probably could. I've seen so many people get uptight about me, about the things that I've done to try to find your daughter, that it probably could. If so, then it's just another zero. Nothing happened that night except I went up there looking for your daughter. If it's a different kind of a lead, then I don't know any more than you do."

"How am I supposed to find that out? They don't tell me anything."

"All I know is that they may be—because they were following me Wednesday and Thursday, okay? And because I was up there before, and I was seen up there, and I was followed on that particular day when I went up and conducted that search on McEwen Road. They know I was up there. They consider me a possible suspect in the case. Maybe this lead has something

to do with me. If it does, then it's a big zero, because I
didn't take your daughter, and I didn't do—you know."

Bindner figured that if somebody had taken Amber to McEwen Road, it had to be a local person,
someone who knew the area.

"Or it's just another one of those stupid coincidences," Kim said. "That's the whole thing. My brain
hurts. And I'm so tired."

They talked about getting together to decide what
the next step might be. Kim said she wanted to hear
what he had to say, and invited him over. She didn't
ask the police or the FBI if she should meet with Bindner. She *told* them that was what she was going to do.

————————

When the search on McEwen road produced nothing,
investigators brought the woman back out to Pinole
and asked her to show them again. This time she directed them to an entirely different area, talking all the
while about a conspiracy—an organization that steals
kids and buries their bodies. They had sexually abused
her all her life, she said, and her parents were part of
the conspiracy.

Further investigation revealed that the woman had
a history of mental illness, was delusional, and made
claims that had no basis in reality.

26

Kim Swartz didn't know how many times she had
walked out Savage Avenue and wandered through the
neighborhood. She knew that time and weather erased
things—a scrap of cloth, a hair from her child's head, a
footprint. Whatever traces of Amber there might have
been were long gone. She also knew that she had to do
something.

The passage of time seemed to diminish the sense
of urgency that others felt. With each new case, the police investigated, then moved on, never giving enough
consideration to the possibility that some of the cases
might be linked. Amber had disappeared four years
ago. Nikki had been gone for six months now. All of
the children were in danger of becoming nothing more
than statistics—entries in somebody's computer.

For Kim Swartz, nothing had changed and nothing would change until she knew what had happened
to Amber. Maybe she couldn't get straight answers

from the Pinole cops. Maybe talking to the FBI was a
waste of time—if they did know anything, they certainly weren't telling her. So she would go directly to a
possible source—the man who had maneuvered his
way into her life, who seemed like the final link between her and Amber. She invited Bindner out to her
house.

When Kim couldn't make some connection with
Tim Bindner—even a brief conversation on the phone—
she felt strangely isolated, lost. Sometimes it was even
worse than that. It felt as if Tim Bindner knew he had
that effect, that hold, on her—and that he exploited it.

The man really had searched for Amber, but what
if he had known exactly where she was? What if he
had known that the whole time he was out there
prowling Pinole Valley searching for her? Some of
what he said made sense and seemed a lot sharper
than anything the cops were saying. But that wasn't
necessarily because he had studied child abductors
and serial killers. She wondered if he could be one.

Kim tried to hold her imagination in check but
found that she couldn't. Nothing Tim Bindner said
was ever unequivocal. He talked about his status as a
suspect, the law enforcement harassment he had experienced, and how unfair, how unreasonable, it all was.
Then he would say that if *he* were a cop, Tim Bindner
would look like a damn good suspect.

Other times he might say, "I didn't take those
kids." But a few minutes later he would be less definitive: "They won't find any evidence. There isn't any evidence to find." How could he know that?

He could be so self-effacing one moment—talking
about how he had tried to help but hadn't accomplished anything—then, the next moment, he'd be running his mouth about how he knew so much more
than the cops.

Bindner frightened Kim. She didn't like the idea of
being alone with him, and felt relieved when the cops
agreed to keep her under tight surveillance. But, fear
or no fear, she would have met with Bindner anyway.

The FBI had a list of twenty-five questions they wanted her to work into her meeting with Bindner. That wasn't any problem. She had a thousand of her own.

She was weeding some flowers in her front yard that morning when a friend stopped by. Kim didn't want to appear unfriendly, but she had to get rid of the woman. She was afraid that if Bindner arrived at that moment, he would smell a setup. As she tried to hurry up the conversation, she noticed his Toyota wagon drive slowly by and disappear down the street.

The friend left, and Kim returned to work among the flowers, wondering if her friend's presence had spooked Bindner.

She never heard Bindner come up the sidewalk, walk across her lawn, and approach her from behind. It was something she felt. She knew that he was there. She turned, and she was right.

If *Kim* hadn't heard him walk up, there was no way that her hearing-impaired daughter would have heard him.

She greeted him, invited him in, and offered him some soda.

"Oh, you drink Jolt," he said, and seemed pleased.

It was a touch that Sagan had suggested. Open the doors and windows and offer him the cola they had found empty cans of scattered all over Oakmont Cemetery.

As Kim and Bindner walked down Savage Avenue to the vacant lot the city had named Amber Swartz Park, Kim described the plans she had for the small area where her daughter had liked to play. A liquid-ambar tree. A gazebo later on.

She was nervous, still jumpy from Bindner's surprise appearance behind her. There was a cop in the house—and a few more, including Harold Sagan, driving around the neighborhood. The Feds were out there, too.

Bindner had come prepared with a list of questions. The first one was about the pink socks.

"As far as I know, that's the only piece of physical

evidence that's ever been found. Where'd they find it? Do you know? It said in the newspaper article that it was in an area that had already been searched."

"It was my understanding it was down behind the baseball diamond down here."

"Along the creek?"

"I don't know."

"Do you know if they were the socks that she was wearing when she disappeared? Did they show them to you?"

"They showed them to me," Kim said, "but in the frame of mind I was in, it was real difficult."

"They didn't tell you exactly where they found them. Did they book 'em into evidence?"

"I would imagine."

"But they didn't tell you whether or not they did. They didn't find anything else down there?"

"They never showed me anything else."

Bindner thought it made sense to do some more searching in the area where they had found the socks.

They crossed the footbridge and walked toward the baseball diamond. "Investigative people, it seems to me, sometimes just don't have it together," he said. "It would seem like they would want to know for sure."

He had more to say about the police, a common theme for him. "I come across so many things where it looks like they're just trying to hassle people and harass people or be egotistical, rather than, 'Hey, let's find out what happened here. Let's do an investigation.' "

Kim was familiar with the theme—Bindner's tales of law enforcement inadequacy or excess. She didn't always disagree. She knew that the cops had harassed Bindner, in part because they considered him a suspect, but it was also a lot like the sick sport of teasing the strangest kid in class.

Bindner didn't seem able to allow Kim her own pain. He would talk about her anguish and suffering, get her to the point where she was feeling it all again, then he would shift gears. His victimization at the hands of law enforcement always seemed to dominate their conversations. He went out to search, and the cops were there to frisk him and run warrant checks.

"They ask me, 'Why do you think she's here?'" Bindner said. "Well, I don't think she's here. I think there's a probability that if somebody might've taken the child and gone in this direction that they might have brought her here. And that probability is no greater than the probability that somebody might've brought her over there, or in two thousand other places that I've already searched. However, I would like to look here. That's what I told them up along Highway 4 across from Franklin Canyon Golf Course when they rousted me out of there. They were just terribly belligerent—terrible sheriff's office guys."

Kim had heard *this* story before, too. Bindner called the two deputies "Mr. Profanity" and "John Wayne's daddy." They had put him in the back of the patrol car—"the cage"—while they ran their checks. He kept telling them that behind the Loprest Company was a prime spot to look. He'd tried to persuade them to go back there.

Bindner didn't know that they had gone there. The deputies had walked out behind the building, found some freshly turned dirt, and dug down. There was a piece of paper buried there, and on it was printed a single word: "Gotcha."

"What I'm saying is," he continued, "every time I go into an area, every time I even come into a case, like Nikki Campbell—I spent six hours looking for Nikki Campbell. Fairfield police department has probably spent six hundred hours investigating me because of that. Ran me out of town and kept my car for two weeks."

Bindner had an arsenal of lines like that. Kim had heard most of them before.

She noticed that as long as he was doing the talking, he made eye contact with her. He seemed animated, speaking rapidly with that slight edge in his voice. When Kim interrupted his flow, shifted the control, his entire demeanor changed.

"What would be the easiest way?" she asked him. "What would make you more comfortable? Because obviously they don't have the manpower to go out and search. And I need help."

"What kind of help do you need?"

"I need to know that every inch of wherever— every clue of anything—whatever the outcome—"

Kim broke off in mid-sentence and gazed over at the hills. "Why?" she asked. "Why would somebody do something like this? I mean, have I done something to somebody? Did she do something? That's what is so mind-boggling. It's going on four years of this. Why? No resolution. No closure."

Bindner looked away as Kim spoke. He didn't say anything for a long time. When he did, he still didn't look at Kim, and he spoke in a softer, almost hesitant way.

"I don't understand it any more than you do. I mean, people do that. Amanda was found dead. And that little girl in Colorado that was taken three years— three days after Amber was found dead. The other one in Texas. I don't remember her name either, but she was found dead. People do it. I don't know why."

Kim couldn't see Bindner's eyes. She could see him only in profile. She didn't know about the kids in Colorado and Texas, but she did know that no one had found her daughter or Amanda Campbell—dead or alive.

She had seen Bindner click out like this before. She had heard him do it on the phone. She knew what dissociating meant, and she wondered if that was what he was doing now. He continued talking, but everything was different. It was as if he weren't the one controlling things anymore. It frightened her, and made her want to immediately redirect the conversation.

Kim asked him about a letter that he had written to her. "I think you left the note in my mailbox," she said, "and you were sitting out here watching the sun come up. You said something about the north hills looking beautiful this time of year. You must have been out here sitting on the rocks, but—I'm going, 'Wait a minute. Where are the north hills?' "

"I'm not sure what hills I was talking about," Bindner said. "I'm not sure where I was when I wrote that, either. How long ago was this?"

"I don't know."

"Kim, I remember one night I got very drunk and sat out by your house. That might be the night. I sat there and looked at the hills. I know I wrote you a note that night, but I was probably talking about the hills where Angela's buried. But I'm not sure."

He was referring to the hills in Briones Park, an area that Sagan and his team had searched for traces of Nikki Campbell. They knew Bindner had been out there; the dogs had tracked his scent all over those hills.

Now Kim gazed at the hill across from Amber Park. "She's out there somewhere. My gut feeling tells me she's not alive. I need to know so I can finally put it to rest."

Bindner stared straight ahead. He didn't say anything.

"Well, I don't know," Kim said. "You don't, either. I hate the idea of thinking that she's not alive."

Bindner encouraged her to keep working, to hang on to her hope. "You probably get people telling you, you gotta let it go," he said, "you gotta cut it loose. It's been four years. You probably get that all the time. 'Go on with your life.' Well, isn't that what you're doing? Isn't Amber part of your life?"

"Exactly," Kim said.

"And if a big part of your life right now is wanting to know what happened to Amber—"

"That's the biggest part of my life," she interrupted. "The sad part is I've just lost so much valuable time with my boys because I concentrate so much on this."

Kim brought up one of the questions the FBI had wanted her to work into the conversation. "Hypothetically speaking," she said, "obviously Angela's in the cemetery now, but do you think they're all connected? Do you think this person may have put them all in the same area?"

She qualified her question. "What I'm thinking now is, if they're connected, could this person be taking these kids and putting them in one place where he would be able to visit them?"

"That's a possibility," Bindner said. "In the Ressler book they talk about stuff like that. They talk about taking jewelry—some of these sexual fantasy type people, like, sexual homicide, like to take a piece of jewelry from the victim and keep it with them as a souvenir. And they like to go back to the place where the event happened or to the place where they left the body. Things like that. Or they might even leave something there and go back and dig it up once in a while. Look at it. There's all kinds of little stuff like that that happens."

They talked about the book, *Sexual Homicide: Patterns and Motives*. Kim wanted to read it, and Bindner thought it might offer her some insight into how sick minds like these work.

"Would you think it was strange if I gave you a memento of Amber?" Kim asked him. "As a peace offering between you and me."

"A peace offering? Aren't we already at peace?"

"Yeah, but I want you to know that. I mean, I have always felt at peace with you. And I don't give things of Amber's away. I don't. That's all I have."

"Well, if you want to do that," Bindner said, "that would be something very special to me."

"I was going through her things last night."

"That must've been hard."

Kim reached into her fanny pack, removed two small objects.

"It was. It was real hard. So, there are two little things that were real special to her. She liked Barbie. She always dreamed of being as gorgeous as Barbie. This was one of her little packs. And when I opened it up, it had one of her favorite little necklaces in it. Just a little heart."

She handed him the tiny pack and the string of hearts and shells.

"She used to wear this?"

"Yeah."

Bindner's voice dropped to a whisper. "That's nice. So you want to give me this?"

"Yeah. I'm sure."

"Thank you. I'll—keep it with me."

"I was hoping you would, because it will be a constant kind of a reminder that I need your help."

"Well, this is definitely something I'll—it's precious to me."

"I was hoping you'd say that."

"I care about you a lot, you know," Bindner said. "I try to do what I can. Sometimes it works. Sometimes it doesn't. Sometimes I get pushed away. Sometimes you get a smile."

What else was there to life, Bindner asked, but caring and loving and being compassionate to others? What other joy could there be in life? "If I could have brought her back to you," he said, "that would've been one of the greatest triumphs of my life. I really wanted to do that."

"You still may be able to."

"When I crawled up on that freeway, I helped save a guy's life up there. That's one of the biggest triumphs of my life. When that fire was burning, I helped these guys—silly-looking fools down there—fight this fire all afternoon, and we saved this school. A whole high school we saved. That was one of my greatest triumphs of my life. You just gotta keep going, 'cause sometimes it's gonna happen to you. And I still want this one to come out right."

They started walking back toward the house. Kim wanted to get the whole thing over with. She couldn't see that she had accomplished much at all.

I'm trying to be a compassionate friend, letting her know that I'm there to help. Letting her know that I care. She accepts me as a friend but still has a little bit of distance between us. And I understand that. She knows I've been investigated and that it's unresolved whether or not I'm the one who took her kid. So that's about where it was. . . .

I would call her once in a while. I sent her a Christmas card every year. I'm the kind of guy that likes to just drop in on people. I'd drop in on her—sometimes just come up and knock on her door, say, "Hi, how you doing?" Talk to her kids and stuff. . . .

It's been several years and all of a sudden there's this bolt out of the blue. All this kindness, and all this closeness that she has apparently carefully avoided during the four years that I've known her, all of a sudden comes out. She wants to be real nice to me, and I'm thinking, "Why? What's going on here?" So it's got to be some kind of setup. They want me to feel guilty. She gives me the necklace. One of their little theories is that the guy keeps souvenirs and trinkets, which I do. Maybe I would take the necklace to where Amber is, or something like that. I can just see their little wheels spinning. A lot of that stuff was going through my head even at the time I was talking to her. Like, what is this? What's going on here? What do they think they're gonna get out of this?

Kim returned to the subject of the books Bindner had mentioned. "I do want to read this material," she said, "because I think it will help me to understand, and hopefully help me to think more like the individual that would commit a crime like this."

"I think it helps me to understand," Bindner said. "Ressler's book categorizes organized offender and disorganized offender. Two different categories. The organized guy plans it out very carefully. This is about murder. He's got his safe spot picked out where he's gonna do the murder—knows how he's gonna do it. It's got what his life might be like. And based on the crime scene, you can tell whether this guy was disorganized or was he organized. Disorganized type guy would be a guy that would take risks, might not know where he was going after he did the abduction."

"A spontaneous type of thing," Kim said.

"He might be the kind of guy that drives a ratty car," Bindner continued. "His whole life is disorganized. And his crime is the same way. So there are those kinds of insights in the book. For example, Michaela."

Bindner was referring to the nine-year-old abducted from near the Rainbow Market in Hayward five months after Amber had vanished.

"I have a feeling that if it was this type of crime that it was a disorganized offender who did it. They said he was a skinny guy. The picture showed him with long, bedraggled hair. They said his car had a lopsided front bumper. He took an extreme risk. He kidnapped her in broad daylight in front of witnesses, so it looks like that type of crime."

"Yet he was careful that nothing be found," Kim said.

"Just because nothing was found doesn't mean he was careful. He could've been very careless but went somewhere nobody knew to look. Unless he went a long ways. That's just one of those examples. Michaela might've been done by a disorganized guy."

"What about Angela and Amber and Nikki and Ilene and—how many others?"

"Well, you gotta have something to place it in order to tell. See, with Michaela we had a description of the suspect, description of the vehicle, the crime scene in front of witnesses. With Amber we don't have any of that. So we can't make any real suppositions about what type of person. With Angela, they found the body, so you can make suppositions from that crime scene."

"What about Nikki?"

"Well, again, Nikki is more similar to Amber from an investigative standpoint. You don't have anything to work with, developing an idea about who did it. Basically, you have a disappearance. Go up and look at the area she was taken from and say, 'Well, maybe this is what happened.' That's what I did when I went out looking for her. Same with Amber. Whoever took her either hit the highway or went out in the valley. That was my supposition. So I went out in the valley. With Amber I did the same thing. It was the same kind of situation. Not as rough a terrain as Pinole Valley is, but rolling countryside, farmhouses. And there are places where you can get off the road really quick—zero visibility areas. Similar neighborhoods, similar terrain, similar types of crime, similar children. But you can't go from there and say this guy's probably an organized offender, or disorganized, or his life is probably like this. You can't do that. You don't have a body, a crime scene. You don't have a description of the suspect or the vehicle or anything. The more that you have, the more you can put together some kind of profile."

Kim figured that was the problem with all the cases. It was the reason that law enforcement kept coming back to Tim Bindner.

"I would think that the less you have indicates it was more an organized type of offender," Kim said.

While it was possible that the perpetrator was disorganized, Bindner concurred. "If nothing's been found after all this time, it's more likely that the guy knew what he was doing and had it planned."

"That's kind of what I've been assuming," Kim said. "I can't believe that this much time could go on and nothing be found, and no one know anything, without it's being well organized."

Kim had a compelling need to know. "Especially after this much time," she said. "What they're doing and how they do it. What this person could be like. To try to understand where this person might be coming from. To try to think like them."

"It's hard to do that," Bindner said.

"Especially when I don't normally think that way," Kim said.

They walked along in a silence punctuated only by

the call of a mockingbird. The sky was clear, a sharp
blue, with only a few scattered, fair-weather clouds.

"If the same person is involved in several cases,"
Kim began, "what do you think the chances are that
they would have the kids all in the same general location? Do you think it's something they want to go back
to? These are all things that have popped up in my
mind."

"Are you talking about murders?"

"Right. Amber and Nikki, say."

"I don't know. That was one of the theories that
the FBI came up with. Maybe if she had been killed,
somebody might've put the body near Angela's grave."

"Oh, really. I didn't know that."

"They went up there with some dogs and did some
searching," Bindner said. "I think because they
thought I did it. But they did go up there and search."

"Where would you put her in a graveyard?"

"You've been to Angela's grave. There's a big hill
up above there, and the hillside going down."

"It backs up against all that park area, doesn't it?"

"There are big areas up there where somebody
could bury something if they wanted to leave it close
to the other kid's grave. If they wanted to come back
and visit those two graves again and relive their crime
in their mind, they could do that."

They walked up through the deep grass toward the
road. In minutes they were back at the front of Kim's
house.

"You can call me any time you want to," he said.

"Well, I don't want to upset your wife."

"The fact that she gets a little bit upset is because
she doesn't want me harassed."

"Right. I can understand that. I'm not harassing
you."

"No," Bindner said. "She thinks if I deal with you,
I'm gonna get harassed by the cops."

"I think if anything, it would ease that, wouldn't
you? If you were doing things behind everybody's
back, I would think they'd be more suspicious. If we're

both being up front, I think it would make things much more open."

"Her mind-set right now is, anything that I go out and try to do, I'm likely to end up in trouble for it. That's been the past experience. It's not necessarily true. I've gone out and fought the fire, to rescue after the earthquake, and I was a neighborhood hero for that, you know. But she thinks if I go out and try to help people I'm gonna get in trouble. And her fear is justified, I think, by what's happened in the past. I lost a job twice. And I got harassed innumerable times, and arrested. It's a real fear. I haven't been convicted of anything, and I'm not in prison or anything like that, but there's still a fear that that could happen."

As Bindner drove off, Kim stood in her house, shaking. "God, I just want to throw up," she said.

27

Bindner's latest chess move included a note.

> Harry,
>   Yes, I'm quite aware of the recent search in
> the Amber Swartz case. Might interest you to
> know I conducted a search of my own up on
> McEwen Road on 8-16-1988—just a cursory
> roadside search, like the one I did for Amanda. I
> found nothing, but it *does* seem like a likely area.
> I hate seeing Kim put through this renewed hell.
>   Tim

Five days later, Bindner had a hell of his own, as
did Sagan, who was awaiting details on an abduction
case in Pittsburg, California, near Antioch.

———————————

On the morning of June 25, Tim Bindner talked to Kim Swartz on the phone. She asked if he knew about the missing child, a six-year-old, taken from her bedroom at 3:15 in the morning. Bindner hadn't heard about it.

"They're putting flyers together and doing the usual stuff," Kim told him. "I'm going to a press conference at four o'clock in Martinez at the police department there. That's all I know right now."

"Was this one a boy or a girl?" he asked.

"Girl. Six years old, approximately sixty pounds, forty inches tall, blond hair, brown eyes. Were you aware of the other two up there over the past few months?"

Bindner was. "You got them back, right?"

"Right."

The third abduction had been in Pleasant Hill, not far from Oakmont Cemetery.

"I clipped a couple of articles about them to put in my file that I keep on stuff like that. But I didn't really pay that much attention to them once I knew they were recovered and that they were safe. They haven't the slightest idea who took them."

Bindner said he figured the cops would just let the investigation lag and probably never catch the guy who did it. He wanted to help with this one. He knew he probably shouldn't, but questions popped into his mind. What kind of neighborhood was it? How far was it to the freeway?

He wanted to go out there, but he expected to get run out of town if he did. "Is it the same person? The kid is about the same size as Angela was, and as Amber was. Is this guy striking again?"

"I know," Kim said. "It's what runs through my mind."

———————

Instead of driving up to Pittsburg, Bindner walked the mile and a half to St. Mary's Cemetery. He stopped at the home of a ninety-one-year-old woman he had met in the cemetery three years earlier. The two had struck up a friendship. He fixed her washer, changed light-bulbs for her, did things she couldn't do for herself. When she couldn't walk in from the porch to her couch, he put his arm around her waist and helped her get through the door.

One day she gave him a photograph of herself. They were looking through an album, and there was a picture of her when she was fourteen or fifteen— maybe from 1915 or 1916. She had been an attractive little girl, and he put the photo in his locker at work.

The only fantasies I had about [her] *were that she was there and she needed me and she was right next to the cemetery where I went all the time. You know, I don't even think it's necessary to call it a fantasy really. She was my friend, and I was her friend, and it was our little secret. And the only reason it had to be a secret was because nobody knew about it.*

It's a ninety-one-year-old woman standing on her porch, winking at me and beckoning me to come up. And she says, "Oh, I'm glad you made it today. Can you do this for me?" You know, change the light on her porch or whatever. And I was so happy to be there, and she was so happy to see me. It was like it was our little secret. It was almost like we had to hide it from some-body. As it turned out, we should have.

On June 25, the two of them were sitting on the couch together. Bindner had his arm around the old woman's shoulder. Her hand was in his, resting against her leg. She was worried about her cat, afraid it was going to die. Bindner talked to her, comforted her.

They were sitting close together like that when the woman's twenty-eight-year-old granddaughter, Erin, walked through the door. Tim Bindner had been stop-ping by for three years, but he hadn't met the young woman before. He remembers that she "freaked out" when she saw him in the house with her grandmother.

She didn't know the history, didn't know the friendship. Bindner admits that *he* went a little crazy, too.

Erin thought that he was molesting her grandmother.

Bindner got mad. "You don't know what you're dealing with here," he said.

He quoted the Bible to her, and told her, "This is about the love of Jesus. You should look at the book of First John."

Erin looked at him as if he were crazy. Bindner knew that he was in trouble. The woman wouldn't calm down. Both of them were angry.

"Why did you let this man touch you?" she asked her grandmother.

The whole scene was getting crazy.

Later, Erin told a reporter for the *Contra Costa Times* that Bindner had said he loved her grandmother, that she was a lonely old lady who needed love. "I thought he was on drugs" Erin said. "He was a really weird-looking man. Evil-looking. I started shaking just wanting him to leave and he would not leave."

When the Oakland cops got there, Bindner left. Then he came back, so Erin called the cops again, and they arrested him.

Erin insisted that Bindner had been fondling her grandmother, that he had molested her. Bindner says he did nothing wrong and that he pled no contest to the misdemeanor—disturbing the peace—because his lawyer didn't talk him out of it and because he was thinking about his elderly friend's welfare. He didn't want the ninety-one-year-old woman to have to come to court and testify against him.

The court placed him on probation for eighteen months. Later, he would characterize his offense as "being nice to an old lady."

Bindner saw the incident as being just like the fiasco at Social Security. He was doing something for somebody—and getting nailed for it. He felt belligerent. What would happen the next time he helped someone? Would the cops or somebody else swoop down on him again? Would he go through life always getting burned?

> *I kinda feel like, catch me if you can, but I'm not do-ing anything wrong. I'm not breaking any laws. It's like, here's another thing I can do that is being nice to people, that is helping people, that is making our world a better place. Now, stop me from doing this. I feel that real sarcastic attitude come into play in my life a lot.*

The night the Oakland police arrested Bindner, the old woman moved out of her house. He sent her two letters asking her to forgive him.

———————

Harold Sagan waited by his phone. He had an open, active investigation into a child's disappearance going on. Pittsburg, Concord, and Pleasant Hill certainly knew that. Every law enforcement agency in the Bay Area knew it.

In each of the three communities, someone had taken a kid out of a bedroom window in the middle of the night. The kids were all back home now, even in the most recent case, and the departments had a sus-pect named Tracy Arthur Stone. Could Stone have taken Nikki? Sagan couldn't stand the wait. He picked up the phone, called, then drove down to Concord.

It didn't take long to determine that Stone had been in jail when Nikki Campbell disappeared. But it wasn't a wasted trip. Sagan had seen an example of good police work. He felt a pang of jealousy, but he had to admire the cooperation among the agencies.

Their six-year-old victim proved to be an excellent witness. She described a tattoo her abductor had on his forearm. A sheriff's deputy went through the county booking files until he found a description of the tattoo, then the cops all landed on Stone. It was damn fine work.

Sagan was wondering if he was up to the task of

handling his own investigation. The stress was getting to him. For seven months he had watched his leads evaporate. He had cleared out all other suspects. Maybe chess wasn't the only game Sagan didn't know how to play.

The detective made his next move in the chess game, and sent it to Bindner on June 30 along with a note.

> I've felt since day one that we have to do a lot more searching instead of waiting for the case to come walking into our plush offices. It probably will surprise you to know, I've employed some of your search tactics, since nowhere in police manuals is that particular topic covered. Most manuals only address known crime scene location searches, but no one has ever addressed the issue of unknown and large-scale search tactics.

In a phone conversation, Bindner told Kim Swartz about his contact with the Fairfield detective. "He's the main guy that's working on the Amanda Campbell case," he said.

"Yeah. I've talked to him a few times," Kim said.

"As a matter of fact, I'm playing a game of chess by mail with him."

"Oh, are you?"

"Yeah. He's beating me." Bindner laughed. "He's got a bunch of stuff that he took out of my car when I was looking for Nikki. You know, they searched my vehicle. One of the things he's got is my search notes from that search that I did. Even though I was only up there one day, I did cover quite a bit of territory. In the last letter he wrote to me he said that he has incorporated some of the ways that I went about looking for Nikki into his ideas about how to do these things. The thing that he wrote to me that really shocked me was, there aren't any instructions or training in any police manual or any training material that he has ever seen about doing wide-scale searches."

"He's absolutely right," Kim said.

She asked Bindner whether Sagan was willing to work with him.

"He's kind of ambiguous with me," Bindner said. "I know I'm still being investigated. Or, at least, I'm still under suspicion. He acts like a friend, but I can see signs that he's doing his job at the same time. Let's put it that way."

"He's got to."

"Yeah. I don't resent the guy. I wouldn't be in correspondence with him, or playing a chess game with him, if I resented him. I did for a while. Every time you get followed around, and you get accused—well, I wasn't accused, but . . . you know you're under suspicion—why, you get a little bit resentful. And I felt that way for a while, but I get over that kind of thing pretty quick."

Bindner said he wanted to return to Fairfield to continue his search for Nikki, but his wife was adamant that he stay away.

"So Sagan's a good chess player, huh?" Kim asked.

"Well, I made a blunder," Binder said. "On my fifth or sixth move, I didn't back up one of my pawns, and he pounced. I don't know how good he is yet because we're only six or seven moves into the game, but I know I'm not very good. This all started when he wrote me a note. He said something like, 'Investigating is kind of like a chess game. You've made some moves and I've made some too.' So I wrote back to him, and I said, 'Yeah. Chess game. That sounds good. Let's play one. Here's my first move.' So he went for it. I think he wanted to keep me writing to him in case I would slip up and reveal something that I might have done. Which, of course, I haven't. I know I'm not going to, but I think that's one of the reasons why he went for it. He wanted to keep me in contact to kind of feel me out a little more."

"Well, he's probably into the game now."

"I think he is," Bindner said. "He's gonna win, too."

Bindner's next move in the game went into the mail in the middle of July. He reacted to Sagan's comments about his search techniques, and told him about his plans for a follow-up search on McEwen Road.

> I do not have any search "expertise," my friend. I merely ask myself, *if* the child has been left in this area, how might it have happened, what are likely scenarios and parameters. Then I go look, where these thoughts direct me. I haven't found any missing kids yet . . . nor do I hope to. I just need to look for them because it seems, after the first week, no one else does. "Find a need and fill it," once again.

Bindner said that he had wanted to do more searching in Fairfield but wasn't going near the city again. That business with the scent dogs had made him angry, and he feared being harassed. "Still," he wrote, "I have images of a little girl's body out there where no one will look, unless someone thinks, 'Well, based on what I know, maybe the culprit put her here.' Not likely to happen."

He closed his letter with: "The Bible has a lot of wisdom in it. Also a lot of foolishness. As do most of our lives. By the way, I never have kidnapped a kid. Trust me."

Sagan captured Bindner's pawn with his bishop by using the Berkeley student's suggested sixth move in the game. On August 14, Bindner sent a short note:

Dear Harry:

> Sorry I can't continue the chess game. Your last move presents an interesting challenge.

However my attorney has advised me not to communicate with any law enforcement people at this time.

If you'd like, may be we can pick it up again later on.

Tim

P.S. good luck on the Amanda case, my heart cries for her, and all the others.

Sagan jotted off a quick note. If Bindner wanted to play chess again, or if he wanted to do some work on the Amanda case, just let him know.

It was a rapid retreat, and Sagan didn't understand it. Was it because Bindner was losing the chess game? He used to be so abrasive—was he starting to get cold feet, to back off? Or was it just that he had decided to follow his attorney's advice? He had a history of complying with his lawyer's directions for varying periods of time, but then he would reestablish contact. That's what he had done with Kim Swartz.

So Sagan waited. He spent night after night sitting in his car outside Bindner's place on Fifty-third Street. Long after the lights went out in the small frame house, the cop sat there trying not to smoke. He would end up lighting a cigarette anyway. Then another.

He also continued his reading. From Ressler's book, he moved on to Geberth's *Practical Homicide Investigation* (another of the books Bindner had read), then to Goldstein's *Sexual Exploitation of Children* and Mundy's *Murder and Madness*. In the early '80s, interest and research in serial crime—sexual assault and murder, primarily—mushroomed as the crimes themselves became part of daily life in most areas of the country.

After Ted Bundy had left Seattle in the '70s, the Green River Killer claimed more than forty victims there, mostly prostitutes in the Seattle-Tacoma area. Police never caught him. L.A. had the Hillside Strangler, two men—Angelo Buono and Kenneth Bianchi—who left bodies strewn around that city. Richard Ramirez, the Night Stalker, who worshipped the devil, followed them. The Zodiac Killer had operated in Sagan's own area during the years before Sagan became a cop. Zodiac sent coded letters to the police, taunting letters. These were the famous ones—along with Jeffrey Dahmer, John Wayne Gacy, Wayne Williams, and Danny Rolling. But there were so many others who weren't famous, and so many unsolved cases.

The early '80s also had brought a new interest in crimes against children. This was the literature that Sagan knew best. He had also made a study of the many forms of child abuse. In the Bay Area, he and the other investigators could be dealing with a hybrid. If the same man had taken Amber and Amanda "Nikki" Campbell, he could be looking for a serial predator who focused on children.

Sagan thought he had probable cause to arrest Tim Bindner, but he wanted the D.A.'s office to file a complaint. Dave Paulson, who was then the deputy D.A., said that it wasn't a convictable case. Maybe a search of Bindner's home would turn up something concrete, some piece of evidence that would allow them to move forward.

The books that Sagan had read suggested that such a killer would keep trophies of his crimes—objects that would allow him to fantasize, to relive his crimes—things that had belonged to his victims. With Nikki, it would have been something she was wearing, perhaps her Santa Claus earrings. Sagan remembered that when patrol officers arrested Joel Rifkin back east, he had trophies all over his bureau.

There hadn't been anything in Bindner's car except Nikki's scent. But what about his house? What about his personal storage areas at work?

Sagan had already assembled an affidavit in support of an arrest warrant. Now the detective decided to pursue a search warrant. The affidavit—a summary of every reason Sagan had to believe that Tim Bindner was responsible for Nikki Campbell's disappearance—

was a complete statement of Sagan's theory of the crime.

He began with the letters to Sheila Cosgrove, the proximity of her home to Nikki's, and the view Bindner would have had of Nikki playing while he was watching for Sheila; indeed, they had found his scent on the Kolob Hills overlooking Sheila's house. They had also found Bindner's scent *and* Nikki's scent at the grave of Angela Bugay, the young girl kidnapped from her home in Antioch in 1983. And they had found Nikki's scent in Bindner's car. He was a suspect in other similar cases, and he had opportunity.

The parts that fit logically together were clear to Sagan, but he was still in the dark about why this guy did what he did, how he thought, what went on inside his mind. That frustrated the detective. He had bits of this and pieces of that, but he couldn't explain the man's thinking.

28

DECEMBER 9, 1992

Almost a year had passed since Nikki Campbell's disappearance.

Tim Bindner had the day off. He read the morning's *Tribune*, then lingered in a hot bath. It was Wednesday, the day he volunteered at Safe Place, a shelter for battered women. Bindner watched the children, played with them, while their mothers and the staff members did chores and determined how to deal with the emotional and legal implications of spousal abuse.

The women there were victims of beatings by the men in their lives. Bindner saw his role as showing the kids that not all men are mean. Home life had traumatized the kids, and they tended to act up. He looked for ways to help them calm down, to get away from their aggressive behavior.

There was one kid in particular, a little boy, who had been a challenge for Bindner. The kid was so hostile that Bindner felt he had to back away and let the kid act up. If he started getting pushy with the other kids, Bindner took him aside—and had even put him on "time-out" once. The kid seemed to accept the structure and became more willing to communicate. Bindner thought the key was for them to talk as equals.

The last time he had been up there, Bindner remembered, the kid had greeted him with a big hug and said, "Let's go to the children's room."

Bindner was out of the bath and drying himself when he heard noises at the front of the small house. As he pulled his clothes on, Sandra met him at the bathroom door.

It was Sagan and some other cops, she said. He had some kind of warrant.

Bindner walked to the front of the house. He didn't know what to think. He didn't know what they were doing there. Then it flashed through his mind—arrest warrant. They were there to arrest him. They were going to put him in the box, the cage.

Sagan handed him the search warrant and explained what it was. "I've put together some evidence and a scenario for what happened on December 27, 1991," the cop told him. "I'd like to talk to you about that part of the case."

Bindner said he wanted to speak with his attorney, made a phone call, then told Sagan that his attorney had advised him not to talk.

Sagan had no choice but to drop the issue, and the officers started moving through the house. Bindner sat on the couch and thought, "They're looking for a reason to arrest me."

These cops believed that he had abducted and killed Nikki Campbell, and they expected to find evidence proving it. He remembers feeling angry.

"I can tell you where I was," Bindner said to Sagan. "I was right in this house the whole day of Nikki's abduction."

"You can't get away with that kind of explanation anymore, Tim," Sagan said. "This is for real now."

What everyone said at Bindner's house that day, how they said it, and where they were when they said it, became a matter of fierce debate. Such things usually do. This time the implications would move beyond the typical dispute between a suspect and the officers investigating him.

Sagan doesn't remember an angry man. He remembers a frightened man. Bindner was trembling. He had a pronounced stutter when he spoke. He looked terrified.

The Oakland man placed another call, this one to Safe Place. "Val," he remembers saying, "I can't make it today."

"Oh," the woman said, "you've been such a good volunteer. You've never missed a day."

Bindner watched the crowd of cops disperse in and around his house. Through the window he saw three times as many media people. Satellite trucks were setting up on the other side of the street; reporters ran around with cameras and microphones.

As Bindner talked to the woman at the shelter, he knew that he would never be going back there. As if there hadn't been enough turmoil in his life before, his whole world was about to change. He thought, "They're not going to find any evidence here of any crime, but I can never go back to that place again."

"Val, I'm sorry, but something came up," he said. "I just can't make it today. Talk to you later."

Bindner knew that the reporters and the TV people lining Fifty-third Street weren't waiting for a sports personality or some movie star to show up. They were waiting for him—waiting to see what was going to happen to him.

Sagan had stepped away, watching as Joe Allio directed a systematic search of the house. The investigators filled evidence boxes with pictures, maps, Bindner's graveyard logbooks, exercises he had done for a creative writing class, twenty-six file folders of his diaries, and newspaper clippings about the missing child cases.

The Bob Larson Ministry was playing on the radio in the house when Dale Myer brought Friday, the big bloodhound, inside. The dog came in with his nose at about knee level, approached Bindner, and raised his massive head. The man looked scared but never moved a muscle. Friday went off toward a draped section of the living room that served as the Bindners' bedroom.

There were sixteen Fairfield officers—three or four working inside the house, and the rest either searching Bindner's car and around the outside of the house or keeping the curious away from the property. In a controversial move, when the Fairfield police department advised other interested area law enforcement agencies about the warrant, they also notified the media by fax. In part, this was to satisfy the bargain from the previous January, when the press had withheld Bindner's identity. But the department also had another reason. If Bindner was the man who had taken Nikki Campbell or any of the other missing Bay Area children, putting him in front of the public would generate calls about the cases and increase the pool of information about the eccentric Oakland man. Another plus was that, with the spotlight on him, if Bindner was their man he couldn't very well go trolling for any more children.

Wayne Galloway, the detective from Pinole, arrived forty-five minutes after the search got under way. The media had been more prompt. Galloway told a TV reporter that he was there only to assist Fairfield; he didn't see anything to connect with the Amber Swartz case.

Trucks, vans, and satellite dishes lined both sides of Fifty-third Street. Reporters had the name and address, and knew that Tim Bindner—dubbed the "mystery man" the previous January—was a suspect in the disappearance of four-year-old Nikki Campbell.

Neighbors stood in front of the cameras. Bindner likes kids, one said—always hangs out with them, acts like one himself. A relative said there was no way Bindner would ever hurt a child.

The media people were already aware of Bindner and his involvement in the other Bay Area cases. When newspaper reporters approached Galloway, he told them that the interview with Bindner regarding the Amber Swartz case had been "routine." He also told the *Contra Costa Times* reporter that Pinole had eliminated Bindner as a suspect. Then what was the portly detective doing on Fifty-third Street? Was eleven hours on a polygraph a "routine" procedure? Why would the Pinole police spend taxpayers' money investigating someone who wasn't a suspect? Was Wayne Galloway on Fifty-third Street simply to assist Fairfield?

Chuck Timm outlined the salient facts of the case for the TV reporters. Bloodhounds had detected Nikki Campbell's scent in Bindner's car. They had found Bindner's scent on the Kolob Hills. And Bindner had been writing to a twelve-year-old Fairfield girl who lived just a short distance from Nikki Campbell. They thought they already had enough to arrest Bindner, but not enough to guarantee a conviction.

Sagan, Allio, and the others worked the place for eight hours. The Fairfield officers searched above the ceilings and in the crawl space under the house. The judge who signed the search warrant had been explicit: Unless they found something clearly related to Nikki Campbell's disappearance, investigators were not to tear into the walls. But if they found the slightest connection, they could dismantle the entire house. The plaster remained undisturbed.

Sagan believed that the man had a stash—files, trophies, erotic or pornographic material—but nothing was ever found. He remembered how Bindner had speculated on January 7 that the perpetrator would keep a souvenir and bury it near the child. That way police wouldn't find it on him if they stopped him. Whenever he went back to visit the grave site, he could dig up the souvenir and have that as a remembrance of the girl.

If the trophies were elsewhere, Sagan reasoned, then so were any secret files. But they would have to be close enough for him to have easy access to them.

Bindner spent the day of the search indoors, occasionally looking out through a window at the activity on the street. In the late afternoon, the police gave him a property list covering what they had seized. The cops left, but the media remained camped on Fifty-third Street. It was over, but it was also just beginning.

———————————

That night's TV news carried the story. "Suspect named in Fairfield child's disappearance." "Oakland man's house searched." "Evidence sought in child's abduction." "Police hunt for clues." In a live feed on the ten o'clock news, Bay Area viewers saw the house in darkness except for the string of white Christmas lights surrounding the words "Merry Xmas" painted on the window.

The fallout from the search hit the papers in the morning. The press attacked Sagan and the Fairfield police department for releasing Bindner's name and announcing the execution of the warrant. One ACLU attorney said, "They are an investigating agency. What is the investigatory reason for doing this publicly, and doing it in the media?"

The *Contra Costa Times* paraphrased a police–media relations policy distributed by the International Association of Chiefs of Police: "A name and other personal information should only be given to the press after a suspect is arrested, an arrest warrant issued or an indictment released."

In Fairfield, residents circulated a petition in support of the department. A few law enforcement professionals also voiced their approval. Of those who criticized the move in the press, some privately called Sagan, urging him to stick with it.

The media coverage was so intense that Bindner was unable to go to his job at the East Bay Municipal

Utility District. His employers gave him a paid, week-long leave of absence, saying they wanted to avoid any disruptions.

The day after the search, Bindner's stepson wanted to walk to a burger place four blocks away. The street was still crawling with reporters, and the boy was afraid to go. Bindner was adamant that he and his family were not going to hole up in their own home, so he made the trip with the boy. Reporters followed them to the restaurant and back. Bindner managed to ignore them until he was back at the house and about to walk inside. He stood in a light rain, his face twisted in anger, and spoke into the microphones that reporters were shoving in his face.

"I've never seen any of these children," Bindner said. "All I've done is gone out and try to find them. I think that if I'm ninety-six years old, laying on my deathbed, there's gonna be an FBI investigator asking me questions, and I'm gonna be answering them as honestly as I can."

In the days that followed, the media coverage was constant. Tim Bindner, the prime suspect, slipped into the role of celebrity suspect. He talked with Marsha Ginsburg and Carla Marinucci of the *San Francisco Examiner*, Yumi Wilson at the *Chronicle*, Ethan Rarick and Joan Morris of the *Contra Costa Times*, and Linda Goldston from the *San Jose Mercury News*. Reporters stopped him on the street. He welcomed them into his home. He even took Ginsburg and Marinucci with him to visit the grave of Angela Bugay. Later he took Goldston there, too.

Bindner was patient, reserved, as he pointed out the ironies, the coincidences that had placed him at the center of so many missing children cases. In an interview with Goldston, he even added to the list that made up the fabric of suggestive evidence. There was everything the cops had already told the media, plus the Christmas card with the picture of the chubby-cheeked Russian girl on it. She was holding up four fingers to indicate her age. Bindner also revealed that he had been in Hayward, just blocks from the Rainbow Market, when a man dragged Michaela Garecht into a car. And the route he drove when visiting Angela Bugay's grave took him past the end of Savage Avenue, within yards of where Amber Swartz had vanished in 1988.

Tim Bindner seemed to be pointing a finger at himself.

———————

Just as Harold Sagan had expected, calls started coming in right away. A seventeen-year-old from Alameda called to say that she had been hanging out in St. Mary's Cemetery the previous summer. There was a strange guy there one night in August. He was sitting on a little girl's grave because, he said, the grave made him feel warm.

The man was wearing a blue sweatshirt, blue jeans, and a baseball cap. He seemed surprised that the young woman hadn't heard of him. He told her that the FBI kept bothering him because he was a suspect in the kidnapping of three little girls. One of them was Amber Swartz.

Later that night she saw him running down the hill in the cemetery. He was making weird noises as he went from grave to grave—always the graves of kids, and mostly little girls.

Another caller was a boy in his early teens who was an avid skateboarder. He had heard that after the fires in the Oakland Hills in 1991, some of the swimming pools up there were empty—making them great places to ride. Three or four times up there he had met this guy named Tim. "Mostly he just hung out," the kid told Joe Allio. "He'd sit in this little green station wagon, or on the hood of his car, drinking beer and watching the sunset."

The kid recognized Tim Bindner from TV. The guy had told him that he had helped put out a fire that was threatening a school up there. "One time, out of the blue, he said that he had time on his hands and was looking for missing kids. But he said the heat was on him—because the cops had figured him for a suspect in those cases."

When he realized the police had taken the necklace of Amber's that Kim Swartz had given him, Bindner called Sagan. He feared they might try to say that it was Nikki's, or somehow discover that it was Amber's and think that he had taken her. He explained to the detective how he had gotten the necklace.

Bindner called again on the fourteenth, and left a message on Sagan's answering machine. He wanted to talk to the detective about an article that had appeared in the previous day's *Tribune*—a story titled "Hero or Fool" that questioned Sagan's judgment in conducting his investigation in such a public manner.

The article had upset Bindner. "I don't consider you a fool," he told Sagan when the detective returned his call. "I consider you very competent. I felt it was unjust the way they portrayed you."

Bindner told Sagan that he wanted to resume their chess match sometime, and maybe one of these days they could get together to talk about Nikki Campbell and the other missing children in the Bay Area.

Sagan was cordial during the phone conversation, agreeing that they should stay in touch. He figured that Bindner was looking for information, wondering what his status was after the search.

Much later, Tim Bindner would deny that he had resigned from the chess game.

> *It was my move, and he took the play sheet as part of his search of my house. How can I make my move in a chess game when somebody else has confiscated the play sheet for that game in a search warrant? I can't. I don't know what the moves are. I don't have them written down anywhere else. My position on the*

*game is that it is in indefinite suspense because I don't
have the moves and can't respond. So all time limits
are off until he gives me back the play sheet and I can
make my proper move. . . .*

*So the game was suspended on December ninth and
it's all his fault.*

On the evening of December 10, George Ellwin
was watching the TV news when he saw police searching the home of an Oakland man, Timothy Bindner—a
suspect in the disappearance of a four-year-old Fairfield girl.

Ellwin saw the reporters hold out microphones as
the man in a yellow rain slicker and baseball cap
walked toward the cameras. The man's hair curled out
from under the hat. Ellwin studied the angry face, his
eyes. He saw the rage in those eyes—and knew that he
had seen them before.

George Ellwin grabbed his phone and called the
Pinole police department. He explained who he was
and told the detective about his earlier calls regarding
the man who had been roughing up the little girl in Alvarado Park on the day Amber Swartz was kidnapped.
"He's on TV right now," Ellwin said. "They raided his
house. He's a suspect in a kidnapping in Fairfield."

The detective thanked him for the call but asked
no further questions.

29

The Bay Area was going Hollywood.

If the onslaught of media attention bothered Bindner, he didn't show it. He agreed to appear via satellite on the *Jane Whitney Show*, a nationally syndicated TV talk show. The original plan was for all the participants—Bindner, Sagan, Kim Swartz, Sharon Nemeth (Michaela Garecht's mother), and Anne Campbell—to fly to Boston. Bindner wasn't comfortable with that because he had never met Anne Campbell.

He expected the format to be one in which he was the suspect. The cop thinks he did it. Both sides receive support from the mothers—Sagan from Anne Campbell, Bindner from Kim and maybe even Sharon. He didn't know there would be a confrontation, a public accusation—but, thinking back on it, he now realizes that was exactly what he should have expected.

Bindner wore his Oakland A's cap and sat in front of the wall of missing children flyers in his living room. He stared woodenly at the camera as he listened to Anne Campbell unleash her rage at him—the man whom she believed abducted her daughter.

Bindner couldn't see what was going on in the studio in Boston, but he could hear it. It frustrated him that he couldn't read the body language of the people as they talked. He was angry. He could understand Anne Campbell's fury, but she was directing all of it at him. He didn't want to come across as angry on national TV, so he thought about what he would say when it was his turn to speak. He tried to keep himself calm, to push the anger away.

Thirteen months after Nikki disappeared, all the terror and anger remained at the surface as Anne Campbell told the story of that day. When she returned home from work, her sixteen-year-old son had met her at the garage door. They couldn't find Nikki. Anne's husband, Jim, had already started looking through the neighborhood.

Later, when she read about the "mystery man" in the *Fairfield Daily Republic*, she felt as if the abductor had returned to observe the suffering he had caused. She knew the reality: Her daughter was probably dead. Now Anne Campbell wanted answers. What did he do to her? Where did he put her? And "he" was Tim Bindner.

Bindner figured that Sagan would have had plenty of opportunity to talk to Nikki's mother. For all he knew, the cop could have told her, "We've got the guy. We're sure that he did it."

When Bindner responded to Anne's accusations on national TV, his voice was flat. "I didn't take your baby," he said. "I tried to find her."

He blamed Harold Sagan for her attitude toward him. "I feel really bad for the children and the mothers of the children," he said. "I want them brought back alive. I want the cases solved."

In what was becoming a familiar refrain, Bindner acknowledged feeling a bit apprehensive but denied any anger about the law enforcement and media focus on him. He said that his public tribunal had aggravated his wife's medical problems, but he had to trust that the Fairfield police were doing a competent job and were honest.

Anne Campbell challenged Bindner about the dog's finding Nikki's scent in his car and at Oakmont Cemetery. "Nikki's never been in my car," he said.

> When you read the affidavit, you discover that the first place the dogs went in the police parking lot after they scented the dogs on Nikki Campbell's dress—I guess they used—was to the Dumpster at the end of the parking lot.
>
> It was in the affidavit. I don't remember if it was in the TV show [i.e., Jane Whitney]. But then, to me that indicates that it's equally likely that somebody at the police station threw her in the Dumpster as it is that she was in my car. I mean, the dog went there first, before it came over to my car. And my feeling about it is that these dogs were following strong odors. Again, people I've talked to say bloodhounds don't do that. They're after a specific scent. But how do we really know that if the dog can't talk to you and tell you what it's after? If the specific scent is there, I believe they can track it. But if it's not there, maybe they just go after strong odors to see if they can detect it. And I'm sure there were a lot of strong odors in my car after being out in the countryside all day, slogging through plants and petting dogs that came up to me and doing all kinds of things out there.

If the dog could testify, maybe he could testify about what he smelled. Or maybe they weren't feeding the animal properly. Bindner couldn't explain it. "All I know," he told the national audience, "is that I did not do it, and the scent was not in my vehicle."

Bindner offered possibilities for why the dogs behaved the way they did, but he was also reacting. The sarcasm was a product of his anger. He wanted to control his responses, but he felt provoked.

Whitney listed the evidence against Bindner and asked him why he thought the police hadn't arrested him. He told her that there wasn't any evidence. Maybe the dog had a bad nose. "There's no real evidence anywhere," he said, "and there never will be."

Bindner defended himself, giving an articulate explanation of the problems faced by law enforcement in the cases. "You need a lot of evidence to arrest someone," he said, "and even more to indict him, and a lot more than that to convict him. We're still at square one here, and we're always gonna be at square one, because I wasn't involved."

Bindner dismissed Sagan's invitation to take a polygraph in the Fairfield case. The tests were "unreliable," he said.

I don't think Jane Whitney was fair at all. They didn't tell me that these people were all gonna accuse me. Well, of course they're not gonna tell you that, but it just got me by surprise. It was kind of an ambush, I thought. The reason I agreed to go on there is because I wanted to get the age-enhanced photo of Amber on the show so people can see what she looks like now, if she's still alive.

In retrospect, I probably shouldn't have done the show at all. But that was my motivation for doing it. I thought, Well, I got these pictures on the wall. They're gonna show 'em. Millions of people are gonna see 'em. Somebody might recognize one of the kids.

Bindner insisted that he felt no anger toward the mothers, no anger that he had been labeled "prime suspect." He had seen the mothers' anguish, especially Kim Swartz's.

Whitney introduced Kim, who briefly described the day of Amber's disappearance. She said she had unanswered questions she wanted to direct to Bindner, cited evidence that implicated him, then fired questions at him. He had been confident that no matter what Kim might ask, he would be able to answer.

But then he heard what she had to say, and he looked stung—as if he couldn't believe what was happening. He said later that he wasn't so much angry at that point as hurt. He wanted to cry.

"You told us we were looking for a dead body," Kim said.

Bindner patiently explained that he had hoped to find a living child to return to her mother, but that he feared that Amber might have become another Angela.

Sharon Nemeth sat studying Bindner's face on the monitor. Whitney asked her about the composite drawing in her daughter's abduction. "I've just been sitting here looking at Tim these last few minutes," she said, "and it's possible that he could look like the composite."

She was talking about a second artist's drawing done much later than the original composite. The shaggy hair remained, but the pockmarks were gone, and the man appeared older. Nemeth reminded Bindner that he had been in Hayward the morning of her daughter's abduction.

"Sharon, at the time your daughter disappeared, I had a big, bushy beard," Bindner said. "I don't resemble that photograph at all when I've got my big beard and my long hair."

"Tim, I was at Sharon's house the day you showed up," Kim Swartz interrupted. "You were taking the fireman's test and you are not allowed to have a big, bushy beard when you're taking a fireman's test. You may have had a couple of days' growth."

Bindner laughed. "That's not true," he said.

Bindner was adamant that he'd had a beard.

On Jane Whitney, Kim said that I just had a two- or three-day growth of beard. That's not true. I had trimmed it down for the fire department interview. It wasn't an interview. It was a physical agility test. I had trimmed it down to maybe half an inch. That's the shortest it was, ever, before I cut it off in April of '90. Most of the time I just let it go shaggy. I was like the

*mountain man. People called me the "wild man" at
work. And my hair was real long, too.*

Bindner was still reacting. It was one confrontation after another. He wanted to get his side out, to
proclaim his innocence, but he wasn't getting much of
an opportunity to do that.

"To say that he is just a Good Samaritan is not
true," Nemeth said. "This man has a lot of darkness
in him."

When Whitney introduced Harold Sagan, the detective mentioned both physical and circumstantial
evidence implicating Bindner. "Once the district attorney gives us the green light," Sagan said, "we will arrest him."

Bindner's attorney, John Burris, sat at Bindner's
side during the show and contributed a scathing indictment of law enforcement. "In my view, this is a
failed investigation," he said.

Burris is bright and aggressive, and he has handled successful civil cases against Bay Area law enforcement agencies. He cited the release of his client's
name to the media, the press conference about the
execution of the search warrant, and the unreliability
of bloodhound evidence. "Even as this man has said,"
Burris went on, indicating Sagan and referring to the
Tribune article, "he could be a hero or a fool. Well, you
don't have a right to be a fool at someone else's ex-
pense. You have a right to follow the law, do the best
job you can, and do it professionally."

The mothers confronted Bindner about his arrest
in San Pablo. The police report twisted that all around,
Bindner said. He never said anything about a bag of
remains. No, they didn't find a love letter to Amber;
that was an expression of the anguish he felt for Kim's
daughter.

He was referring to the note that San Pablo
Sergeant Mark Foisie had found in Bindner's van on
the evening of the arrest near Adobe Liquors:

I love you, Amber. You are my first, and I
tried so hard for you. Tried + cried and still ache
in my heart. They will always try to pull me back,
but I never will. They don't know about us.
They've never heard of us.

"Do you know if the dogs were used in my daughter's case?" Kim asked him.

"I don't believe they were," Bindner said.

"Well, I know they were. Do you know whether or
not my daughter's scent was picked up in your van and
at Angela's grave?"

"I know that your daughter's scent was not in my
van, 'cause I've never met her."

"Well, that's where you're wrong," Kim said, "because my daughter's scent was picked up in your
van—and at Angela's grave. And no one knows that. It
has never been released before, and I'm telling you I
know it."

"Well, now I know why bloodhound evidence is
not admissible, because they've made several mistakes," Bindner said.

Sharon Nemeth is a quiet, thoughtful person. After Michaela disappeared, Tim Bindner had written to
her a few times, and she had written back. She wanted
to maintain contact with him for the same reason that
Kim did. She considered him a suspect.

She studied Bindner's face, and she listened to his
words. "One thing that I have learned in the last four
years of my life," Nemeth said, "is that most of the pain
that people inflict on other people comes from their
own pain. You know that you have a dark side. And if
you are responsible for any of these children, I want to
ask you to set yourself free, and set the rest of us free,
by telling us what happened to them. And I want to say
that if you have that pain, and if you have that darkness, just don't inflict it on any more children."

Bindner said that if there were any way he could
tell Sharon what had happened to her daughter, he
would. "I have a conscience," he said. "With all this

pressure on me, if I was guilty of any of these crimes, I would've broke down and confessed long ago."

Bindner tried to continue—to talk about the searching he had done for the kids—but Nemeth cut him off. "But, Tim, in private, and to some extent in the press, you do say things that lead us to believe that you know, that you are responsible. That's not fair."

Bindner said that his words had been twisted around. The press was trying to make him look guilty.

There was no arguing that it was an exciting and mysterious case. The media had jumped on it and run with it. Cemeteries, missing children, coincidences, bloodhounds, an eccentric suspect willing to be a celebrity. It was the stuff of fiction.

John Burris educated the audience about the difference between public opinion shaped by the media and evidence presented in a court of law. "Given the evidence that we have," he said, "despite all the public opinion, despite all the efforts by the police department to focus on him, there isn't really the kind of evidence that would cause a jury of fair-minded people to find him guilty."

Burris was eloquent and cogent, but just another voice in the media trial of Timothy Bindner.

Bindner and Sagan also appeared on a segment of CBS's *Street Stories*. Bindner was more comfortable with the one-on-one interview format of that show. He and Sagan traded accusations and explanations in separate interviews.

Richard Roth, who did the interviewing for the segment, sat with Bindner in his home and walked with him through St. Mary's Cemetery. Roth stood with Sagan at the grave of Angela Bugay and on top of the Kolob Hills.

The first time the public heard the evidence against Bindner was on national TV. There were too many coincidences, too many bits and pieces of information that seemed to implicate this one man. But no one had arrested him. Eccentricity is not evidence of crime.

The calls continued to come in to the Fairfield Police
Department. Joe Allio returned one to Nathan Moore,
reaching Moore's daughter, Louisa, instead. But that
was okay. The message about Tim Bindner had to do
with her anyway, she said.

She remembered that when she was in kindergarten—probably about 1982—the kids in her class
had all put their names on cards and attached the
cards to helium balloons as part of a class project. Not
long after that, Bindner contacted the school to in-
quire about the project. Somebody at the school gave
Bindner's address to Louisa, and she wrote a short
note thanking him for picking up the balloon and noti-
fying the school.

About every three or four months after that, she
received a letter from Bindner. They began with him
thanking her for writing to him, included some information about himself, and said that he had found
the balloon while walking through a cemetery. He
said that he often went to cemeteries to pick up
litter.

"He also sent some coins," Louisa told Allio.
"Sometimes even dollar bills. After the first few notes,
he started writing long, rambling letters. He talked
about cemeteries and about religion."

In one letter, Bindner said he was going to Lake
Tahoe and would stop by their house. He said that he
had been playing the lottery for her and had won a
small amount of money. He showed up a few days
later driving a blue van.

Louisa and her mother were both there when he
drove up. He gave the child $30 or $35, then invited her
out to sign the inside wall of his van. She did that, and
then Bindner asked Louisa's mother to take a photograph of the two of them standing beside the van.

Louisa remembered when Amber Swartz disappeared. "I received a letter from him saying he hoped

that we would remain friends even though he was a suspect in Amber's disappearance. He said he wasn't involved, but he was being investigated. Until I got the letter, I didn't know the police considered him a suspect. There wasn't anything on TV or in the newspapers about it."

After the letter about Amber, Bindner wrote less often, although he did send Christmas and birthday cards. They had been pen pals for a couple of years, but then her parents became concerned and withheld Bindner's letters.

Louisa's mother didn't remember much about the letters, or what had alarmed her about them, other than the man's saying that he was a suspect, and his strange ramblings about his personal situation, his religious beliefs, and his concerns for children.

Another woman, Gloria, called the investigations unit. She had a sister who had died in 1937 at the age of fifteen. She said that from sometime before 1980 through 1983 someone had left coins at her sister's grave in St. Joseph's Cemetery.

"The coins were from 1937 or 1922," the woman said, "the year my sister died or the year she was born."

Gloria's mother used to collect the coins, but she died in 1983. Gloria left an anonymous note at the grave thanking whoever had left the coins. She wrote that her mother had passed away and that it had been important to her that someone was remembering her daughter.

Gloria returned to visit her sister's grave in September 1983 and found a note written on the back of hers. The author said that his name was Tim; his nickname was "Wild Man." He said he enjoyed walking in the cemeteries and was sorry to learn of her mother's death.

It was another of Bindner's fantasy giveaways, more of the mysterious and seemingly innocuous incursions into others' lives. Bizarre, perhaps, but still not evidence of a crime.

As Harold Sagan worked to digest all of the information coming into the department after the search and the media exposure, he received a call of support from an unexpected source. A bailiff at one of the courts in Contra Costa County called to convey a message from Tracy Stone, the man arrested in the Pittsburg abduction case. "Stone says he realizes he's made his mistakes," the bailiff said, "and now he has to do his time. He said to tell you you're on the right track. He says you have to get Tim Bindner."

Sagan thanked the guy for the call, then sat at his desk and wondered what the hell the world was coming to.

SIX

ESCALATIONS

30

Tim Bindner walked out of his house on Fifty-third Street in Oakland. His arms seemed excessively long, apelike. Even the way he moved his body—in quick, jerky motions—was simian. He walked to the end of his short driveway and surveyed the street—what he thinks of as his neighborhood, his people. He wore a dark T-shirt and jeans, and his trademark ball cap, and he stood in the shadows, where he was difficult to see.

But Harold Sagan saw him. The cop sat in his parked car half a block away and watched—as he had for so many hours on more than a hundred nights since Bindner had become a suspect.

Bindner walked up the block, away from the unmarked cruiser. He was good at picking up surveillance. He had been doing it for years, but he hadn't picked up Sagan.

The gray-haired cop watched the slender, wiry man move down the street, then pulled his car out onto Fifty-third no longer listening to the background chatter of the radios. He knew Bindner's destination, so he made a turn, then another, and drove there.

Sagan parked, switched off his lights and ignition, and sat in silence outside the walled enclosure of St. Mary's Cemetery. He checked his watch. Within minutes, Bindner jogged by on the opposite side of the street, hesitated only a moment, then vaulted over the five-foot-high stucco wall into the cemetery.

Sagan got out of the cruiser, straightened his 6'1" frame, and looked at the sky. He operated by a single rule: If there was less than a quarter moon, he went in. He didn't want to cast a shadow. He didn't want to be seen. This night the cop had the cover of an overcast sky, and he knew there was only a sliver of a moon up there somewhere above the clouds.

He gave Bindner five minutes of lead time, then crossed the street and climbed over the wall. He moved quickly away from the lights on the street, into the dark shadows of the trees and shrubs along the perimeter of the cemetery. As he had expected, it was black, and almost silent. The only sound he heard was the man ahead of him padding his way over the grass.

The headstones were unreadable at night, but Bindner didn't need to read them. He knew exactly where Mildred's grave was. He knew how to find Florence. He stopped to visit with her, talked to her, said a brief prayer. Then, with his usual jerky motion, he moved off to another grave and lingered there.

Sagan watched. He moved closer. In the darkness, the almost impenetrable night, he moved to within fifty feet of Bindner. Then forty feet. He couldn't make out the words, but the man's mutterings carried on the night air.

Thirty feet.

Two decades earlier, Sagan had spent nights crouched in a jungle in Vietnam, listening. He had remained motionless, a human statue in the lush vegetation, waiting for a sound. He knew the routine. The army had trained him to reach out through the thick night air for the enemy, and to kill him silently. Efficiently.

Twenty-five feet.

It would be so easy. So quick. So silent. Other nights when he had been this close to the man, he had thought about talking to him—considered walking up and starting a conversation, man to man. Maybe this was the night when he would let Bindner know that this silence and this field filled with the dead were familiar to him, too.

Twenty feet.

The cop was downwind. No scent. No sound.

Bindner was kneeling and mumbling at a grave.

Even as Sagan could imagine taking the necessary steps, snapping the man's neck, he also knew that he wanted Bindner alive. He *needed* the strange little man alive, and had to protect him, keep him safe for the day when the cop might tell him he was under arrest. Then it would be up to the courts.

Bindner stood and resumed his monkey-hopping among the gravestones. Sagan watched him zigzag through the night, certain that he could hear the man singing to himself. Then, in the distance, Bindner began to howl—just like the monkeys in the jungles of Vietnam had so many years before.

———

Sagan's office at the Fairfield police department is neat. He puts things away. There are a few photographs, a few awards, some memorabilia—all orderly, a model of organization. It is a working space. He wants files where he can find them, reports where he can place a hand on them.

Sagan reviewed the list of what had been seized from Tim Bindner's home. Most of it was written material—logs, journals, diaries, copies of letters. The investigative team would check and cross-check the dates, times, and places. They had already shipped the physical evidence seized during the search to the California Department of Justice for analysis.

Now Sagan scanned some of Bindner's papers. The handwriting was never neat but usually readable. Sometimes it was a scrawl, causing the cop to wonder if Bindner had been drinking when he wrote it.

Bindner wrote about the bizarre coincidences in the Bay Area cases and their impact on him. He wondered if the cops were setting him up. Maybe the Fairfield police had confiscated his car because he was getting too close to something. Maybe *they* had something to do with these abductions. He had said the same thing to Kim Swartz.

Shrines seemed to be important to the man. The living room wall plastered with posters of the dead or missing children. Was it reverence for the dead or a fascination with death and its emblems?

Bindner wanted to establish the legitimacy of his search efforts and to have someone—law enforcement?—recognize the viability of what he had done. Was it still his rescue fantasy, the desire that he'd had as a young man to be a CHP officer? Sagan suspected that it was something more complex.

Bindner had researched the subject of serial murder. He knew the difference between organized and disorganized—the categories of offenders used in the FBI's criminal profiles. He had listed the characteristics of the organized offender for Sagan, then said that he fit them. He had done the same thing with Mary Ellen O'Toole. Was he doing his own amateur investigation, or was he studying the literature, educating himself about what cops look for?

He'd had the opportunity to act on his rescue fantasies during the Loma Prieta earthquake in 1989, then again when wildfires swept the Berkeley and Oakland Hills in 1991. Aspects of even those rescue efforts seemed to be a defiance of authority. Bindner had to operate alone. He had to demean others' efforts. He didn't seem capable of accepting any authority.

So much of his writing denigrated everyone's

efforts but his own. He had an exquisite sense of his own suffering but no one else's—just the pain experienced by Timothy Bindner.

He kept insisting that love and compassion were what motivated him. Did those words have some idiosyncratic meaning for him? Love. Compassion. Biblical references to the first book of John. Then why taunt the agencies that were trying to do the same thing that he professed to be doing? Why put all that energy into misdirection and equivocation? If he was innocent, as he claimed, he could so easily cooperate with law enforcement and clear himself.

He made fun of the bloodhounds, but he wondered why the police hadn't used them in the Amber case. That was before his confrontation with Kim on the *Jane Whitney Show*.

They think I kill little girls. Let me amend that. They suspect that I might be involved in the abduction and/or sexual assault and/or murder of little children, and they are investigating the possibility of that having occurred. . . .

Somebody throws a rock, breaks a window in the schoolhouse, and he runs. The person that didn't throw the rock stands there and watches. Who's gonna get blamed?

And what if he thinks it's very pretty to watch that window break? And what if the first person who comes out to investigate says, "What happened?" And he says, "The window broke. Isn't that pretty?" Well, shit, you're convicted, man. . . .

I don't even know at this point which children they think I killed, which children they think I abducted, which children they may think I have raped, what my motives may have been. They're just trying to put something together on me regarding children. Meanwhile, I have to continue to do what I'm put here to do.

It was late in the afternoon when Harold Sagan sat with his long legs extended out onto the coffee table in his living room. He thought about the case—and Tim Bindner. The guy was enjoying the limelight. He was getting off on all the publicity.

Sagan watched tapes of news clips. The *Jane Whitney Show*, the *Street Stories* segment. He hit the stop button on his remote control and switched off the power to the TV. The house was silent. He sat there, allowing his mind to drift over all that he knew about the case and about the man who had become the focus of his investigation.

Bindner wasn't just involving himself in the investigations, he was including himself in the lives of the victims' families. Was he trying to be a member of the family? He wanted their acceptance, but the exchanges on the TV show had chilled some of the relationships he had established. Even so, Sagan knew that Bindner had written to Sharon Nemeth—and against the advice of his attorney, he was also still writing to Kim Swartz.

Sagan figured that Bindner was enjoying the media attention and his newfound status as the Bay Area's celebrity suspect. It was time to bring the situation under control, but more and more, Sagan felt as if he were the only cop actively working the cases. Since the search of Bindner's house and the publicity that followed, even fewer of Sagan's phone calls to other agencies were returned. He had the support of his own department, but there was information out there that he needed—incident and interrogation reports—and no one was providing them. There was no cooperation, and no indication that anyone else was considering possible linkage among some of the Bay Area cases.

Kim Swartz trusted the detective and relied on his judgment. He was the only one who seemed to care enough about the cases to stick with them, to go after every lead, every piece of information that came along. She stopped answering Bindner's letters. As a group, the parents stopped commenting publicly about Bindner. Sagan curtailed all official statements about Bindner's status as a suspect, and any reference to the Campbell investigation included only that it was continuing.

Bindner still wrote to Sagan on occasion, but the cop had shifted gears. He wanted to go proactive—push the guy's buttons, force him to react. He wanted to point out Bindner's inconsistencies, remind him of his fantasies, challenge his pseudo-expertise at searching for missing children. The cop had to be reasonable, but he wanted to keep Bindner off balance.

If Bindner was the man, Sagan thought, his celebrity status was maintaining him at a level where he felt invulnerable. Everyone was leaning in Bindner's direction. It was time to get *him* to do a little leaning, make him give in order to get.

Bindner wrote to Sagan on February 11, 1993, saying that he never should have done the Whitney show. He accused the detective of turning the mothers against him. "God wants me where I am," Bindner wrote, "and he has a purpose for me. I came only to try to find these missing children. I wonder what your role is. I don't see it as loving or compassionate. If you are involved in the evil acts, you will be found out eventually. Leave me and my family alone, you have caused enough anguish."

Sagan answered the letter the next day. He assured Bindner that the mothers had minds of their own, and wrote: "Trying to turn the tables on me concerning 'evil acts' is a shallow attempt at covering up the futility of your situation. Again as stated in the past, the investigation is not a personal vendetta against you, may the facts present themselves as they will."

He told Bindner that he had spent the previous week looking again at a suspect from early in the Nikki Campbell investigation. "I was able to prove the man didn't take Nikki," Sagan wrote. "I have gone through the same process with you untold times, but unfortunately I can not clear or eliminate you."

Bindner wrote back on the seventeenth.

You mentioned the "futility" of my situation. My efforts, although they have not produced results in missing children cases, are not futile. The evil acts *have occurred*. I did not do them. Too many coincidences exist. It is that simple, yet I don't suppose you would want to work with me on *that* angle, would you? Hey—if so, let me know! I am not nearly done yet, I *will* tell you that. I am *just getting started*, man.

I have gained strength, and I believe God has put me here for a purpose. No one, now, can stop me.

Your letter was well-written. It almost makes me think you are real. However, you do not seem to have any respect for my wife or my children. They are my most precious. Yet you seem to think they don't exist.

Bindner wrote about his searches for Amber and Michaela, the one day that he was able to spend looking for Ilene Misheloff, and insisted again that he had not taken Nikki Campbell.

There will be another one, my friend. Are you really on my side? God, I hope so. Another little girl will "disappear," "vanish," and probably die in pain and anguish.

I will try to be there to look for her, and to apprehend the criminal.

Look elsewhere, my friend, I did not take Nikki. I love her.

The angry tone of the letter concerned Sagan. Again, he thought, someone reading it could interpret the man's curious statements in a variety of ways: "I am not nearly done yet. . . . I am just getting started. . . . I have gained strength. . . . There will be another one." Sagan submitted the letter to the FBI for analysis.

31

FEBRUARY 28, 1993

It was eleven days after Bindner's last letter to Sagan.

At five o'clock in the afternoon, Sharon Peterson and her three-year-old daughter visited the grave of a relative at St. Mary's Cemetery in Oakland. A cool breeze drifted through the flowers that other visitors had left behind. The smells of blooming acacia and eucalyptus leaves drifted on the chilly, late afternoon air. There was still some daylight, but most of the visitors had gone.

Peterson's daughter wandered off the paved walkway toward some bushes and fallen trees fifty feet away. That didn't worry her mother. They visited St. Mary's often—and, while Peterson occupied herself with her thoughts, the child usually went off to explore.

This time, within just a few moments, a man emerged from the brush near a row of fallen trees. Sharon Peterson looked over at him, noticing that he was short and wiry, wearing a baseball cap. Then she remembered having seen him on TV.

"Stay away from my daughter," she screamed. "Leave us alone."

The man spread his arms wide. "What the hell's going on?" he said. "I ain't doing anything."

The woman screamed again. "I know you, Tim Bindner," she said. "Leave us alone. I know you."

With his arms still extended out from his sides, he backed away from the obviously distraught woman. "Hey, I'm not gonna hurt you. I'm not gonna do anything to you."

Bindner had been in the adjacent Mountain View Cemetery visiting the grave of a relative, and now he was going to chill out with a couple of beers. He was a frequent visitor and volunteer at St. Mary's and other cemeteries in the San Francisco Bay Area. He enjoyed repairing broken statuary and gravestones, and resetting monuments that had been knocked over by vandals or undermined by the rain. He walked toward Sharon Peterson, thinking that he would warn the woman not to let her little girl play among the gravestones on the downhill slope. Some of them were very old and loose in the ground. They could tip, fall over, and crush a child. He had read an article about a cemetery where that had happened.

Peterson moved past him, grabbed her daughter by the hand, and ran. Peterson was moving so fast that she kept losing her grip on the child, who was desperately trying to keep up with her terrified mother.

Bindner watched them go—the mother hysterical, the kid running to keep up. If he'd had any intention of grabbing the child, that would have been the time to do it. In her hurry to get out of the cemetery, the woman was almost leaving the kid behind.

Bindner said later that he didn't have any thought about grabbing the kid, despite what they said about him on national TV—that he had abducted this child, or looked like the man who had abducted that child; that he had a dark side. He felt as if the cops and the media had ambushed him, marked him indelibly as some kind of pervert.

Bindner took his beer and walked through St. Mary's to one of the mausoleums. Kids gathered there at night to do their drinking, and sometimes he would talk with them, asking them not to damage anything on the grounds.

He had a personal interest in cemeteries—he saw them as places of beauty, places filled with history and the souls of the people who had made that history. When he repaired their gravestones, he fashioned his own tools and concocted his own cement. He subscribed to journals—*Stone in America* and *American Cemetery*—about stone and monuments and graveyards.

This time, though, he wanted to be alone with his thoughts, to have some peace. The cemetery was the best place in Oakland to accomplish that. So he sat next to the mausoleum and drank. If the cops were going to come, let them find him here. Why should he go out and allow them to grab him on their turf? Let them find him in the cemetery. He hadn't done anything wrong.

———————

The episode had frightened Sharon Peterson. When she ran, she had found a phone and dialed 911. That's when the confusion began. That guy who was on TV, the one who they think took that kid in Fairfield, he's in St. Mary's Cemetery—he came out of the bushes near her daughter, she explained, adding, "But he didn't do anything."

"Is your daughter with you now?" the dispatcher asked.

"Yes."

The dispatcher called out a possible 207—a kidnapping. A "kidnap suspect" and a three-year-old had emerged from some bushes. Four patrol units responded to the cemetery.

It took Bindner a half hour to finish his beer. He stood up and walked back through the cemetery, out onto Pleasant Valley Avenue. He didn't know what to expect. If the woman had called the cops, they would have come in after him, he reasoned. It didn't seem likely that they would wait out here for him.

He got into his old Toyota and pulled away from the curb. He turned the corner and got as far as the 1900 block of Pleasant Valley Avenue. An Oakland police car approached from his rear. A motorcycle cop blocked the road in front. Both cops approached the battered, lime-green station wagon. They ordered Bindner to get out.

"Let me pull it into the curb," Bindner said, remembering that his hand break didn't work properly.

The engine was still running. His car rolled forward a few inches. The motorcycle cop repeated the instructions. "Throw your keys out on the ground and get out."

Bindner started to do as he was told. "I haven't done anything," he said. "What the hell's going on?"

One of the cops grabbed him and pulled him out of the car. The cop forced Bindner up against the vehicle, frisked him, and handcuffed him.

The patrol sergeant, Thomas Hogenmiller, sorted things out. He knew that Bindner had been on national TV and that he was a suspect in the Bay Area abduction cases, but there were no warrants for his arrest, and he hadn't tried to do anything to the Peterson child. The guy smelled of beer and appeared intoxicated. Later, his blood test would show an alcohol concentration of .20, more than twice the legal limit in California. The cops arrested him for driving under the influence.

Within days, Bindner was back on the front pages. The article in the *San Francisco Chronicle* read: "The incident marks the latest twist in a bizarre story involving the police, the FBI and the parents of several missing East Bay children."

———————

Harold Sagan's idea that publicity about Bindner could be contained had received its first rude shock. Tim Bindner was a walking news story. There seemed to be no way to keep him out of the limelight.

32

Kim Swartz came home from work at the foundation and unlocked the front door of her Savage Avenue home. The house was silent.

She walked to Amber's room and looked in at her daughter's bed, the dolls, the electric candle in the window—a light to guide her child home.

Something was wrong. At first the room didn't look any different from the way it had looked the hundreds of other times she had stood in the doorway, sat on the bed and wept, or just held something of Amber's and stared into space.

Kim moved slowly through the room—not touching anything, just looking. The closet doors were open. She had left them shut. Paperwork, books, the phone on the desk—all had been moved. On a little table there was a pocket rosary with religious medallions attached to it. A friend had given it to Kim shortly after

Amber disappeared. The rosary was in two pieces; one of the medallions was missing.

She walked through the house. Lights were on in the garage, the kitchen, her bedroom. Her own phone was on the floor, and someone had pushed a button so that anyone who called would get a busy signal. Her bedroom window was open, and the drape was hanging outside—as if an intruder had brushed against it as he was making his exit.

She called the police to report the break-in, then stood in the empty house wondering why the medallion was the only item that had been taken.

———

Harold Sagan continued to study Bindner's writings. His first impression was that Bindner had written the materials for an audience. The FBI had searched his place in 1988 and removed boxes of documents. Sagan didn't know what was in this material. Later, he would find out that most of it had never even been examined.

Sagan figured that Bindner must have expected the FBI or some other agency to descend on him again—to scrutinize his journals and his search logs. The stuff was intriguing, bizarre in many respects, and an educational journey into the mind of Timothy Bindner. But none of the materials contained anything that immediately struck Sagan as incriminating.

The man was obviously obsessed with children—their lives and their families—as well as the anguish suffered by families when a stranger abducts a child. He had become a self-educated expert on the subjects of child abduction and sexual homicide. He also had an insatiable interest in death and cemeteries. There was nothing new in any of that.

For years he had remained at the center of these tragedies and made no effort to avoid or alleviate the controversy. Whenever his various attorneys advised him to back off, he would follow their advice for short periods of time, then jump back into the middle of things. He especially couldn't seem to stay away from Kim Swartz.

He had confided in her. "I tried to work with law enforcement after Amber disappeared," he'd told her. "I still ended up being apprehended and questioned. I didn't get arrested, but I still ended up being under a very severe scrutiny even then, while I was trying to work with them."

Sagan knew there was a grain of truth in that statement. What was missing was the rest of the story: He blew the polygraph, demeaned the machine, dumped on the dogs, and refused to do anything to clear himself. Under the law, he had no obligation to clear himself; the burden wasn't on him. He professed much love and anguish for the children and their families, said he wanted the responsible person to be caught, so why didn't he take that extra step? He could clear himself, do his searching, work with the families, and set law enforcement free to pursue other avenues of investigation. Instead, he kept the pot stirred, equivocated, basked in the media glow, and guaranteed that police would focus on him. After his polygraph in the Amber Swartz case, Bindner had even urged friends and family members not to talk with law enforcement people.

Sagan reread his own reports and the few summaries that he had received from other jurisdictions. He studied everything Bindner had written.

Bindner insisted that he was in sympathy with the mothers. Then why did he keep reminding them, especially Kim, of their pain? Every time he wrote to Kim, every time they talked on the phone, every time he went out to Pinole, he reminded her of her suffering, her pain, her anguish.

Sagan tried to put it together.

If mothers aren't feeling pain, he thought, perhaps they should be. A man could take the children, then punish the mothers with constant reminders of their tragedies.

Why? Were these the vengeance fantasies that

Sagan had read about in Ressler's book? A man can't punish his own mother.

Is the world such a harsh and dangerous place?

Tim Bindner had told his first wife that there were too many children in the world. Sagan wondered, could a man possibly believe that dead children—the ones already buried in the local cemeteries and the ones stolen, killed, and concealed—would constitute a family? Would such a man abduct children and take them to visit Angela Bugay, or would he go there himself to report to her? Would he want them aware of their kinship?

One subject about which Bindner was unequivocal was his emotional attachment to Angela. That didn't mean that he'd had anything to do with her death. Besides, Antioch had a solid suspect in that case. So what did it mean? That Angela was a child for whom he felt great love and compassion? Or, could the events of her death have set Bindner in motion? The bloodhounds linked Amber's and Nikki's scents to Angela's grave. Sagan wondered if the 1983 homicide was a trigger case for Bindner, a catalyst that transformed thoughts into action.

He presents himself as a martyr—like Jesus. He thanked Kim for helping him clarify his religious thinking. He once gave her a tape—"Jesus, Here's Another Child to Hold." Kim said he liked the title song best.

In the hypothetical that he was considering, Sagan asked whether it could possibly be a kindness to send children to Jesus. The one who truly loves the children removes them from their suffering and delivers them to the Lord. And this way they remain children forever.

Something was coming together for Sagan, but it was even crazier than he had imagined. If Tim Bindner was their man, he was a solid suspect, a narcissist, a cunning predator who required attention, who always needed to be in the spotlight. Could he be dissociative, like Ted Bundy? Able to split himself away from his rage, to compartmentalize the different lives he led? Could he be that delusional? Could he really believe that he was doing good works?

The detective needed help. Reading the books was one thing. Dealing with a man like Bindner, attempting to investigate him, was something else. He had said it on *Street Stories:* "This is the kind of guy they write books about."

Sagan spent $150 of his own money for an hour with a psychiatrist at Stanford. It was money wasted. The therapist knew his Freud, all right—but he had no understanding of evil.

Tim Bindner liked to walk the streets, to talk to people. He knew how things were on the streets—one guy ready to kill another because of a look, an expression.

He figured most people were good. They wanted to get married, have kids, live their lives. The few that didn't were the ones who needed someone to take them off the street and put them in cages. Of course, the media played it up as if the country were going to hell and everyone was crazy. He went through the neighborhoods—from Oakland into Berkeley—jogging two miles to work every day, three miles to a game at the Cal-Berkeley campus. Yet nobody bothered him. People saw him coming through day after day. After a while they waved to him.

The media made it sound as if all people were evil. They were pushing this "don't talk to strangers" thing. Bindner hated that, because he was the stranger who wanted to talk to kids. He wanted to say "Hi" and find out what was going on. If the kid wanted to talk, that was fine. Some of them pulled back. He didn't know why they did that, but sometimes they did. Sometimes they ran away from him because they recognized him as "the kidnap suspect."

Many kids didn't answer him when he talked to them. They looked at him, but they didn't say anything. He was the stranger their parents had told them not to talk to. So he moved on.

33

JUNE 9, 1993

Six months had passed since the search of Bindner's house.

At a press conference in his Oakland office, John Burris announced that his clients, Timothy and Sandra Bindner, were filing a $25 million claim for harassment against the city of Fairfield and Detective Harold Sagan. The claim was the first step in a lawsuit, and the city had forty-five days to respond.

"When you get falsely accused," Burris told reporters, "you never get a chance to defend yourself. It's been six months, and no evidence of a crime has been put forward. If they have credible evidence, they should come forward."

Bindner and his wife claimed that the Fairfield police, and particularly Harold Sagan, had violated their civil rights, compromised their right to privacy, and destroyed their reputations.

"The real killer," Burris said, "is walking around free, elated.".

The court had dismissed the DUI charge against Bindner. This fact, Burris said, was more evidence of the damage his client had suffered. The court had ruled that police had no probable cause to stop Bindner. He wasn't driving erratically. He wasn't speeding. They'd pulled him over because of his notoriety, because of a complaint from a woman who, despite being upset, said that Bindner hadn't done anything. The media had blown the episode out of proportion with their attention to his client.

Three days after the incident with Sharon Peterson at St. Mary's Cemetery, police again had detained Burris's client, this time at Mountain View Cemetery. Bindner was in the same general area where he had run into the Peterson woman, where the trees had blown down and knocked over some of the gravestones. He was mixing a batch of glue and getting ready to repair one of the broken markers when the cops arrived. Someone had called and said that there was a man with a backpack in the cemetery acting weird. They detained Bindner, verified his identity, searched and released him.

The claim alleged that as a result of Fairfield's actions, the Bindners had experienced "hatred, ill will, harassment, ridicule, and condemnation."

Bindner's neighbors had accused him of murder. As he was walking on Fifty-third Street a few days after the search of his home, a woman called from the other side of the street, "Hey, did you kill that little girl?"

One man had even threatened to shoot him. Bindner had been walking back from a social justice committee meeting at his church one night. There was a full moon, so he decided to go up and walk around St. Mary's Cemetery. He passed a house where a man and woman were arguing on the porch. The man broke off his harangue at the woman and stared down at Bindner.

"There's that Bindner guy that molests kids," he said. "That's all I need."

Bindner answered him. "No, I don't hurt anybody. I never molested any kids."

"You come back down this street again, I'm gonna shoot you."

Bindner ignored him and continued walking to the cemetery. The man called after him. "And if you trespass in the cemetery, I'm gonna call the cops and have you arrested."

Bindner climbed the gate and went into the cemetery, just as he had been doing for years.

Within minutes, three police cars responded. The cops were down around the gate with flashlights. They walked up to the new mausoleum on the hill and then over to the mausoleum between St. Mary's and Mountain View. By this time, Bindner was at the east end of St. Mary's, so he crossed into Mountain View and slipped out the back way. He didn't want the cops to detain him again, or possibly arrest him. He was doing what he had done for a dozen years, but he didn't think that would matter to the cops. The next day, as Burris had advised, Bindner filed a police report about the man's threat.

Kids threw rocks at him. Sandra's chronic ulcers worsened.

Bindner told the press conference: "On December 27, 1991, I was with my family in Oakland, forty miles away from Fairfield, so they made a mistake. I hope they do find the guy who took that girl."

In Fairfield, Sergeant Chuck Timm's reaction to the claim was succinct: "We believe Mr. Bindner was involved in the abduction of Amanda 'Nikki' Campbell. Filing a claim doesn't change our investigation."

Sagan's comment was equally brief. "Nothing has changed," the detective said. "He's still the prime suspect."

Sagan knew that if Bindner *was* their man and they didn't get him the first time, they would lose him forever. He wanted something more, something conclusive and compelling. And the Solano County District Attorney was demanding a "convictable" case.

Sagan was still trying to understand Bindner. Before the search of his home and his subsequent notoriety, Bindner was introducing himself to others as a suspect in child abduction cases. After the search, he had basked in the notoriety of the media attention, granting interviews to anyone who happened by.

Sagan viewed the claim and the imminent lawsuit as hindering Bindner's ability to do what he wanted to do when he wanted to do it. Burris had told him not to do any searching, not to communicate with any of the mothers. This time the financial incentive might just keep him in line.

But Bindner was still making his nocturnal visits to St. Mary's, and the detective was still on his heels.

After the press conference, Bindner joined a group that was going around Oakland to homicide scenes and conducting prayer vigils. He told one woman, "Watch TV tonight. You're gonna see me on TV."

He started talking about missing children, and he spooked the woman when he explained who he was. It was as if he were bragging. The woman thought she ought to call the police. She called Harold Sagan.

In California, municipalities do not pay punitive damages awarded by a court. Individuals named in such actions must pay them. "I'm taking up a collection on the twenty-five million," Sagan quipped. "I'm playing Lotto regularly now. Maybe I'll get lucky."

He told Chuck Timm, "I'm kind of disappointed. I

thought I was worth more than that. But I'm thinking I'd better have a car wash and a bake sale."

Bindner sent a note to Kim Swartz postmarked June 15. He admitted that his attorney would not approve, but he wanted to let her know that he was thinking about her. He included his phone number in case Kim needed his help with anything. He also wrote: "Just checked out *Uncovering the Mystery of M.P.D.* by Dr. James Friesan; it's supposedly a good Christian perspective on the subject."

Kim hadn't known that Bindner had any interest in multiple personality disorder (MPD) until the day she told him that she was going to speak at a conference dealing with Satanic rituals in abuse situations. Some of the victims, she had told him, suffered from MPD.

She had wondered before if Bindner was dissociative. Now she wondered if he was a multiple. The guy was so smooth. If he could just split away—and she thought she had seen him do that—it would make a great defense if police ever arrested him. She believed she had heard him do it during their phone conversations: He would just drift away. He also did it that time when they were out walking in her neighborhood, and it had frightened her.

The Pinole police had asked Kim Swartz not to communicate with Sagan. She ignored them. When she faxed a copy of the note to Galloway in Pinole, she also sent one to the Fairfield detective.

The reference to MPD puzzled Sagan. Was Bindner dropping hints? Was that what he was about? Was it another diversion? He had long felt that whatever Bindner said, the opposite was probably true. "If he points to a certain spot," he told Chuck Timm, "look somewhere else, because it won't be at that spot."

The lawsuit strengthened Sagan's determination. "I don't give a shit what happens," he said. "I'm going to continue going after him until he's either cleared or in jail. If he thinks I'm giving up, he's sadly mistaken. If anything, now I've got even more reason to continue working on him. Now it's personal."

The detective worried that if Bindner was playing a cat-and-mouse game with police, the lawsuit helped create a convenient smoke screen behind which he could thumb his nose at law enforcement.

In May, Sagan had attended a workshop on psychological profiling in Las Vegas. He cornered a well-known Chicago detective there and outlined the case for him.

"Could this be someone who hasn't done anything?" Sagan asked the cop, who had been through FBI training in profiling. "Could it just be a fantasy thing?"

The veteran homicide detective's response was quick and unequivocal: "No. A person like this has committed the act. They don't display all these behaviors unless they have committed the act."

Sagan pushed. "Well, the people who taught you said that it could be nothing more than a fantasy trip."

"They're full of shit," the cop said.

———————————

Kim Swartz received a note from Bindner. He enclosed a small medallion. She held the object in her hand and gazed at it. She wondered if it could be the one that had disappeared from Amber's room four months earlier. She couldn't be at all positive, but the thought unsettled her. She reported it to the police, but they didn't seem to think too much of it.

———————————

In August, the city of Fairfield rejected Bindner's claim. Burris filed the lawsuit.

I still didn't do it, and you still haven't filed any charges. Let's drop all that stuff, okay? It's not real. It didn't happen. Let's drop it all. I'm ready to drop it all. You come up with theories. You come up with connections. You come up with viable theories. You come up with suspects. There has to come a point where you say, "We have a case," or, "We don't have a case." Well, if you have a case, file it. I offered that challenge to Harry the day after he searched my house. I said, "Put up or shut up, man." I'm not gonna back down from that challenge. Put up or shut up. If you got a case, file it. If you don't, leave me alone. That's the essence of our lawsuit.

Most of the time, after they made a case, the investigators dissected the crime to get into the mind of the bad guy. This time, they had to do it with a suspect as the case evolved—and do it without a crime scene, without a corpse.

———————

The calls came to Sagan about once a week. Sometimes the women identified themselves. Most often, they delivered their messages and hung up. "Please don't quit," they said. "This is about more than just the girls who are already missing—this is about those who *will* be missing in the future. People support what you're doing."

That was good to hear, but the calls increased the size of the burden the detective was carrying. He had some vacation time coming up, and he was going to Germany to visit relatives. He relished the idea of getting away from the case and the pressure for a few weeks.

He got on the phone to Germany to arrange his visit. It was good to hear the voices he hadn't heard in so long, and Sagan slipped comfortably into his native tongue.

It was clear to Sagan that his strategy of containing Bindner had failed. The guy was a walking media event, a man who attracted attention wherever he went. "I'm the guy you saw on TV," he might say. Or, "I'm the one they think took those kids."

The cop knew that a different approach was necessary, but he wasn't going to think about it until after he returned from Europe.

34

SEPTEMBER 21, 1993

George Ellwin had watched the TV news in early June. He'd listened as Bindner and his attorney described the claim and pending lawsuit against both the city of Fairfield and the chief investigator on the Nikki Campbell case. Ellwin had had it. His calls to the Pinole police were a waste of time. So he called Kim Swartz.

It was in the San Pablo–Richmond area, he told her—at Alvarado Park on June 3, 1988—more than five years before. Ellwin described the man he had seen. The guy was acting suspicious, he said, and he was handling the little blond girl in a rough way.

Ellwin was apologetic. During all those years he had felt as if he should have done something more, should have tried to help the little girl. He told Kim that when he learned of her daughter's abduction, he had called the Pinole police. "I gave them the license number of the car," he said. "It was light blue, maybe two-tone—kind of beige on top and light blue on the bottom—a 1966 Pontiac Bonneville, four-door."

He described the man—white, about forty, with shoulder-length hair somewhere between dirty blond and brown. "He grabbed the little girl by the back of her neck and the seat of her pants, threw her into the front passenger side of his car, then he pushed her down onto the floor."

Ellwin told Kim about staring at the man's face. "When the guy started to drive out of there, his head snapped around and he glared at me. His eyes just locked on me. I could never forget a face like that."

Kim asked about the timing. Ellwin had gotten off work that day at about 3:30. By the time he had picked up his daughter, bought ice cream, and driven to the park, it must have been between 4:30 and 5:30.

It was nine months before Detective Phil Pollard responded to the call Ellwin had made to the Pinole P.D. "He wanted to know if I was sure about the license plate," Ellwin said. "I was only ten feet away when I wrote it down. He said it came back registered to a different vehicle, one that was junked down in L.A. I didn't hear from anyone after that. But when I saw the news broadcast of the search of this Bindner guy's house in Oakland, I called again. I told the detective that Bindner was the guy I saw in Alvarado Park that Friday in 1988. But I don't know what, if any, action they took on that."

This was the first that Kim was hearing about any of it. After all the reports of sightings of Amber, the crank calls, she was skeptical. But George Ellwin sounded so torn up about the whole thing, she thought this call might be for real.

"I had my little girl with me," he said. "I couldn't do anything. He was driving that big car. I couldn't follow him. I was driving a Toyota. I couldn't have kept up with him. Or he might've driven me off the road. It's bothered me."

Something else that convinced Kim Swartz of the man's sincerity was that he had left a trail—his calls to the Pinole cops. The police could easily verify them. George Ellwin sounded like the genuine article.

"I don't think the police did anything with what I told them," he said. "When I saw the news yesterday about the lawsuit, I decided to call you directly."

Kim was fuming. She called Harold Sagan, the one cop she trusted, and told him about the call she had received from Ellwin.

Two days later, George Ellwin directed Harold Sagan to Alvarado Park and showed him where he had seen the man's vehicle. "I grew up around here," Ellwin said. "I'm very familiar with this park and the whole area."

"Do you know where the Social Security Building is in Richmond?" Sagan asked, referring to the office where Tim Bindner was working in 1988.

"You mean the main building, the red-brick one?" Sagan nodded.

Ellwin looked to the west. "It's over that way. If we were at a higher elevation, we could see it from here."

The two men walked through the parking area toward the locked gate leading to the forest fire staging area. "About your identification of Timothy Bindner," Sagan said. "Was that based on seeing him on the TV broadcasts?"

"I saw him in June 1988," Ellwin said. "That's what it's based on. He's the man I saw. Seeing that, the way he treated that child, made such an impression on me. And his face when he was staring at me, I'll never forget that. I asked my daughter if she remembered that day. She says she does. She remembers seeing him get out of the passenger side first, but otherwise, what she said is pretty much the same."

"Why didn't you contact me directly?" Sagan wanted to know.

"I called the Pinole police because it was about Amber Swartz. I figured they were investigating it, so that's who I should call. I thought they'd talk to you. When I saw the news about the lawsuit, I was afraid they hadn't done anything with it since 1988. That's why I called Kim Swartz."

"Would you be willing to take a polygraph to corroborate what you've told me?"

"I'll do anything I can to help," Ellwin said. "If I have to establish my truthfulness, that's all right, too. I know what I saw."

The man seemed almost too good to be true.

On September 30, Sagan interviewed Ellwin's daughter, Elaine, a bright sixteen-year-old. She told the detective that she remembered the man and the little girl who had been in the park in San Pablo five years before.

"We drove past the car," she said, "and I saw the man letting the girl out of the car. Then we turned around. He grabbed her and threw her back in when he saw us. He had his hand over her mouth because she was kicking and screaming."

"What did the girl look like?" Sagan asked.

"She had blond hair. She was younger than I was." Elaine shrugged.

Elaine Ellwin would have been eleven at the time.

"What about the man?" Sagan asked.

"He was skinny. He wasn't tall, but he wasn't short either. Brown hair, I think."

"Did he have a mustache or a beard?"

"I don't know," Elaine said.

"What about the car?"

"Light blue or light gray."

Elaine Ellwin had heard that someone had abducted another little girl, this time in Fairfield, but she hadn't seen any of the TV news accounts, nor had she seen any pictures of the prime suspect.

The next day, Sagan called George Ellwin's sister. The woman remembered her brother's visit, the newscast about the missing child, and the shocked expression on her brother's face. He had told her what he had seen at Alvarado Park, and she had urged him to call the police.

Sagan asked the required questions. Did George Ellwin have a history of any mental problems? Was he the sort of person who would exaggerate or embellish things?

The woman said no. "George is very levelheaded. He's an unassuming guy."

———————

At noon on October 5, Sagan again sat with Elaine Ellwin. This time he explained what a photographic lineup was. She wasn't under any obligation to identify anyone. She shouldn't guess or assume that one of the pictures must be the right one.

Sagan placed a six-photo array in front of the teenager. She studied the pictures for a long time. "They all look so much alike," she said. "Numbers two and three look most like the man I saw. Number two looks more familiar than any of them. His hair is most similar. I think it was curly, and just above the shoulder. I'm not sure."

The detective asked her to put question marks above numbers two and three. Then he asked her again about news accounts or photos of the suspect. Elaine was sure that she hadn't seen anything like that.

Sagan carried the photographs with him out to his car and looked again at the array. Number two was Tim Bindner.

———————

On Friday, October 22, Sagan called Detective Wayne Galloway. He went over the situation with the Pinole detective, reminding him about Ellwin and letting Galloway know that he wanted to have the man polygraphed. "This is your case," Sagan said.

The Pinole cop said he would look into it and get back to Sagan. Sagan never heard back from Galloway, so he made his own arrangements to have Ellwin tested by a retired Department of Justice polygraph expert, Robert C. Liberdy.

Liberdy was the consummate professional. A polygraph examiner with the DOJ from 1973 until his retirement in 1992, Liberdy had administered more than seven thousand polygraph examinations in felony criminal investigations, with a quarter of those involving murder cases.

On November 2, Liberdy conducted the examination of George Ellwin. During the pretest interview, Ellwin went over his story again, this time fine-tuning some of the details. The man he saw had been about 5'11", 165 pounds, wearing a plaid wool shirt and jeans. He was certain now that the time was 4:45 P.M.

As the monitors measured Ellwin's responses, Liberdy began the questioning. "On June 3, 1988, did you see a man you have identified as Tim Bindner with a young blond-haired girl parked at the Alvarado Park?"

"Yes," Ellwin said.

"On Friday, June 3, 1988, did you use any force or violence against Amber Swartz?"

"No."

"On Friday, June 3, 1988, did you see Tim Bindner force a blond-haired girl onto the floor of a blue-and-beige Pontiac?"

"Yes."

"On Friday, June 3, 1988, was Amber Swartz ever alone with you?"

"No," Ellwin said.

"To the best of your knowledge, has your statement to the police about what you observed on June 3, 1988, at Alvarado Park been completely truthful?"

"Yes."

Liberdy's opinion was that Ellwin was telling the truth, but the examiner's conclusion included a word of caution. The questions about Ellwin's seeing Tim Bindner with the young girl were based upon Ellwin's perception. He believed he had seen what he described. But there was the possibility that he was honestly mistaken in his identification.

Sagan had gone as far as he could go with it. Despite the lack of cooperation or interest from Pinole, it was their case. He sent everything he had down to Galloway.

35

It was a week after Harold Sagan had met George Ellwin at Alvarado Park.

At 10:30 P.M. Sagan was sitting in his car on Fifty-third Street in Oakland listening to the background chatter of his radios. Tim Bindner had gone into his house earlier and stayed there.

In Petaluma, thirty-five miles west of Fairfield in Sonoma County, twelve-year-old Polly Klaas and two friends were having a slumber party. As Polly's mother and six-year-old half sister slept in an adjacent bedroom in the modest, single-story house, Polly and her friends played the board game Perfect Match.

In 1984, Ronald Reagan had filmed his "Morning in America" campaign commercials in Petaluma. The city of 45,000 was portrayed as picturesque, a peaceful

American city. Petalumans worked hard, saved, persevered. It was a community for families, a safe place to bring up kids. The ads didn't show the two parks in Polly's neighborhood—Walnut and Wickersham—that were inhabited by the homeless, alcoholics, and drifters.

At 10:30 that night, a heavyset, bearded man—armed with a knife—let himself into the house in Petaluma where the girls were playing.

Polly wanted to retrieve some sleeping bags from the living room. When she opened the bedroom door and saw the man standing there, she stepped back into the bedroom with her friends.

The man warned the girls that if they said anything, made any noise, he would slit their throats. He told them to lie down on the floor, where he bound them and pulled pillow cases over their heads. He talked, kept reassuring the girls. He wasn't going to hurt anyone, he said. He just wanted money.

"Which one of you lives here?" he asked.

Polly said she did.

The man asked about valuables in the house, and Polly told him there was $23 in a jewelry box. He told Polly that she was going with him, then directed Polly's friends to count to one thousand. By then, he said, Polly would be back with them and he would be gone.

The man never came back, but neither did Polly.

The two girls managed to untie the ropes that bound them, and they ran down the hall to awaken Eve Nichol, Polly's mother. A man with a knife was in the house, they said. He took Polly. Polly's gone.

Eve ran through the house searching for her daughter. At 11:03, she dialed 911.

While Petaluma police officers were searching Polly's house and neighborhood, and interviewing Eve Nichol and Polly's two friends, thirty-nine-year-old Richard Allen Davis was driving his white Ford Pinto into a ditch in Santa Rosa, twenty miles north on Highway 101. Sonoma County Sheriff's Deputies Michael Rankin and Thomas Howard responded to a call from the property owner, and they questioned Davis. The burly, bearded ex-con said that he was "sightseeing." It was after midnight.

The deputies searched Davis's car, gave him a field sobriety test, then helped him push the Pinto out of the ditch and released him.

There were no outstanding warrants on Davis, and the deputies weren't able to access his lengthy criminal record from their car. Also, it was a heavy night for radio traffic. The two officers were operating on a different frequency than the one that was carrying bulletins about the kidnapped child.

Later, when the deputies heard about the kidnapping and saw the first composite drawing of the suspect, they didn't think of the midnight tourist. The sketch didn't look like him.

———————

Harold Sagan's phone began ringing the next day. The calls were from newspaper and TV reporters—did Sagan see any connection between the Polly Klaas abduction and the Nikki Campbell case?

Sagan kept track of the news from Petaluma. The FBI was working with the county sheriff's department and the city police. Petaluma had become a showcase for high-tech law enforcement equipment. The level of interagency cooperation Sagan saw in that investigation was foreign to him.

———————

A local print shop became the center of the volunteer search effort in Petaluma. Hundreds of men, women, and children searched neighborhoods and fields, and distributed millions of flyers. Kim Swartz and her people from the Amber Foundation were among those helping out.

Residents wrapped lavender ribbons around all

the light poles in downtown Petaluma. Lavender was Polly's favorite color.

America's Most Wanted aired a segment on the kidnapping. *The Home Show* featured daily updates and live reports from the command center. *Eye to Eye with Connie Chung*, and *20/20* did segments on the story. Actress Winona Ryder offered a $200,000 reward for Polly's return. According to *People Magazine*, Polly Klaas, the twelve-year-old who loved drama and music, was "America's child." The same article called her abduction a "new kind of crime."

Kim Swartz wondered what they were talking about. Kids had been disappearing from the Bay Area at a faster clip than anywhere else in the country. Nationwide it was almost one child per day—close to three hundred a year. Kim felt strongly that the Klaas case deserved all the media attention it was getting—but every other case did, too.

She bridled at the notion that child abductions were something new. And for those who seemed most shocked and appalled at the violation of the sanctity of the child's home, there was a name: Tracy Stone. He had been arrested in Contra Costa County only fifteen months earlier for home intrusion abductions in Pleasant Hill, Concord, and Pittsburg.

The search continued. The flyers went nationwide via computer and fax. Volunteers answered the phones in the nerve center twenty-four hours a day. Nothing.

On October 27, twenty-six days after the little girl was taken, Polly's grandfather Joe was working the phones at the search center when one of the volunteers approached him and said that there was a man calling who insisted on talking with Marc Klaas, Polly's father. Joe took the call.

He thought that the man had said that his name was Ken Bender and that he was an investigator of lost children. The caller said that the last case he worked was the one involving Nikki Campbell, the child who was kidnapped two days after Christmas in 1991.

"I was doing a lot of work on that case," Tim Bindner said. "Then I got into trouble because they thought I did it, and they arrested me and impounded my car for two weeks. My lawyer says I've got to stop doing these kinds of investigations."

"Where are you?" Joe asked him.

"I live in Oakland."

"Will you give me your phone number?"

Bindner did.

"Are you a professional investigator?"

"I work in a sewage treatment plant," Bindner said. "I'm not a professional, but I've done a lot of work in this field."

Joe Klaas asked him for his address, and Bindner gave him the number of his post office box in Richmond.

"I don't search like other people," Bindner said. "I go where they don't. I use an AAA map. And when they go in one field, I say, 'Why wouldn't she be in the next field?' So I go in the next field. I do more outlying areas. I worked on the Michaela Garecht case in Hayward. Have you heard of that?"

"I think so," Joe said.

"She was taken from her scooter in broad daylight. I worked on seven searches in all. I don't know if I can work on this or not. My lawyer told me because I got in trouble on the Nikki Campbell search that I shouldn't do this anymore."

"Well, what are your methods?"

"My searches are based on supposition and observation. I just go into outlying areas where nobody else looks."

Joe Klaas was thinking how weird this guy sounded. He had something on his mind besides volunteering for something his attorney wouldn't let him do.

"I've got about fifty flyers and I'm gonna send them to my friends in prison," Bindner said.

"Oh, you have friends in prison?" Klaas said. "I work with lifers in Soledad."

"Lifers?"

"Yeah, I do AA at Soledad. I coordinate the AA meetings there. Why do you do it?"

"I'm a Christian," Bindner said, "and it's just my way of spreading the word. I'm gonna send this to my people."

Inmates don't like the kind of person who would do a crime like this, might have served time with him, and would inform on him. Bindner had other pen pals, too, and planned to send flyers to them.

Joe Klaas thanked him for his call, then phoned the FBI. He thought the whole conversation was strange, as though this guy might have had something to do with Polly's disappearance and he was calling to find out what the authorities knew about him.

Marc Klaas called John Burris and asked that he have his client refrain from contacting the center.

Bindner was angry. He had defied his attorney's advice by calling the Polly Klaas people, and then they rejected him. They knew who he was, he thought, and probably considered him a flake. It was a situation like the old ad for an exterminator. The bug crawls out from under the sink and gets slammed.

He had a right to help people. He was an American citizen. It's a free country. He wanted to assert that right.

It was a big part of what his lawsuit was about. By their accusations, the Fairfield police had destroyed many of the things he did, and enjoyed doing, to help other people.

Bindner thought of himself as an Andy Dufresne, the character in Stephen King's *Rita Hayworth and Shawshank Redemption*. Dufresne goes to prison for a crime he didn't commit, but there's all this circumstantial evidence that makes him look guilty.

Law enforcement had an investment in seeing Bindner locked up. After the Amber investigation, the metaphor he always used was that of building a box. Once the FBI had built their box with him inside, they would put the lid on, and he wouldn't be able to get out. "And they build it one board at a time," he would say. "Every time they get a board in place, they go reaching for the next one. And I keep telling people they're never gonna get the lid on, 'cause there is no lid. But they've got some boards."

First it was the FBI and Pinole. Now it was Fairfield. There still wasn't any lid for the box, but they had him grounded. He ached to go searching for Polly Klaas, but he couldn't.

His take on the crime was that whoever had grabbed Polly was an organized offender. When he snatched the girl, he was careful. Intelligent. It was a well-planned abduction, controlled every step of the way. Bindner had the itch, had a search plan in mind, and had even checked over some maps. Then he got shot down.

Once again, Bindner was feeling his own pain. Exquisitely.

———————

Within days, the story had made its way onto the pages of the *San Francisco Examiner*—SUSPECT IN PREVIOUS KIDNAPPING OFFERS TO HELP SEARCH. John Burris cited his client's wish to help in finding missing children and acknowledged that volunteering his searching skills in such cases was not in Bindner's best interest. "He becomes involved in the issue and it distracts efforts of law enforcement and other people," Burris told Marsha Ginsburg.

When Harold Sagan heard about Bindner's call to the Polly Klaas Center, he figured that Bindner was itching to play his usual games. He's a suspect, but he searches. He's so willing to move beyond his persecution, his pain, and offer his services.

But Sagan knew that the man didn't have a clue what real pain was. Anne Campbell knew. Marc Klaas and Eve Nichol knew. Kim Swartz, Sharon Nemeth, Susan Bugay, and the Misheloffs—they, along with too many others, knew well the torture of losing a child.

36

Kim Swartz divided her time among the Polly Klaas Center, her family, and George Ellwin. She called Wayne Galloway at the Pinole police, but either he didn't call back or he called while she was in Petaluma.

Kim met other volunteers at the Polly center, people who had come from Petaluma to Pinole years earlier to help in the effort to find Amber. Kim was a different person from the one they had known back then. Through the Amber Foundation, she had established a model in the Bay Area for the work the Polly Klaas volunteers were now doing. She had talked to groups in different parts of the United States and Canada—lecturing on child abuse, cults, sexual abuse, child abduction, and ways to organize search efforts for missing children.

She also had learned how law enforcement agencies investigate abduction cases, and their methods didn't impress her. Kim believed that cooperation was essential. Any effort was better than nothing at all, but so much more could be accomplished if only all the agencies would work together for a change. And law enforcement had to start leveling with the parents. When plunged into the horror of a stranger abduction, families were quick to accept whatever the authorities had to say, yet they ignored the advice offered by others who had experienced the same horror. It made sense for people to trust authority when they were vulnerable. But Kim had done exactly that, and she'd learned that it didn't work. Carrying a badge didn't make someone God. Also, the political pressure to solve a case fades fast. Resources shift elsewhere. Everything hinges on an investigator's personal commitment to a case.

Kim's experience had taught her that the FBI and the local police pressured families to believe everything they said, even when they weren't getting anywhere. Even as months turned into years, law enforcement people expected the parents to accept on faith that they were "following leads." That was crap, and Kim knew it.

Most of the time the agencies involved didn't bother talking with their counterparts in other communities who had been through the same kinds of investigations. She had talked with Sagan about this, and he'd agreed. "Every time a child is abducted," the cop said, "we reinvent the wheel."

The previous summer, Kim and the Fairfield detective had driven out through Pinole Valley to Oakmont Cemetery. Along the way, she had vented her feelings about the way law enforcement conducted investigations. "Nine times out of ten the offenders are pedophiles," she said.

Predators seeking child victims cruise neighborhoods, traveling a certain distance—a few miles to hundreds of miles—from where they live. "The FBI says they consider that," Kim told Sagan, "but they want to look at all the evidence where the crime happened. If you want to find out who this is, and do it efficiently, you need to reach out to other cities and counties, ask them to search their registered sex offender files. All area police departments need to work together, instead of always relying on FBI agents who don't live in the communities, who don't know the suspects, but who think they can do it all."

She got no argument from Sagan. The cop knew all about linkage blindness—the failure of an agency to see the similarities among crimes that were happening in different jurisdictions—and the resistance within the law enforcement community to the idea of cooperation. All the pieces of puzzles may be there, but if the cops don't come together the puzzles may never get solved.

One day when she was talking to Joe Klaas, Kim pointed out the lack of cooperation. "Nobody's contacted Fairfield. They have an open case, and they have leads."

"They're not checking those things out?" Joe asked.

"They may tell you they're doing that," she said, "but they aren't."

She knew that no one had called Sagan, despite the open case on Nikki Campbell. The FBI claimed they did these things and more, did things people would never dream of, never realize—but Kim Swartz didn't buy it. That certainly had not been her experience. They'd even dragged her back for another polygraph two years after her daughter's abduction.

She felt strongly that there needed to be a permanent task force with at least one representative from each of the departments in the Bay Area. That group would deal only with the issue of child abduction. If any officer leaked information, which seemed to be the primary excuse for not cooperating, that officer would be replaced.

"It's horribly frustrating," she had said so many times. "They could have officers who live in the towns, who know these people, know the vehicles they drive."

Ever since 1989, Kim had been hearing about a

"protocol" for abduction cases—some sort of guide for law enforcement agencies to follow. She had never seen the document and had no idea what it contained. It made sense to her that the foundations should know what was in the protocol since it could affect their ability to assist law enforcement. But the pros tried to keep it a secret, for cops' eyes only. However, that didn't deter Kim. She picked up a copy at a conference.

The document was a combined effort of the FBI and the National Center for Missing and Exploited Children (NCMEC). Most of it turned out to be material that she had seen before. There was a 1987 article by the FBI's Ken Lanning: "Child Molesters: A Behavioral Analysis." It was a good summary, but old, the same generalizations that she had been hearing for years. Kim knew that not every pedophile was a child molester and that not every child molester abducted children. Most of those who did released them alive after acting out their sexual fantasies.

Kim read Lanning's section on what he called the "inadequate" child molester. The FBI agent's description included eccentricity, a man who was a "social misfit." Children didn't threaten him; he could relate to them on their own terms. He idealized children, emphasizing their innocence and purity. He was passive, denying all anger—or allowing it to accumulate until he exploded (usually in a frenzy of sexual violence directed at a child). The behavior was repetitive and persistent, with the man focusing his attention, energy, fantasies, and money on kids.

Bindner always said that he loved children—the dead ones, the living ones. He said he would never hurt a child. Yet he collected the posters of missing and abducted children, clipped stories from the newspapers about the tragedies kids experienced. He said that he felt anguish for all of them. But did *he* place them in that danger, Kim wondered, or was he the rescuer he said he dreamed of being?

Appendix H of the "Investigator's Guide to Missing Child Cases" immediately caught Kim's attention. It

included a child abduction investigative guide that had
been prepared locally in 1989. The names of the con-
tributors were familiar: Mary Ellen O'Toole, Duke
Diedrich, and Larry Taylor of the FBI. Phil Pollard and
John Miner from Pinole. Rich McEachin, one of the
Antioch detectives assigned to the Angela Bugay case;
Ken Gross from Hayward. Officers from Dublin,
Vallejo, Sacramento, and San Francisco, along with
representatives of the Department of Justice. The
document was the product of sixteen hours of meet-
ings in March 1989 on Coast Guard Island in San
Francisco Bay.

It read like an instructional manual for someone
organizing a business hierarchy. The emphasis was on
administration. Kim knew that the lead time in abduction cases was one to three hours at best. So much had
to be done in so short a time—and, increasingly, police
were looking for bodies, not injured and frightened
children.

Kim didn't understand the secrecy surrounding
the manual. It didn't contain anything that she hadn't
already read or heard. Maybe they knew that she
would take issue with the lack of emphasis on immediate search efforts, or ask questions about the section
on interjurisdictional cooperation that no one ever
followed.

A request for interagency assistance required that
an abducted child be "in great bodily danger." This pro-
vision generally excluded parental kidnapping in custody disputes. A second criterion was that the child's
disappearance had to fit a profile for an abduction that
could be expected to result in murder. Kim knew that
unless someone had witnessed the abduction, or the
child was incapable of wandering off alone, making
that kind of determination could take days.

The third criterion included "extraordinary criminal violations"—a perpetrator who was a suspected serial killer, or the shooting of a police officer. Kim was
well acquainted with both.

In their introduction to the document, special

agents Ronald Hilley and Mary Ellen O'Toole said they had discovered an "unexpected theme" during their meetings on Coast Guard Island: "Law enforcement must work as a 'team.' Secrecy, power struggles, lack of cooperation and the persistence of old stereotypes—for example, 'This is my case'—will damage these cases more than any poorly designed investigative strategy could ever do."

Were they really that blind and hypocritical? San Francisco's FBI office seemed to know only one team—its own. The FBI was more immersed in secrecy and intransigence than any other law enforcement agency she knew.

The rest of the section dealt with victimology and described interviewing techniques to be used with parents, neighbors, other potential witnesses, and suspects. Kim figured that was O'Toole's contribution. The investigators were told to interview family members and neighbors "expeditiously" and "in as much detail as possible," and to discover everything they could about the child. What were the child's normal patterns of activity, who were her closest friends, and had there been any behavioral or physical changes? What were her hobbies? Were her diaries and school papers examined? Was there any history of running away or of any discontent in the home? What about drugs, alcohol, sexual activity? Investigators should then use such information to determine what type of offender was responsible.

While the cops checked their checklist and filed their forms for computer entry, the clock kept ticking. Amber was seven when she disappeared. Nikki Campbell was four. Use those initial, critical hours to search for the child, *then* do your offender analysis. This was one area where Kim Swartz agreed with Tim Bindner: Get out and beat the bushes.

The protocol referred to the first six to twelve hours as the "critical phase," but of eight areas of emphasis, "searches" was number eight—and didn't show up until page 31. The first order of business was to determine that they were, indeed, dealing with a valid abduction. The second was victimology. Even the process of looking at registered sex offenders was not a high priority.

———————

Despite John Burris's advice, Bindner continued to write to Kim Swartz. He assumed that copies of his letters went to the police or were analyzed by Quantico, but that didn't deter him.

Kim went up to Bernie's grave in Rolling Hills Cemetery. She loved how quiet it was there—peaceful and meditative. It was one place where she could clear her head and write.

> Tim,
>   It's taken me awhile to be able to sit down and answer your letter. I won't plead busy schedule. There's been confusion, mixed feelings, anger. Mostly it's being just plain mad.

She wrote about closure, emotional relief, and the clarity sometimes afforded by anger. She defended Harold Sagan. The cop was doing his job and sticking with it. That was more than she could say for most of the cops she had dealt with.

> I'll be short and sweet. In court they'd have to prove you guilty. The defendant doesn't have to prove a thing. There has been such a cloud over you for so long. I'm telling you, you have to reverse the way it works in court. Clear yourself with the cops and then you can do your searching and no one will hassle you. Then we can work together, resurrect our friendship. It can't hurt. It might even add to your punitive damages (I'll be the first to hit you up for a donation), or do you take some perverse satisfaction in being in the center of the storm?

Please don't mistake this for passing bitter-
ness or sour grapes. I've had enough bullshit for
2 lifetimes. You never seemed to hear me when I
said that to you all those times. You just changed
the subject and talked about your problems with
the cops and the F.B.I. Hear it this time. Tim. I'd
like your friendship. I'd like to see you working
to help people. But words aren't going to cut it
this time. It's going to take some action.

Get out from under the cloud once and for
all, then let's talk.

Kim was in the middle of things at the Polly center
when Bindner's response arrived on Savage Avenue.
The letter included a fail-safe clause: "There *are* certain
areas of inquiry that I cannot and will not enter, but if
you have questions, *let's get them cleared up*, please!"

Kim wondered, if Tim Bindner had nothing to do
with Amber's disappearance, or any of the other kids,
what couldn't he discuss?

It was a long letter, mostly a rehashing of things
that he had said before—all about the search for Amber,
his suffering since the search, his vow of nonviolence.
"So there is a horrible anguish," Bindner wrote, "when
a man publicly accuses me of killing a child when he
has no evidence whatsoever that the child is dead. Our
lawsuit is not a 'game of lotto.' It is a demand for justice, and for accountability by the police."

Bindner swore he had never abducted, killed, or
injured anyone, and offered to answer Kim's questions. Her next letter would be an easy one to write,
but it would have to wait until she could devote
enough time to word it exactly right.

———————

As she drove to the Polly center, Kim Swartz saw the
hundreds of volunteers spreading out through the once
peaceful city of Petaluma. "Idyllic," the newspapers

had called it. That was just the way she used to think of
Pinole—as a great place to bring up kids.

The team of volunteers searched fields and wooded
areas, parks and vacant lots. They were participating
in the most widespread search for an abducted child
that any organization had ever conducted.

Kim drove through the business district, under the
banner stretching from side to side: PLEASE LET POLLY
GO! Polly's friends at the junior high school had put it
together.

Kim and others answered the phones and distributed flyers—eventually, millions of them, all bearing a
picture of Polly Klaas as well as the composite drawing of her abductor.

On November 30, almost two months after Polly's
disappearance, police arrested thirty-nine-year-old
Richard Allen Davis on a parole violation. One of the
flyers had drawn police to the Coyote Valley Indian
Reservation near Ukiah, seventy miles north of
Petaluma. Someone there said the picture resembled
the heavyset, bearded man staying in a shack on the
reservation.

The volunteers continued with their work. Police
told them nothing. Kim heard about it only because
she had happened to be talking to a reporter from
Channel 7.

On December 4, Davis confessed. Investigators followed his directions and found Polly's body under
some wood, off the side of a road in Cloverdale, fifty
miles north of Petaluma.

The search for "America's child" ended after sixty-
four days.

37

Harold Sagan heard of the discovery of Polly's body on the radio. When he got to his office, there was a message from Anne Campbell. She was crying.

"The Petaluma police finding Polly's body hit her hard," Sagan thought. "This brings it home. Polly's dead, so Nikki must be dead, too."

The Polly Klaas case had hammered Sagan as well. All the hopes, prayers, and wishes for the child's safe return, all the flowers and lavender ribbons, the photographs of the smiling twelve-year-old—it had come down to nothing but the flickering of a single candle in a storm. And it had given every parent of a missing child one less reason to hope.

Sagan drove over to see Anne Campbell that Sunday morning. He was driving and thinking, "Where have I screwed up the case? How many times have I screwed up the case?"

Anne probably wouldn't ask, but she would be

right if she did: "Why haven't you done what Petaluma's done?"

Had Sagan shut down potential resources because his approach to the investigation had been so unconventional? What did he have? What physical evidence did he have that tied Tim Bindner to the case? He didn't have a shred. He had some dogs, a theory, and some circumstantial evidence. That was it.

Days passed before Sagan could shake himself out of it.

―――――――――――

On December 9, a crowd estimated at more than two thousand people gathered outside St. Vincent de Paul Church in Petaluma to attend a memorial service for Polly Klaas. Eight hundred got inside, including Governor Pete Wilson and U.S. Senators Dianne Feinstein and Barbara Boxer. Joan Baez opened the service by singing "Amazing Grace." U.S. Representative Lynn Woolsey read a letter from President Clinton and Hillary Clinton. "We can best honor Polly's memory by dedicating ourselves to preventing such senseless deaths in the future," the Clintons wrote.

Tim Bindner watched the memorial service for Polly Klaas on TV. All the local networks gave it uninterrupted coverage. It was the kind of media treatment reserved for dead presidents, Bindner thought.

Bindner enjoyed the choir's singing and tolerated what he considered inappropriate political posturing by Wilson and one of the senators. Overall, though, he considered it a beautiful service, a wonderful tribute.

> Who would ever think that a twelve-year-old girl would end up—well, would end up dead, first of all— but would end up being the reason that a seventy-minute religious service would be broadcast without commercial interruption on all the local TV networks?

He had to love Polly just for that. The whole Bay Area was looking at love—and looking at God.

There Harold Sagan was again, sitting in his car on Fifty-third Street looking at Bindner's house. Once the broadcast started, the detective drove to a sports bar and watched it on TV. Anne Campbell was at the service, and seemed to be doing well.

The pain that Polly's death had caused was heart-wrenching to watch. Everyone had tears in their eyes. Even a few guys in the bar were crying.

After the broadcast, Bindner attended a charismatic mass at his church and spent the rest of the evening singing, swaying, being together with forty other church members and sharing joy. He could feel it in the room. Believing was good for the soul.

He thought about the man who had killed Polly Klaas. After grieving for the child, Bindner had to jump the fence—to Richard Allen Davis's side. He hoped the state wouldn't kill him. Bindner believed that any man, no matter what he had done, could use the rest of his life to make the world a better place. He wanted Davis punished—wanted him locked away for the rest of his life—but he didn't want to see him killed. Bindner had protested California's use of the death penalty and was opposed to the whole idea of capital punishment. He could not condone killing in any form, he said.

Over time, his thoughts about the crime and about Davis had changed. At first the crime had seemed so organized, methodically planned and executed. Now it seemed to transcend the FBI's categories. Davis had had it together when he took Polly. Everything became disorganized after that, as if he just lost it. Maybe his carefully laid plan of where he planned to take her fell apart, so he fell apart. He ran his car off the road, into a ditch. He even dumped all the incriminating evidence out in a field somewhere—without bothering to bury it. Polly was hidden in some bushes when the cops came—she was practically under their noses. Then Davis went back to get the kid—and, in the process, left evidence all over the place. Sloppy.

The press reported that Davis had cursed the woman who owned the land when she came down there to find out what was going on. She responded by going back to her house and calling the cops. If Davis had wanted to make a discreet exit, he should have been civil to the woman—pleasant and cordial. He should have been in control.

After all the risks he had taken at Polly's house, Bindner thought, Davis should have been able to handle the situation with the landowner without any difficulty.

The guy claimed that he was doing drugs that night. Maybe he was. Maybe the anticipation of what he planned to do to Polly had him so excited that he blew up when he saw that being thwarted. Maybe he had known exactly where he was going and what he was going to do, but then his car ended up in the ditch and his script had to be abandoned. He would have been furious about that, Bindner thought.

Bindner wondered what made the guy tick, what went on inside his head. Did he realize what he had done? Did he feel anything?

As early as 1977, psychiatrists were calling Richard Allen Davis a classic sociopath, a man for whom the rules meant nothing. He had spent his entire life moving in and out of correctional facilities and mental institutions. He described "tensions" that had built up in him, urges that he needed to act on, mainly because he had sensed that his victims (kidnapping, sexual assault, robbery) *wanted* him to do "something" to them.

Psychiatric evaluators had concluded long ago that Davis would not profit from treatment in any mental health facility. If Davis was released from jail,

the clinical experts said, they fully expected him to resume his pattern of criminal behavior. They considered him "extremely dangerous."

He had proved them right.

———————

Three days after the service for Polly Klaas, Harold
Sagan was working another case. A man had taken a
baseball bat to his two-year-old son. As soon as doctors removed the boy from life support, it would be the
detective's thirteenth homicide of the year.

———————

Kim Swartz continued to leave messages for her elusive detective. Galloway finally returned the calls.

"I just want to know what you're going to do about
Ellwin," she said.

"Ellwin?"

He sounded as if he didn't know who Kim was
talking about. "Ellwin," she repeated. "The one who
says that he saw what happened to my daughter that
day. He saw who she was with."

"Kim," Galloway said, "he describes Bindner, and
I saw Bindner a few days after he says he did. There's
no way it could've been him that Ellwin saw."

"Look, Galloway, I remember what he looked like
the day he came to Sharon Nemeth's door. He's telling
me that he had a beard then. But when I saw him, he
had only a few days' growth."

The guy had a talent for changing his looks, Kim
thought. It was uncanny. Galloway and the others obviously didn't understand that.

"Ellwin called in with the information five years
ago, at the time of Amber's abduction," she explained
to Galloway. "He was interviewed, then he was reinter-
viewed nine months later. He didn't talk to anybody
again until the search warrant was being served on
Tim Bindner last December. He called the P.D. again,

and Terri Price talked to him. He told her Bindner was the guy he had called in about before. This guy he was looking at on TV was the same one he had seen with Amber that day. 'Thanks a lot,' she says, and hangs up the phone."

The detective told her there wasn't anything more they could have done with the original information.

"What about now?" Kim demanded.

"The description doesn't fit," Galloway said.

They weren't going any farther with it.

"On your message you sounded really upset, Kim," Galloway said. "Like you think we're not doing anything. I know you must be real frustrated now that Petaluma has made an arrest."

"Look," she said, "I'm not upset that they made an arrest. I'm thankful they did. I'm upset because my local police department has someone here that they should be taking a closer look at, and they're not doing it. I'm not stupid. I *know* he has been a suspect."

"Well, we still haven't ruled him out," Galloway said.

That was different from what he had told the media in front of Bindner's house the day Fairfield was conducting the search. "He was not developed as a suspect," he had said.

Galloway told Kim to stop by his office; he had some photographs he wanted to show her.

Kim was angry. They were trying to make it look as if they were making progress when they weren't doing a damn thing.

When she finished with Galloway, she just sat there, fuming. She had been putting in long hours in Petaluma, tried to keep up with her boys, and had worked hard to stay on top of the situation with Ellwin. If she couldn't get the Pinole police to investigate this lead, she knew that she would have to go public with the story.

The same thought was careening through her mind over and over: George Ellwin had seen Tim Bindner with her daughter at Alvarado Park on June 3, 1988.

Kim Swartz never thought that northern California would turn out to be like this. It hadn't seemed so unpredictable or so violent when she was growing up. She had heard others say, "We have to keep moving until we find a safe place." But she knew that no such place exists.

Her answer was always the same: "You can't run from it. It's just not going to work that way. Somehow you've got to get people together and drive those forces away from you."

————————

Newspaper reporters and the Channel 5 news team interviewed Sergeant Chuck Timm in Fairfield, then drove south to Pinole. Ellwin was willing to talk to the media, but he had requested anonymity. He didn't want his daughter placed in any danger and he didn't want Bindner coming after him. He knew what he had seen. He had told the cops all about it, and now he was ready to tell the reporters the same thing.

Some of the Bay Area stations and newspapers picked up on the story. Most of them didn't. The coverage of Polly Klaas and Richard Allen Davis dominated the news.

Of course nothing ever came of it. Most of the local media wouldn't touch it. It didn't have any validity, and the Pinole police said, "No, we're not gonna talk about it. This is something we will not discuss." And we're talking about the police that are investigating the crime. And they said, "We won't touch this. We won't talk about it." They were afraid they were gonna get their butts sued if they opened their mouth. So Fairfield is the one that opened their mouth, as they usually do. It was ridiculous. It was just another lesson in media stupidity to me. They never should've ran that story, because it was nothing. . . .

The scenario doesn't make any sense. And I think the Pinole police realized that. What the man saw was

*probably what he thought he saw originally—a parent
dealing with a kid he was mad at. You know, he was
mad at the kid and said, "Get in the car," and threw the
kid in the car. And there was no other children reported
missing around that time, so I think that's what it was.
I think it was a dad and his daughter.*

Lieutenant Miner called Kim Swartz. The Pinole
police had set a meeting for later that week. Miner,
too, said there was no way that Ellwin could be right.
The Pinole police had talked to Bindner on June 4 or
June 5, and he had had straggly hair and a full beard at
that time.

Kim knew that Bindner had been in Reno getting
married over the fourth and fifth. When she met him
June 6, he was scruffy-looking but had no beard—just
as Ellwin had said. Were the cops trying to drive her
crazy? She knew what she had seen.

She told Miner that she wasn't the only one who
had seen Bindner that day. Others remembered him as
being without a beard.

"Maybe he shaved before he went over to meet
you," Miner said. "Either way, Ellwin can't be right."

The lieutenant said they were looking at several
other suspects who couldn't be ruled out. They hadn't
even ruled out Tim Bindner yet, but they didn't have
enough on anybody to make a charge stick. If they arrested Bindner, maybe they would get a few days of
play in the press, but they'd be taking the risk of
getting slapped with a major lawsuit, just as Fairfield
had been.

That's what had happened to Sagan, the lieutenant
suggested. His fifteen minutes of fame was over, and
now he was getting his ass hauled into court. The Fairfield detective had gotten too personally involved. He
was narrow-minded. The guy couldn't see beyond Tim
Bindner. That can happen in cases like these. You investigate, work your way through a list of suspects until you have it narrowed down. Sagan had snapped at
Bindner like lightning at the top of a barn.

Kim didn't want to hear it.

She knew that Sagan wasn't wearing blinders. He was always ready to look at any suspect, to consider any possibility. He had done that with Tracy Stone and Richard Davis. He cleared suspects, but he couldn't do that with Tim Bindner.

"See you Friday," Kim said, and hung up.

Sagan was in the city council chambers, venting. It was a large room with an echo. He paced up and down. Chuck Timm, the only other person in the room, listened.

Sagan felt that the Pinole cops were trying to blame him and his department for creating an issue when none existed. They were telling Kim that they had other suspects, *real* suspects. In the best of times between the two departments, they never discussed any suspects beyond the few that they had already looked at and dismissed.

The man Pinole had generated something on was Tim Bindner. Then they dropped it. They even made a public statement that the Oakland man was not a suspect. But every time Fairfield got something going with Bindner, Galloway was right there.

Pinole's situation was similar to Fairfield's. Even if they were to decide that they had enough evidence to make an arrest, the district attorney did not consider it enough to convict—even with George Ellwin. The Pinole police contradicted his whole story.

Kim Swartz couldn't get it out of her mind. Ellwin said it was Tim Bindner. She called Ellwin and asked him the same questions all over again.

"Kim, I know what I saw," he said. "This man looked right at me. Because of the circumstances, it's a face that I would never forget."

He had gotten only a few glimpses of the little girl, enough to know that she was the right size and age— but he was off on the clothing. He remembered the pants as being pink. Maybe the shirt was pink, too.

And maybe George Ellwin had seen what he had originally thought he had seen: a heavy-handed father disciplining his own little girl.

38

DECEMBER, 1993

Kim took her mother with her to the meeting at the Pinole police department, but the cops said she'd have to wait for Kim in the lobby. Kim didn't understand why Amber's grandmother couldn't sit in on their discussion.

The chief, the lieutenant, and two detectives were there. One of the cops placed a photograph on the table in front of Kim. It was a picture of three people—a Pinole cop whom she recognized, a woman she assumed was FBI, and Tim Bindner. They were standing beside Bindner's blue van. Kim was allowed to look at the picture, but told that she couldn't pick it up.

The cops told Kim they had taken the photo on June 6, 1988. They also said that was the same day the dogs had picked up Amber's scent in Bindner's van. They had brought Bindner in. He was at the station that day.

Kim knew that wasn't right, but she was nervous

and confused. In the photograph, Tim Bindner had a full beard. Was Ellwin wrong?

She was trying to concentrate. June 6 didn't sound right. Bindner had been at her house that day—mid to late afternoon. She knew that a Pinole officer had stopped him for a routine check, and she thought that he had gone out into Pinole Valley to search after that.

She had been in a state of shock at the time. Maybe she was wrong. Maybe she was wrong about the beard, too.

The room was so hot, Kim was having a hard time following the discussion. Different cops talked. They would have done something if only Fairfield had come to them. They would have shown them the photo. But there was other information they weren't going to share. Fairfield was just going to have to trust what they were saying. That was it.

"They tried to reach you," Kim said. "You didn't return their calls."

"You should have come to us," one of them was saying. "If you don't like the treatment you're getting, you can always go higher up."

"How am I supposed to know you're doing everything you can be doing?"

"You're just going to have to believe us."

"I'm sorry," Kim said. Her head was starting to clear. "That's not good enough. You have no vested interest in my daughter. You want to get this over with. You want me off your back. I feel like I'm constantly handing you guys things, but I'm just a thorn in your side because you don't want to deal with it."

The chief said, "I think you understand the way you handled this with all the media and everything was not the right way. You're not going to get anything accomplished by doing this. You might get a little bit of attention and sympathy, but that's about all you're going to get."

Kim was angry. "I'm getting to sit here and tell you what a bunch of assholes you are," she said. "If that's what it takes to get a meeting with you, then I guess that's what it takes. I don't want anybody's sympathy, and I certainly don't want your attention. What I want is someone's help."

When Kim Swartz left, she decided that if there were any more meetings, she was bringing an attorney. She also decided that her next stop would be the mayor's office. The cops didn't want to hear it, but she wasn't going away. What were they going to do, throw her in jail?

As they walked out of the police station, Kim told her mother what had gone on and mentioned the photograph the cops had shown her. Although her mother remembered seeing Tim Bindner at the house on Savage Avenue on June 6, 1988, she didn't remember any beard.

When Kim told Sagan about the photograph, he had to wonder about it. They could have provided him with a copy. That wouldn't have gotten them sued.

Sagan was also bothered by their claim that the picture had been taken on June 6. That would have been the earliest possible date, but for some reason, June 8 stuck in Sagan's mind. He knew that there were photographs of Bindner from shortly after he had injected himself into the case, but Sagan didn't remember anyone saying anything about a beard. And why hadn't Kim been allowed to touch the picture?

The same dog handlers had worked Pinole, Hayward, and Fairfield. Of those who saw Bindner during the Amber Swartz and Michaela Garecht investigations, none remembered a beard. In Hayward, he had looked grungy, as if he hadn't shaved in four or five days.

Sagan could put no stock in what Pinole was saying now. He knew that in the summer of 1988 Tim Bindner had been at the top of their short list of suspects.

Everyone who had any involvement in the case knew who he was. They were tossing him into the back of cruisers on a daily basis, interrogating him for hours at a time, maintaining around-the-clock surveillance on him. He wasn't just one of fifty people they were looking at. They had worked him so hard, it became common knowledge out in the valley and among the staff at Oakmont Cemetery that this guy was their primary focus.

Then there was George Ellwin. Sagan had no doubt that the man was telling the truth. He saw what he said he saw. But was it Bindner or a look-alike?

When Bindner was in Fairfield on January 7, 1992, Sagan swore he'd had a smirk on his face when he said, "Cops don't talk to one another."

The man was right.

———

Sagan spent his evening on Fifty-third Street in Oakland, thinking about the strange man inside the old house.

Sagan remembered a story that Bindner had written; it had been among the papers seized from his house during the search. It was a fantasy piece about a naked little girl on a hill in the rain at night. The guy in the story was chasing her but also rescuing her. The fantasy seemed to be erotic, but there was nothing explicitly sexual about it.

"Is it real?" Sagan wondered.

He had read and reread the piece. He could visualize a place, a ridge area at Briones Park adjacent to Oakmont Cemetery. It was one of the ridges where Bindner would have had the clearest view of the cemetery—and of Angela's grave. Sagan and the other investigators had searched those areas because of their theory that the dead children needed to be within sight of one another. The bloodhounds indicated that Bindner's scent had been all over the hills out there.

Sagan could visualize Tim Bindner standing on another hill, this time in the light rain, looking down

at Sheila Cosgrove's house—waiting for a glimpse of
the girl. "What if his stash place is inside his mind?"
Sagan thought. "What if he records some partial things
in his files, but the real stash is inside his head? How
does a cop get his hands on *that*?"

39

At their annual Christmas party, Dale Myer and the other bloodhound handlers put out a container labeled NICKELS FOR SAGAN. There was a printed sign beside it: "As you know, our good friend Detective Harold Sagan has been named in a lawsuit by Tim Bindner and a collection basket at Fairfield P.D. raised $3.65 toward the $25 million goal. With your help and support we plan to match that amount tonight. Please give generously."

The handlers presented Sagan with $4.09 and a painted thermometer similar to the ones used in United Way campaigns. "You're almost there," Myer said.

Sagan knew that the Pinole police and the FBI had seized Social Security records when they searched Bindner's home in 1988. He had heard that they were computer printouts. Lists. They were the primary reason the SSA had fired Bindner the second time—more unauthorized computer searches.

The Fairfield detective also knew that Bindner had run a computer search for Susan Bugay on June 2, 1988, and that he had run a search on another abducted child (whom police had subsequently rescued). In May, Sagan saw the printouts of Bindner's computer inquiries for June 2 and June 3, 1988. At 2:48 P.M. on the day before Amber Swartz was abducted, Bindner had accessed Susan Bugay's file. On June 3, he'd accessed his regular case load at 11:34 A.M. and 12:39, 1:35, and 1:43 P.M.

Sagan looked at the printout. There were two more inquiries on June 3—one at 7:45 P.M. and one at 7:49 P.M. Bindner had maintained that he had punched out of work at around 4:00 P.M. that day. Then, he said, he had visited St. Joseph's Cemetery, arriving home in time to see some of the A's game on TV. Yet he—or someone who knew his access code—had logged back onto the computer that night. If it had been Bindner, the computer records made a shambles of his alibi.

Beyond that, he didn't know what was in the records, and no one was sharing any information about them.

After appearing in the *Street Stories* episode on CBS, Sagan received a call from an ex-cop back east whose daughter had received a card and a gift from Bindner in 1988. It sounded as if Bindner had run the same fantasy game again, the one that had gotten him fired the first time, in 1985. That time, authorities had identified thirty-nine recipients of Bindner's generosity, all of them young girls.

> *In '88, when they interviewed me, they found a bunch of computer printouts in my van, and they contacted the Social Security people and said that they had found these printouts. Then they found out that I had been accessing these files that were not on my case list. So they fired me for not a violation of law but a violation of policy that says you can't do this.*

You know, basically you're not supposed to dip into this stuff unless it's part of your workload. But the funny part about it is that the printouts they found in my van—those were discards that people had thrown in their trash can. I was using the back of them to make banners for the baseball games. You know, signs like "Go A's" and stuff like that, to put on my van for the game.

So it had nothing to do with nothing, and I don't know how many hours they spent analyzing the printouts. But there was nothing there that had anything to do with anything.

"All his money is tied up in his fantasies," Sagan thought. "Some of us go out and buy a new car or a new sofa with liquid assets. He sends a kid fifty bucks."

Bindner was doing the same thing in the Bay Area—writing letters to kids. Following the search and the accompanying publicity, Sagan had gotten a call from a CHP officer. "I always thought it was strange," the cop told him, "but I allowed him to write to my daughter."

All of the girls on the list had received $50 bills from Bindner before his firing in 1988—all, that is, except one.

Judy Lyman was living in Sparks, Nevada, when her gift from Tim Bindner arrived in April 1989. It was a check for $50 drawn on Mechanics Bank in Richmond. She saved both the check and the letter. Bindner had written that this was his last shot at being involved in a fantasy gift-giving. He said that he wouldn't be contacting Judy again, and he asked her to please not call the cops. He didn't want another hassle like the one he had experienced before.

Pinole and the FBI had cleaned him out in 1988, yet he was still able to write to this girl in 1989. How could this be? He'd had no access to his lists after July 1988, and he had left his Social Security position in August.

"Where did he get the name and address?" Sagan wondered.

Sagan knew that a man interested in children might also keep a stash—sometimes child pornography, sometimes other materials that he considers erotic. The latter might be collections of photographs of children, clippings from catalogs, printed materials, or even the man's own writings. The collection would contain items of significance to the man, things he finds exciting. Often his stash is the most important thing in this type of man's life. Would Bindner's files, if they existed, fit that category? If so, Sagan had to figure out where they could be. No collection was inside the house. It wasn't inside the house, so where was it?

"They're not going to be on-site," Sagan thought. "They're going to be removed, but close enough to give him ready access. He has to be able to get at it twenty-four hours a day, seven days a week, because when the urge hits him, he has to be able to act."

Sagan pushed himself back from his desk. "St. Mary's Cemetery," he said aloud.

The cemetery was close to Bindner's house, and he knew every corner of the place. He had moved some of the stones there, repaired them, reset them. That gave him legitimacy. He could be in the cemetery at any hour of the day or night.

St. Mary's, Mountain View, and the Jewish Cemetery abut one another and create a sanctuary of more than three hundred acres in the urban sprawl at the north end of Oakland. Sometimes, at night, the cemeteries become a shrieking wilderness of feral cats, skunks, red fox, and racoons. The animals move down from the eastern foothills and prowl among the stone markers, the marble angels with their wings unfurled, the granite children in postures of prayer.

One time an escaped monkey screeched its way along St. Mary's paths, through the rows of pine, cedar, oak, and eucalyptus trees. People in the neighborhoods heard it for several nights—no one saw it— then the wailing stopped. No one knew what had happened to it.

When Sagan tracked Bindner there, there were times that the man had disappeared into the woods. Ten or fifteen minutes would pass before he'd reappear. Would it be a thirty-gallon trash bag that he had to dig up? Or would he get off just sitting next to it?

By California standards, St. Mary's is an old cemetery—a mix of headstones, crypts, and mausoleums. Bindner was more familiar with all of that than most people, including those who worked there. Before he began attracting so much attention, he could have easily created a vault for himself. Some of the areas are so old that no one visits them anymore. What if Bindner had removed one of the granite blocks that had a recessed area behind it? No one else would be dismantling any of those crypts.

Anything I put in my file cabinet right now, or anything I put in my house right now, I anticipate the possibility that it will be scrutinized. It's like a filter you have. Do I want the cops to look at this? Before I put it in the folder, I realize that it may be looked at some day by some investigative people. Do I want this in here? . . .

I had some stuff hidden outside. I had some files hidden outside, and after the search on December 9, 1992, took the duplicates of that file—it was a photocopy of some of the stuff I had here at the house—and after the search took the original, I tried to retrieve it, but it was all mushy from the rain. I couldn't read it, so I threw it away.

It was in a couple of plastic bags folded over, but it had been in the ground for a couple years, and moisture seeped in and took it away, so I just threw it. I just wanted to have it, 'cause it was notes that I wanted to have. It was basically some of the daily log files about the missing children. . . .

I don't have anything I really want to keep secret anyway, to tell you the truth. The stuff that I duplicated and hid was not because I wanted to keep secret. It was

*because I wanted to have it. In case they took it, I
would still have it.*

Sagan visited St. Mary's again so he could walk
around the cemetery, thinking in terms of conceal-
ment. The cemetery had a million hiding places in it.
The detective thought back through all his long, black
nights of surveillance. Bindner did frequent some favorite places—graves that he liked to visit, places
where he often cut through the woods. Sagan walked
around in there, letting his mind wander. If he were
Tim Bindner and he had something to hide, where
would he put it?

————————

Tim Bindner loved St. Mary's at night, especially in the
rain. He socialized with the kids who drank up there,
talking to them and engaging in their little sparrings
with each other. Some of them dabbled in Satanism,
and sometimes they broke into crypts.

Once the kids broke into a family mausoleum that
had an iron gate in front of it. On each separate crypt
there was a marble facade. They got the lock off the
iron gate, then smashed the marble. They pulled the
casket out and put it on the floor of the mausoleum
and opened it.

The next morning, when Bindner jogged through,
he noticed the damage and stopped at the office to report it. "Somebody broke into the Stagnaros' mausoleum last night," he said. "Maria's casket is laying on
the floor."

It didn't look as if they had taken anything.

Most of the kids weren't any problem, but some
nights Bindner wanted to be alone. He might sit up on
the hill—drinking or not drinking, thinking or not
thinking—looking at the sky and listening to the cemetery's noises. If it was raining, he would enjoy the
heightened pleasure of the fragrance of the trees and
flowers.

Bindner has done cemetery repair work in Utah, Idaho, and Montana—but he always comes back to St. Mary's. Florence's grave is there. She died in 1923 at the age of eighteen months. That was twenty-five years before Bindner was born. There's a picture on her grave. Those are the ones that always grab him—the ones with the pictures. He visits Florence and talks to her, tells her that he's sad that she didn't get to live out her time in this world, and says how much he wishes she were there with him right now.

Bindner read an article a long time ago. Maybe it was a section of a book. It had to do with cults and how they dispose of the bodies of babies after making human sacrifices. They get rid of them at night in cemeteries—at the bottoms of graves dug for the next day's funerals. All a person had to do was jump down in the open grave, dig a couple of feet, cover the body over, and tamp it down. The next day there would be a funeral. The casket would be lowered down on top, and nobody ever would find that body.

Northern California has mostly loam soils at the surface, with clay deeper down. A man could dig six feet before hitting clay. Sometimes the loam will go for ten, twelve, or even fourteen feet. Or he could hit clay at three feet. It all depended on location. On a hillside, like those they have at Evergreen Cemetery, he might even hit rock.

If workers have shored up a grave and covered it with boards for the next day, and a man jumps down in there with a flashlight, he can see what he's going to have to deal with. If there's a concrete vault lining the grave (which is optional in California), he knows he can't dig there, and he moves on. If he's going to dispose of bodies in that manner, he needs to hang out at cemeteries, learn their policies, know what he's dealing with.

As long as he digs down deep enough to cover what he's burying there, nobody will notice. He's got all night to work it, to get it right.

St. Mary's digs the day before. So does St. Joseph's

in San Pablo. They often leave the setting of the vault until the morning of the funeral.

Once the interment is completed, no one could go down and pull that casket up and look underneath it. Even if the cops suspected something, they would have to get an exhumation order from a judge, and for that, they would need probable cause.

Any cemetery could have bodies buried without benefit of religious ceremony. It was that simple. You could hide anything in a cemetery.

> By two o'clock the next afternoon, people are going to be praying over that little baby, and there's going to be a casket and a vault on top of it, and at least eighteen inches of dirt on top of the vault. And it's all gonna be down there. It's gonna be way down there.
>
> And they might even come to the funeral. The person that did that might even come to the damn funeral the next day. The person that's being buried has absolutely no relationship to the person that has been prematurely interred. So they can come, and say they were an acquaintance of the deceased, and attend the funeral, and just enjoy the whole spectacle. . . .
>
> You're protected. You're not only protected, you can sit there and laugh while people are praying. . . .
>
> When I think about something like that, I think about the kids I went out and looked for. I think about Amber. I think about Michaela. I think about Ilene. I think about Nikki. Any one of them could be up in any one of these cemeteries that I've been to—could be in any one of those graves.

Late on the night of January 1, 1992, the bloodhounds had howled their way through Oakmont Cemetery tracking Nikki Campbell's scent. Harold Sagan had turned to Special Agent Mary Ellen O'Toole, asking her if a killer would bury a victim in an existing grave.

It was possible, the agent had said.

SEVEN

TASK FORCE

40

At a press conference, Jim Freeman of the San Francisco FBI office announced the formation of a "Crimes Against Children" task force. Its mission would comprise eight unsolved abductions in the Bay Area since 1983.

The Polly Klaas case prompted the formation of the task force. Investigators had amassed data on sex offenders, primarily child molesters, and were cross-checking that information with other data bases. Freeman's announcement acknowledged that the information had not led them to Richard Allen Davis, but they expected that it would help with the other Bay Area cases.

"It is believed that with a coordinated effort," the press release said, "law enforcement would be in a position to share similar modus operandi (MO) and intelligence on suspects, and thereby be that much closer to solving difficult cases."

The FBI was also establishing a "specific protocol" for its coordinated response to crimes against children. More than sixty law enforcement agencies in northern California were joining the effort.

Among the seven specific objectives Freeman listed were two that addressed interagency cooperation and the sharing of information. An ongoing law enforcement dialogue was essential—because "violent sex offenders and/or child kidnappers are often serial offenders and they commit crimes in many jurisdictions." They would share the data gathered with all law enforcement agencies.

When news of the task force hit the media, the names of the victims and their communities were familiar to most Bay Area residents. Amber Swartz in Pinole. Michaela Garecht in Hayward. Ilene Misheloff in Dublin. And, the most recent addition to the rolls of unsolved disappearances, Nikki Campbell in Fairfield.

Harold Sagan was out of town when two local FBI agents, Dave Heinle and Kimton Zane, stopped at the Fairfield police department. Chuck Timm met with them. The two agents wanted to get to work on the Campbell case again. Timm told them the investigation had never stopped, never broken stride. He said that they should come back and talk to Sagan.

Harold Sagan considered the visit politic. The furor over the Klaas case had led to the creation of the task force. But Heinle and Zane weren't task force; their office in Fairfield was a satellite operation for Sacramento. Sagan figured they probably had been contacted by San Francisco. He had worked with the two agents many times before. He got along well with both men. The problem, as he saw it, was their lack of connection to San Francisco—and that office's unwillingness to share the voluminous information it had collected on the abduction cases even with its own people.

Just how far out of the San Francisco loop the two agents were would soon become apparent.

Chuck Timm's attitude was similar to Sagan's. "It's

our case," he said. "We will do what we need to do. If the FBI wants to assist us in that process now, fine."

Both cops had been working the Nikki Campbell case for more than two years with virtually no assistance. If they had to continue that way, they would. Sagan and Timm shared a distaste for the politics of law enforcement and wanted only to catch a killer. They wanted real cooperation, not an illusion—not something transient that would disappear when the media attention ended.

———————

Kim Swartz was selecting a new check style for the Amber Foundation. She settled on the one she felt was most appropriate: a ransom check. Why be politically correct about it? she thought. Besides, paying the bills to keep the foundation going was a lot like paying ransom.

Kim's increasingly assertive manner concerned some law enforcement people. She also had instant access to the media and the ability to create a storm in a hurry. She had done that with George Ellwin, but media coverage of the Polly Klaas case had diminished the impact of Ellwin's story. Then Pinole had snapped back at her. That one wasn't over yet.

She believed they were long past the point where there was enough suggestive and circumstantial evidence to force the agencies to sit down and make a decision about whether to arrest Tim Bindner. She was three months away from another anniversary date, and was starting to feel creepy about Bindner again— as if the guy were around, following her, watching her. She knew that wasn't true, but the feeling was there nonetheless.

Kim had known in advance that Freeman's announcement about the task force was coming. Some of the parents felt the approach had been used before and produced nothing, so why bother? Special Agent

Larry Taylor seemed concerned that Kim might share that attitude.

"Take the edge off," she told him. "I'm not going to blast you guys in the media. At least you're trying something. It's better than not doing anything. Who knows if it's going to work? You don't know until you try."

She *did* share the attitude that this was an old tactic, and she had little confidence in the FBI. But an approach like this offered avenues they might not have explored before. "We have to find out if there's anything common in the cases," she said in her statement to the press, "to see if anyone's name has come up more than one time, to look at the MOs, to see if there are situations over the last twenty years that maybe haven't been looked at before. Anything's better than doing nothing, and it always gives us new hope."

Kim wanted a standing task force of community agencies, not another ad hoc effort locked behind federal walls. She'd read the protocol and a glossy new manual distributed by the National Center for Missing and Exploited Children. But Kim was painfully familiar with the administrative inertia that afflicted bureaucracies.

She also wanted something done about Tim Bindner. His was the one name that kept coming up. Rule the guy in or out. Kim didn't want to hear that it was just a coincidence that Bindner had gone looking for Amber, that her daughter's scent was in his van, that he had failed the polygraph. It was a coincidence that he was in Hayward at the precise moment that Michaela Garecht was dragged screaming into a car. It was a coincidence that the bloodhounds had tracked two of the kids to Angela Bugay's grave in Oakmont Cemetery and found Bindner's scent on the hill overlooking the Cosgroves' house in Fairfield. Everything that connected him to anything was a coincidence. She wanted that aspect of the case worked. Make an arrest or leave the man alone.

The story about the federal task force broke in the *Tribune* and *Chronicle* on March 31. Five FBI agents would reexamine all the cases. Bindner couldn't see them going out and scouring the countryside. They wouldn't want to get mud on their shoes. But that's the way you find bones. People have to get out of their cars and walk around.

The newspaper articles had said that the task force would be doing computer searches. They were going to track registered sex offenders—to see if they were in a place where a child had disappeared. Bindner considered that tedious, and probably unproductive.

Some abductors would grab a little girl, then release her later—send her into a store and say, "Go call your mama." That was the early stage. Later on they might get into the violence part of it. Once that happened, there was somebody out there killing kids, and how do you stop it? With computers? They hadn't stopped Richard Davis. The state had 65,000 registered sex offenders free or on parole, and 6,000 of them were in the Bay Area. If the guy was the type who would kill just to get pleasure and thrills, then he would do it repeatedly. There wasn't any reason to stop. And such a killer wouldn't be the type to advertise his identity.

The most recent case was Nikki Campbell in 1991. It was all stale now, Bindner thought. The task force was going to have to dig through moldy bread to find the spoor that started it. It was too little too late. Why weren't they doing it five or six years ago? Instead, they had followed *him* around, harassed *him*, investigated *him*. The rest of the agents were probably sitting in front of the Russian embassy.

The task force was sure to come sniffing around, knocking on his door. He was apprehensive. His role as a suspect had become a way of life for him. Even so, he thought that maybe he should curtail his walks near any of the elementary schools. There might be a car on his corner every day and every night.

Bindner thought that the agents should want to talk with him. He had conducted searches in seven of the damn cases. But the more he considered the possibility, the more he felt that he didn't really want them coming around.

41

The spirit of cooperation at the heart of the task force announcement died on the vine.

The city attorney's office in Pinole sent Fairfield Chief Douglas Milender a letter breaking off the working relationship between the two police departments. They wanted Fairfield to return any hard copies of documents in the Amber Swartz case that Pinole detectives might have shared with them. If Fairfield developed anything relevant to their case, they were to deal directly with Pinole's chief and obtain his permission to pass information along.

Milender, a capable administrator and normally an easygoing man, fired back his own response. No one was going to tell him how to run his department. Despite having received virtually nothing from Pinole, the Fairfield department had provided Wayne Galloway with information relevant to his case. That was over.

The consensus in the Fairfield department was

that Pinole was insulating itself from the threat of a
Bindner lawsuit. What had energized Fairfield's investigation had sent Pinole scurrying for cover.

To Sagan, it looked like the task force had an even
bigger task. The San Francisco FBI office had to know
about Pinole's action. The city had worked closely with
the Feds on the Amber Swartz case. "If these cases get
made," the detective thought, "it's going to be in spite
of Pinole."

Somebody was killing kids, and the cops were all
too busy pissing at each other to do anything about it.
There was a black eye waiting in the wings for someone. The only question in Sagan's mind was who was
going to get it.

———————

While the Pinole city attorney was composing his letter to Chief Milender, Kim Swartz was writing a note
of her own. Hers went to Tim Bindner. She had received a card from him the week before. Again he told
her that he had done nothing wrong and that he
wanted to clear up any questions she might have. So
she asked where he was the day that Amber disappeared, what type of vehicle was he driving? Did he
have a beard then? What time did he get home? When
and how did he find out about Amber? Why was Amber's scent in his car and at the Oakmont Cemetery?
They were the same questions that had gone without
definitive answers for six years.

Binder wrote his response the day he received
Kim's letter. He told her that he had considered calling
her but was worried that the cops might have his
phone tapped. It wasn't that he had anything to hide,
just that what they had to say to each other was nobody else's business.

Bindner told her about driving his van up to St.
Joseph's Cemetery that day after work. Yes, he'd had a
beard. He had gotten home sometime between 5:30
and 6:15—he couldn't be more specific than that—and

heard about Amber on the news that night. He couldn't explain the dogs. Either they were wrong or it was a setup. Her witness at Alvarado Park was wrong.

In early August, Binder sent a card.

> As always at this time of year I am thinking of Amber.
>
> I am sorry Kim; I am sorry I couldn't find her, and I am so sad she is still missing.
>
> Mainly I just wanted to tell you that I care about you and your family and, that, despite all the *stupidity* that has occurred, I am here for you.
>
> I will do anything that I can to help you find your daughter, and I know you will too, I have seen your efforts. I am serious, in that—let me know if there is any way I can help.
>
> I'll say a quiet prayer for Amber on her birthday. A few tears may fall. . . . I'd rather be searching: If, I knew, where.
>
> In *my own way*, I love you.

Kim wrote back to Bindner on August 19, Amber's fourteenth birthday. She thanked him for the notes, but said that there were still some things she didn't understand. If the cops had his phone tapped, somebody must suspect him of something. Why had they still been following him in 1992? How could he be so sure that there wasn't any evidence? A setup? If somebody had wanted to frame him, he would be in jail, she said. And then she hit him head-on.

> Tim, you have spent a lot of time trying to convince me that you didn't take Amber. I know of a way and it would not interfere with your lawsuit against Fairfield, so your lawyer should have no objection. A private polygraph. You can choose the place, no police, only you and I get the results and I'll pay for it. Since you have nothing to hide, it should clear the air and cost you only a morning or so of your time.

Bindner responded by announcing that he was finally going to take his attorney's advice and refrain from contacting her.

She sent a final, furious note. In it, she quoted the letters in which Bindner had claimed to have nothing to hide and had promised that he would answer her questions truthfully.

> Please understand this. I want the truth and I will get the truth no matter how long it takes. If you had anything to do with Amber I will know that because I am going to find out what happened to her.
>
> You conducted 7 missing person searches. I lost one 7 year old child. Pain, frustration and nausea are all too familiar to me.

Tim Bindner didn't answer that letter. He felt that Kim was asking the same questions that she, the Pinole police, and the FBI had asked before. There wasn't any point in continuing to go over the same ground.

> *She thinks maybe I did it, that I'm playing with her. You know, maybe she thinks this is part of the cat and mouse game. If I had taken her daughter, it would have to be a pretty sinister cat and mouse game to have going on all these years.*
>
> *If I had killed her daughter, I must be one of the most devious, evil, diabolical persons in the world. To have that kind of relationship with her, you know, and to go out and search for her daughter for two and a half months, to talk with her children, to make friends with her children, to be so close to her for years. And if I had killed Amber, it would make me so evil and so diabolical.*

42

Following the brief media flurry about the task force, there was silence. There was nothing in the papers about the group's progress. Nothing about the Bay Area cases at all.

Tim Bindner knew the task force would be taking a close look at him. They had to. His name had surfaced repeatedly in the investigations they were reexamining. So he started looking over his shoulder, watching for the surveillance that he knew would come.

The Pinole police, the Contra Costa County sheriffs, and the FBI had been all over him in 1988. He was sure the FBI had followed him back from San Bernardino in 1991. They were on him again after the search of his home in December 1992. They had even planted a transponder device on his car.

This time his wife was the first to spot the surveillance. Sandra Bindner had watched as her husband jogged off to work in the first light of morning. A dark sedan moved slowly down Fifty-third Street behind him. She waited, then called him at work.

When Bindner left the EBMUD facility that afternoon, he looked for them. It didn't take him long to pick up the surveillance—three, maybe four, cars—playing their game of tag as they passed him, slowed down, then moved quickly away only to reappear. "Here we go again," Bindner thought.

> Some of their surveillance techniques seem very amateurish. It's very obvious when you're being followed, very obvious when they're covering up what they're doing. It's like, "Whoa. What kind of movie am I in here, guys?" I felt that several times when I knew they were following me. This is a movie. You guys are weird. I wish I had my camera. You could tell. I can't prove that that was FBI agents surveilling me, but I know goddamn well it was. So some of their surveillance work is a little bit shoddy, amateurish, I think.
>
> It gets to a point where you just feel enough is enough. You guys think you're smarter than me, and I think I'm smarter than you. You think I did it, and I know I didn't. And we're all playing games with each other. Let's just drop all that shit. Sometimes I get a little bit angry about the way they approach me, and the games they do, the entrapments, the enticements, all the stupid stuff they've done over the years. I get tired of it, 'cause I haven't hurt anybody. I haven't done anything to anybody. They probably spent $100,000 of the taxpayers' money trying to box me into a corner, trying to get me to jump at some bait. I've never jumped, and I've never been boxed into a corner. So I get tired of it, and I am tired of it. And if this task force is going to use that same kind of approach on me, they're not gonna come up with anything. They're just gonna embarrass their damn selves just like the rest of 'em did. Just like Harry Sagan's got red on his face right now. They're not gonna find anything 'cause there's nothing there.

Although Harold Sagan considered the task force a political gesture, he knew that the San Francisco office had a new special agent in charge (SAC), Gordon MacNeil, a working cop. He had been on the streets of Miami and had survived a shootout there in a case that had made national headlines. Maybe they *would* do something. Maybe there would be some cooperation after all the months of silence.

San Francisco's public position was that Tim Bindner wasn't a suspect in any crime. But Kimton Zane and Dave Heinle had shown interest in Fairfield's case, and they wanted to know more about Bindner. They were working the case, assisting Sagan whenever they could.

Sagan routinely asked them about intelligence that San Francisco had gathered in some of the other cases. The two agents passed along the requests for information, but nothing came back.

———————

Tim Bindner didn't know what was going on with any of the investigations, but he sensed Sagan's isolation.

> *I have this feeling in my own heart that the FBI people kind of wanted to distance themselves from what Mr. Sagan was doing. He put his foot in his mouth, basically is what he did. By running his mouth too much, by making all these public accusations. The FBI doesn't work that way. The times they've come to my house—and they have been to my house several times—it's been very discreet and very respectful, and I don't think they wanted any part of what he was doing.*

Sagan heard about the surveillance on Bindner. It had to be FBI. He hadn't ordered it, and nobody else would have. "He's not a suspect?" Sagan said to Chuck Timm. "They have said that he's not a suspect. Well, if he's not a suspect, what are they doing putting him under surveillance? They're wasting taxpayers' money."

"They're just rattling his cage," Timm said.

"He's not going to take them anywhere now," Sagan said. "To him it's a goddamn game."

Sagan called Heinle and Zane. They didn't know anything about any surveillance, but the local agents said they would check with San Francisco.

Sagan continued to fume. That kind of surveillance sent Bindner a message; it told him something. The guy thrived on information. When he couldn't get it—when he didn't know what was going on in the investigation, or even if there *was* an investigation—then he might be vulnerable. But when they followed him around, it was like sending the guy a telegram.

The official position of the San Francisco office was that there had been no surveillance. They didn't know what Heinle and Zane were talking about. But at lunch with other agents, the men from the Fairfield office had overheard a conversation between two young agents. They were talking about tailing Tim Bindner in Oakland.

Sagan blew up. The Fairfield department was getting zero cooperation from San Francisco. The agency was lying. To Harold Sagan, this was law enforcement at its worst. He had a case to work.

On February 14, 1995, a memo from the San Francisco FBI office made its way through the Sacramento and Fairfield offices of the Bureau and landed on Sagan's desk. It purported to be answers to questions that Sagan had asked them months earlier.

The electronic surveillance at the grave of Angela Bugay on July 8, 1988, had provided "no recording." Sagan had heard that the lawn sprinklers went on. If Bindner was saying anything to Angela, the agents were listening only to the hiss of spraying water.

The memo continued: On July 17, 1986, Bindner's mother had given title of her 1967 Dodge van to her son. On September 22, 1987, more than a year later,

Bindner obtained the LOV YOU license plate. That was DMV stuff.

There was more on Angela Bugay. The FBI's behavioral science unit hadn't done a profile in that case because the Antioch police had developed a suspect, and because they had consulted a private psychologist. The memo from San Francisco also stated that Antioch's investigation was at "a very sensitive stage, and any information is closely guarded. The FBI does not have jurisdictional interest in this case beyond domestic police cooperation."

The San Francisco office had nothing more to add, "other than to say Tim Bindner has been eliminated as a suspect in that case."

Bindner had told him the same thing in 1992. He'd said the FBI told him that in 1988.

Tim Bindner had written to the Antioch police about the case. He had hung out at the child's grave. He had offered theories about how the crime happened and why it should be viewed as the possible work of a serial killer.

Then more kids had disappeared, and two of their scents could be tied to Oakmont Cemetery.

Even though Antioch and the FBI had eliminated Bindner as a suspect, Sagan felt that they didn't grasp the importance of the case. Sagan believed he needed to investigate whether the sexual assault and murder of the five-year-old could have served as an excitor for Bindner—a trigger. His obsession with the case—the visits to her grave, the apartment complex, and the crime scene—remained critical to Sagan.

Sagan continued to believe that Angela's grave linked Amber and Nikki.

43

With the passage of time, Tim Bindner had grown less concerned with what Harold Sagan was doing. He figured the FBI had muzzled the Fairfield cop and forced him to take a back seat to the task force. Sagan had presented his theory to the world, and Tim Bindner was still walking the streets. The cops were running around in circles, but he was a free man.

He was also still mulling over the possibilities in the case that had started everything for him, the abduction and murder of Angela Bugay. The child continued to be a significant presence in his life—the dead girl who had crashed into his life via his dreams.

I was up in the cemetery today and it was raining, and I was walking around. It was a nice rain, and it was warm up there, and I was thinking about it. "Sure smells good up here. Smells so sweet. It's sweet and it's quiet." There was nobody up there.

And maybe that's what he needed—for it to be quiet and nice and smelling good. It brings out the smells of all the plants and stuff. It's not just the water itself, but it's the smells, too.

The guy who killed Angela did not kill her because he wanted to kill a little girl. He killed her because he didn't—well, I think he killed her because that was the only way of getting rid of the completion of his fantasy. He lived out his fantasy, and then he had to get rid of what happened after that. . . .

I wasn't there, but—what I'm saying is, the fantasy itself is not going to encompass what happens after it's completed. The fantasy may include the murder. But after the murder's done, you're not gonna fantasize about how you dispose of the body and how you cover your tracks. If you're so caught up in your fantasy that your fantasy is going to be realized, then you realize that "Oh-oh, what do I do now?" It's not planned. Now I have to improvise.

If the fantasy, the masturbatory fantasy becomes the focus of his escalating activity, that would make sense to me that it doesn't really necessarily include what happens after. What happens after can be an absolute bungle job. . . .

Now as far as Angie, I don't know. Maybe the same thing happened. "I gotta get rid of this now. I'm done." Maybe it wasn't so controlled. Maybe it was the same kind of deal. We've talked about that Angela was not supposed to be found, and that the ones later were hidden better. Well maybe it wasn't that way. Maybe it was like he did his thing and after it was done it was like, "Well, here it is." And it gets done, and he's gone. "I got rid of her. Okay. I got away with it."

Bindner was also thinking again about Oakmont Cemetery and the possibility that someone might have buried the bodies of the children up there in open graves. He had been the one to suggest a possible connection between Angela and Amber. Then they had done their thing with the dogs, and the Nikki case came along. Oakmont had become the hub of all the cases. Now he wondered if the task force would investigate the possibility that the cemetery was also a killer's dumping ground.

> *I go into all these cemeteries, and I see these open graves. They sure as heck do dig 'em the day before, and they stay empty all night. The other thought that occurs to me is, say if Nikki's body or Amber's body is found in Oakmont Cemetery. I'm dead. I've had it. I didn't do it, but I'm gone, man. . . .*
>
> *There's nobody down there. There's no little kid buried underneath any of those graves up there in Meditation. I really believe that. And if there is, I may end up somehow being the victim of a very, very bizarre coincidence.*

There was more when all the theories of the case came together, and he knew it.

> *I guess I have to come back off my innocent, arrogant pedestal and say, "Who could possibly look at the evidence in this case and not have a theory, hey, this guy may have done it. It certainly looks like he may have done it."*

On the morning of April 12, 1995, Ron Homer called Sagan. The FBI polygrapher from San Francisco had been talking with Special Agent Larry Taylor. "We've got to get working on these cases," Homer said.

The aspect of the investigation that involved Tim Bindner was still at square one: Either eliminate him as a suspect or make the case against him. Fairfield had the most information on the guy.

Homer figured the lawsuit was preventing cooperation among the agencies. Sagan respected the polygrapher and didn't contradict him, but the lack of cooperation antedated the lawsuit by more than a year.

Special Agent Larry Taylor, who was familiar with

all the cases and served on the task force, was working exclusively on the child abduction cases. Taylor had interviewed Richard Davis, and had been in the group that found Polly Klaas's body. On the nineteenth, Taylor and Sagan sat in the Fairfield detective's office, talking generally about the status of the investigations. The Bureau had worked a number of weak suspects in the other cases, Taylor said. Tim Bindner was still a solid suspect.

Sagan and the FBI agent agreed to exchange information and compare what they had. It had taken a long time to get to this point, but maybe the investigation was finally going to move.

On May 26, 1995, a federal court judge dismissed Tim Bindner's lawsuit against the Fairfield police department and Harold Sagan. He remanded the case to state court.

The judge ruled that the search warrant had been valid. The psychological theory described in the affidavit, and the reports of the bloodhounds' behavior, complemented the facts in the case, the ruling continued. The state court in Solano County could weigh the defamation issue, but there would be no further discovery.

Tim Bindner greeted the news with detachment. He trusted John Burris, was confident that his attorney would make the best possible decisions.

But he no longer expected the city to settle the suit, especially with a guy they believed abducted and murdered a child. The prospect of a trial was not appealing. In its own defense, Fairfield would drag out all of its evidence against him. He figured they would hit him with everything, and he no longer knew what everything was. The risks seemed high—not the least of them was a repeat of the media saturation—and it would be a hard case to win.

44

Tim Bindner couldn't shut up, and he didn't want to. He said that he was willing to die to express himself and to try to solve some of the cases. He was the prime suspect, the celebrity suspect, the man the Feds followed. Despite this status, if he had a lead, some kind of a clue, he had to put that forward, he said.

> I have to put it out there and see what happens. If it points a finger right back at me, that's too bad. I didn't do it. We got to find a way to brush that off and go elsewhere.

He didn't consider his feelings a death *wish*, but he knew that his own persistence or some strange set of coincidences might cause his death.

> What it becomes is a resolve to find these children, or to find out what happened to them and to say,

"Damn anybody that gets in my way." I'm going to try to go my direction and do what I need to do to find them or to find out what happened to them, and if that causes my death, then I'm willing to do that.

Bindner could image some prison official telling him it was his day to die.

"Oh, but I didn't rape her. I didn't kill her," he would say. "Somebody else did."

He would say the words, but he would know that it was his time to die. If his efforts to solve the cases resulted in his being killed by the state of California, then he would dedicate his life to Amber and Angela. He said he had already told them: "I would die for you girls."

You know, the phrase Stephen King—the operative phrase he used in his novels was "You bought the fucker." You know? In other words, didn't you know what was going to happen? Didn't you look at it? . . .

I have always looked at it and said, "Well, what's the worst that can happen?" So I know what the worst is that can happen, and if it happens, well, I bought the fucker, you know? I may have to pay for it. I may not. But I bought it 'cause I put myself out there.

Tim Bindner continued to speculate about all of the cases. Would the guy responsible for the missing kids hit again? Would he choose a town away from the Bay Area—one not sensitized to the issue of child abduction? Ukiah, on the north coast, was a possibility. But there was nothing to prevent him from hitting in the same place again.

An abductor that has gotten away with this in a certain area will feel comfortable with that area. He may have done it in a place where he knows certain roads, certain hillsides, certain places where nobody else would generally ever go, unless they had a specific purpose for being there. But it's his hangout, his safe place, his hideout, whatever. Even just the place where he goes up to watch the sunset, drink a beer, or to go after work to be by himself. It's certainly conceivable if he's successfully done this, and gone through that ritual, done something in these places, that he would come back again, especially after this length of time, and want to revisit his places, and want to relive that experience with another child. So I don't see anything precluding that from happening again in any of these places.

Because Bindner had long believed that the settings where Nikki and Amber had been abducted were places where there aren't a lot of kids constantly around, he reasoned that a killer would have to sit a while, bide his time, cruise around. He would plan what he was going to do.

Bindner alluded again to the quiet neighborhoods in Pinole and Fairfield. He didn't see these cases reflecting an "ostentatious" personality. He expected the killer to indulge himself in more of a "private pride" kind of feeling, even if he were arrested.

I can't see a guy like this making any kind of deal unless he's sure he's nailed, unless he's sure they've got a conviction—be it the death penalty or a murder conviction with some other penalty. If he's not sure he's gonna get convicted, I can't see him pleading.

He's gonna want to make them work for it. Whatever they get, he's gonna want to make them work their asses off for it. He's not gonna just hand them anything. That's the feeling I get.

If he's been doing these, and doing them so efficiently all this time, and not having any of it found out—some of it finally does get found out, why, there's probably still gonna be this pride there that says, "Dang it. I goofed one. But I sure did a good job on this one, that one, and the other one." So I can see a motivation there, a pride motivation, a superiority motivation to hold on to that, not to just give it to them. Or, if you want to use that in the power sense, to give little hints and tidbits and make 'em chase around. Let 'em find it a little bit at a time. I see that as more likely than the guy just coming out and saying, "Okay, I can put all these minds at rest. I can help you out. Let's make a deal." I don't see that happening.

Bindner continued to try to put himself into the body and mind of a predator who operated like that. He said he couldn't imagine himself going to work the next day if he had just killed a child.

Some kind of dissociation has to happen. But that's just the way I would respond to it. I mean, to even do something like that, dissociation perhaps comes first. And then the whole act and what comes after it may be on a different level of reality or whatever. I just don't know. It baffles me. There's got to be some separation between that reality—what you actually did—and your daily life, and dealing with people and laughing, drinking coffee and going about your duties on your job, dealing with your family at home. It's—I couldn't do it without dissociating somehow. Completely.

45

In 1988, Amber Swartz's birthday was the first, impromptu, Amber Day. In 1995, Amber Day again fell on August 19, Amber's fifteenth birthday.

After seven years, Amber Park finally had been landscaped—an intricate arrangement of railroad ties, a patio of stone blocks, and a central location to plant the liquidambar tree. A volunteer effort had transformed the overgrown field where Amber had collected bugs and rocks. That morning, a few yards from where her daughter had disappeared, Kim lifted a shovel of dirt and covered the tree's roots. Her message to the foundation's supporters and the media representatives was the same as it had been for seven years: Care for our children, and keep them safe.

Harold Sagan drove into the parking lot at the rear of the Ellerhorst School. He talked briefly to Kim Swartz and Dale Myer, who was there with his bloodhound, Friday.

The Fairfield cop was restless. He crossed the road in front of the school, found a well-worn path up the steep incline, then followed trace trails, climbing through some low brush and the overhanging branches of evergreen.

Sagan had been thinking about retirement, now less than three years away. The bureaucracy and politics of police work were getting to him. Maybe it was time to move on. He had been surfing the Internet one night when he saw an advertisement for a position as a professor of law enforcement in Munich, Germany. It seemed to have been designed for the bilingual doctoral candidate, but the timing was wrong. Besides, leaving the Nikki Campbell case would be like ignoring an open wound.

He still talked with Anne Campbell once or twice a week. It pleased him to watch her grow stronger. He was impressed with all that she had accomplished since her daughter's disappearance.

After climbing about two hundred feet, he left the trail and stepped between two trees. He could see the school, the playground, then, up through the field, he looked at Amber Park, Kim's backyard, and Savage Avenue. He didn't even need binoculars. Amber, skipping rope in her purple pants and white shirt, would have been just as visible from this vantage point as Nikki Campbell would have been from the Kolob Hills, walking alone in her pink ski jacket.

Sagan descended the hill and drove out of Pinole through the valley to Oakmont Cemetery. He turned in, driving up the hill to the Meditation section, where he wandered among the graves. The connection was here, he thought, as he approached Angela Bugay's grave. Yet Sagan anticipated that the Antioch police would arrest and indict Larry Graham, who had been their main suspect in the Angela Bugay case all along.

The grave hadn't been tended recently. Weeds extended out over the flat, bronze plate. The left side of Angela's ceramic picture had been chipped almost away.

Sagan lifted the flower holder, finding cobwebs beneath it. No one had been there in a long time.

No, Tim Bindner had not killed Angela Bugay. But the connection is here, he thought, gazing off at Mount Diablo in the distant haze.

The Monday morning after his visit to Oakmont Cemetery, Sagan presented a case review for members of his department, two representatives from the D.A.'s office, the local FBI agents, and Special Agent Tim Bezik from the San Francisco office. The Fairfield detective's investigation had uncovered information related to cases other than Nikki Campbell, including Amber Swartz, Michaela Garecht, and Ilene Misheloff—all cases that the FBI task force was reexamining.

Sagan presented that information first, then outlined his plans for continuing the Nikki Campbell investigation. Bezik arranged a follow-up meeting with Sagan and Larry Taylor for a more thorough comparison of their case materials.

Taylor had spent months struggling with the Bureau's files in the missing children cases. All the information was in sequential order; as leads came in, they were placed in notebooks. The Michaela Garecht file had grown to thirty-seven volumes, Amber Swartz's to thirty-four volumes. All of this had to be reviewed page by page.

When Taylor and Bezik returned to Fairfield, Sagan set them up in an office with the detective's own case files and a directory. All they had to do was choose the piece of information they wanted; the directory indicated the file and the page and line numbers.

Even after four hours, Taylor knew he would have to come back. There were thousands of pages dealing with cases all over California. It was also clear that Sagan's investigation had not been confined to the Golden State.

As they walked out through the sally port, the

three cops talked about the view from the hill opposite the Ellerhorst School in Pinole. "Have you been up on our hill here?" Sagan asked.

Once more the Fairfield cop climbed the Kolob Hills. He pointed out the cul-de-sac where Nikki had been playing with friends in the fading light of December 27, 1991. He showed the two agents the view of Larchmont and Salisbury, the intersection where the bloodhounds had indicated that someone had taken Nikki into a vehicle. And there was Sheila Cosgrove's house at the foot of the hill.

When Sagan had been on the hill taping *Street Stories*, he had described a man whose head would be filled with fantasies. Then Nikki Campbell walked into view. The fantasies exploded in a great mushroom cloud. Perhaps it wasn't the most articulate expression of his theory of the crime, but it got the point across.

Now, after three and a half years of investigating his own case, of being pulled into the other Bay Area cases—after all the research, the reading, the conversations with experts—Harold Sagan believed he understood the requisite predatory state of mind. He knew that the essence of it all was the nature of a man's personality.

The professional literature dealing with the sexual predator suggested that there was seldom a single motivation at work. A stalker, a predator had many aims and goals. From this vantage point above the neighborhood, a man could scan the streets, evaluate his possible moves, assess the risks that might be involved in abducting a child. He could exert absolute control, and no one would know he was there. No one would know that he watched.

Sagan believed that there was a simple projection: a victim will feel about me the way I imagine her to feel about me; she will want me to come and get her. It was also more complicated than that, the detective thought. Such a man could take a child, sexually assault her, dispose of her. The violence was instrumental—a means to an end.

Sagan's research also suggested that once the decision to act was made, there was little chance of any backing off. According to the FBI's own studies, an abduction was rehearsed in fantasy countless times. With the first touch, an assailant went on fire. This guy would know that he was with a little girl, a stranger. But, to him, she would be more than that. She represented something or someone to him.

Vengeance, maybe. Once the child was dead, who suffered? The mother.

The payoff for this kind of assault would go on beyond the excitement of those few moments. Punish mothers. Play games with the authorities. He would have no emotional attachment to the victim, but he would have an intimate emotional involvement with the image, the memory of her. He could become involved with the hysteria surrounding her disappearance—the searching, the ministering to the family's needs, the investigating.

However he might dispose of the child's body would become another example of his own perfection. She would be so gone that no one could ever find her. He would be confident, expansive, willing to be suspected, interrogated, followed. He couldn't lose. He would see himself as invulnerable. He could afford to be contemptuous.

"Do you see the similarities between this and the Pinole case?" Sagan asked.

The agents nodded.

Sagan reminded them that intelligence they had generated about Timothy James Bindner suggested that he was a creature of habit. "He sat on that bluff at Oakmont Cemetery watching you guys watch him," Sagan said.

He asked Taylor about Lone Tree Cemetery in Hayward. Sagan knew that Bindner had applied for work there even before he'd begun practicing for the firefighter's test in 1988.

Lone Tree was an old-style cemetery on a hill, the agent said, up above the Rainbow Market.

Sagan sensed the agents' interest. It was the beginning of a new working relationship. In some ways, the Fairfield detective was starting all over again, returning to that cold, rainy December morning when he first gazed up at the Kolob Hills. This time, though, he and his investigative team weren't alone.

46

Tim Bindner thought he would make a good juror in the trial of Richard Davis for the murder of Polly Klaas. He knew what police and the media could concoct. He had experienced their zealous excesses. He believed that he could go into the trial with an open mind, not being swayed by what had been said on TV or in the newspapers.

> If I went out in Pinole Valley right now and found Amber's bones, the first thing you'd see in the media was that I'd led police to her remains. There would be an analysis of why I felt the guilt at this time, and why I couldn't stand it anymore, and all this stuff.

The forty-seven-year-old Bindner sat in a motel room in North Oakland opening a bottle of beer with the blade of his knife. Despite his feeling that he was still the only suspect in the Bay Area child cases, he said he had begun walking through his neighborhoods again. Children ran from him. Parents called their kids indoors. They peered out at him through windows. One man threw a rock. An elderly woman confronted him.

"The rumor's going around that you're a child molester," she said, "and you took that little girl up in Fairfield."

"You don't know that," Bindner had told her. "I can answer anything you want to ask me."

"Well, the dog knew that the girl was in your house because the dog detected her scent in your front yard."

"That's one I haven't heard." Bindner laughed. "Where'd you get that from?"

"That guy on the news said that," she responded.

"I'll tell you what that dog did in my yard. He smelled another dog and he peed on a bush."

Of all the cases, Nikki Campbell's was the one that just wouldn't go away. Bindner had to admit that it was a persuasive case. He could even see a jury buying into it. He knew that he could never convince the police that he hadn't done it. Bindner wanted only to get to the point where he could say, "They're not gonna be able to get anything more that I have to worry about."

He still didn't think that he would be arrested: "The bottom line is that there is no proof. There is no reality."

Slipping through the mirror to Looking-Glass World, there was no reality. There was only the distortion—twisted images appearing in unexpected contexts.

As he sat drinking and reminiscing, Bindner tried to remember the Loprest Company, the place where sheriff's deputies had dug up the "Gotcha" note. He said he didn't think he had ever gotten behind there. He also said he didn't think he would have left a note like that. "Must've been a hot day with a lot of beer if I did that," he said.

To do something and not remember that you've done it—to have no recollection—then you wouldn't know. If somebody comes back and says, "Hey, you did this," I go, "No, I didn't." "Yes you did. Here's the proof." And you look at it and go, "Oh, shit."

Tim Bindner continued to maintain that he had a clear and conscious memory of where he was when Nikki Campbell was taken. He knew that the cops viewed the blackout theory as a possible explanation—that he could have committed these crimes and not remembered. But he didn't buy it, he said.

Nor did he buy the idea that he could have planned and executed a child abduction and homicide in such a way that he would never be caught.

The image of me doing something right to hurt somebody—taking a child and killing a child so that nobody would find out—I used to think about that. To think that somebody would think that of me, that I could possibly do that—that hurts.

I'm telling you, it's not possible. It may have been at one time, but it's not now.

Sometime back in my past when I didn't know any better, it may have been possible. It didn't happen, and it never will, and now it's not possible.

I haven't done it. I'm not gonna do it. No matter what. There.

Intellectually, Bindner accepted the notion that circumstances capable of eliciting sexually aggressive behavior might occur. If that happened to him, he said, he would withdraw, move out of town, kill himself. But nothing like that was going to happen to him. He wouldn't allow it to happen.

Maybe that could've happened if I had gone wrong, if things had gone wrong in my life. Motivation. Desires. Fantasies that had gone in the wrong direction. But it didn't, and I know it's not. I guess what I'm trying to say is, I know where I'm at, and I know where I'm not going. To say philosophically, you could do that. You could kill a child. No, I couldn't. Not now I couldn't. Maybe I could have. Maybe there could have been something that made me do that. It's not gonna happen. It can't happen. Didn't happen.

It remained difficult for Bindner to be unequivocal. The possibility of something like that happening to him seemed to fester. "The idea that I could is so odious," he said.

But Tim Bindner did experience fantasies about young girls. A "little fantasy girl" had grown up with him having fantasies about her. He said he never touched her, never forced anything on her. All he had were the fantasies. He wasn't going to cross the line. Yes, there was sexual excitement associated with the fantasies. And, yes, in indirect, nonintrusive ways, he had acted on the fantasies. But he had never been coercive, he said. Never abusive.

He had drawn a line—what was acceptable behavior and what was not. He admitted that the line was movable, but insisted that he had nothing to be ashamed of, nothing in his past to hide.

One of Bindner's fantasies about Amber Swartz involved finding her in a gully beside Pinole Valley Road. She would have a broken leg, and he would carry her home to Kim.

In a fantasy about Nikki Campbell, he's driving down the street when he sees her out there, all alone in the encroaching darkness. He's going to take her by the hand and walk her home.

When Bindner talked about this fantasy, he gazed off into a corner of the small motel room. It was late. His boss had called to tell him to report for work in the morning—what was supposed to be his day off. Maybe it was all of that and the cumulative effects of an evening's drinking that made him seem to drift away somewhere. But maybe it was something else, too. His voice was soft, his sentences short and disjointed, his tenses confused. He was like someone talking in his sleep.

*Walked her home. Warm her up. Give her something
to eat. Make sure she was okay. No reason to take her
in the car with you if she was cold. But she must've
been cold. Don't know where she lived. She couldn't tell
me. I'd take her home and warm her up. Then I'd find
out where she lived. Wouldn't necessarily call the cops.
Make sure she was dry.*

Was this dissociation? Kim Swartz thought she
had seen it. Ron Homer had listened as his polygraph
subject seemed to drift into the reliving of an experience. Bindner had talked about it, read books about it.
Was this the way he moved from one side of the
Looking-Glass World to the other? From one reality to
another?

*If I wanted to take her into my car, and I needed to
do that—you know, to make sure she was all right—
that scenario doesn't make sense 'cause she was old
enough to talk. She could've told me where she lived.
And I would've just took her by the hand and walked
her home. But if conditions were such that I had to take
her in my car, I would do that. Make her comfortable.
Warm her up. Make her dry.*

Bindner's eyes drifted back from somewhere beyond the walls of the musty room. He seemed disoriented, glancing at the floor. "I don't know what else to
say," he said. "I wish I'd been there so I could've done
something."

He acknowledged that he was trying hard to understand what everything meant—what had happened to
the children and what went on in his own mind.

*Probably one of the things that I spent too much
time doing was trying to convince everybody that I
didn't abduct, rape, kill, or do anything else to hurt
these children. I should just realize that I can't convince everybody. There's a lot of people that are never*

gonna believe that. Spending all the time and effort trying to do that probably takes away from my own perspective.

He pushed the last of his empty beer bottles onto a table, stood, and prepared to leave. "I think you have to let it go sometime," he said at the door, then walked away down the hall.

POSTSCRIPT:
STALEMATE

47

Tim Bindner still talked about the types of people who abduct children and whether such people could voluntarily stop that behavior.

> *I think it's like anything else in life. You assess the realistic possibility of what's gonna happen. Say you have a job. Say you have a family. Say you're the Boston Strangler. You're going into town and you're killing somebody, and you're coming back home and playing with your kids and living with your wife. Then all of a sudden something comes up, or it looks like maybe they're on to you. You stop, right then and there. Okay. And say you stop, and then they don't realize, or they don't take any action because they don't have enough evidence to take any action. Then you realize, well, hey, they backed off. Then you can—maybe you think you can start going out and doing it again. But you're a little more careful when you do it again.*
>
> *I think that the person that's doing these things makes an assessment at every point as to the risks*

involved. I don't think it's so much impulse. The impulse is always there. It's like, how do I put this into action without getting punished for it? It's like stealing a candy bar in a store, man. Is somebody watching me? Can I get this in my pocket without being seen? And you got it in your pocket now, right? Can I walk out the door? Did somebody see me put it in my pocket? If you think somebody saw you put it in your pocket, you go down the aisle and you just take it out of your pocket and you lay it down and walk on out. Then, if they apprehend you, they don't have the evidence.

I used to do that. I used to try to steal candy bars. If I thought I was being watched, ditch 'em, okay? It's the same damn thing.

Not all of those who abduct a child assess their risks through every step of the act. Some are careless, Bindner said. But if someone has gotten away with it more than once—even it he attracts law enforcement attention—he won't stop, but he will change the way he operates.

You're gonna do it more careful. And you're gonna do it in a different place. And you're gonna change your vehicle, your mode of operation. The whole thing is gonna change. . . .

Doesn't everyone have their own temperament, their own way they respond to things? It depends on the motivation of the person. But I feel there are some who would do that—who would take that second heat and say, "Well, screw you, guys. I'm gonna do it a different way. And you're still not gonna catch me." And that might be the guy who's prowling the Bay Area and taking these kids, and then he left. He left after Nikki. He went somewhere else.

FBI Special Agents Larry Taylor and Tim Bezik had continued to visit the Fairfield police department and to review Harold Sagan's voluminous files on the

Bay Area child disappearances. On a Monday in January, the two agents spent five hours going through case material, then grilling Sagan.

Bezik viewed Bindner as a "unique situation."

"We can't rule him out of any of these cases," the agent said, "but we can't actually put him *in* any of these cases."

Evidence of Bindner's eccentricity continued to come in. A former neighbor from Fifty-third Street told police that Bindner's habit of leaving out large bowls of food for the neighborhood's stray cats had created a nuisance. When neighbors complained, Bindner said, "I have to do it. God told me to do it."

"He told me he was a suspect," the former neighbor told the cops. "He said the authorities had placed him within a half hour of Amber Swartz's disappearance."

Then Bindner had complained about his suspect status. "Stop injecting yourself in these fucking cases," the neighbor had told him, "making a pain in the ass of yourself to the cops. Your problems'll go away."

But Tim Bezik was right. The evidence of something more sinister just wasn't there.

Harold Sagan had begun to consider a new approach to the problem of the suspect he couldn't rule in or out of the Nikki Campbell case. The California Department of Justice and the Solano County District Attorney's Office had both been using voice stress analysis (VSA) as an investigative tool.

The results of VSA, like those of polygraph testing, are not admissible in court, but they are used to corroborate or disprove existing evidence or statements. Unlike a polygraph subject, the VSA subject does not have to be attached to a machine. Audio tapes are sufficient to provide accurate readings. The VSA equipment measures microtremors in the larynx (voice box), which quivers under the stress of attempting to be deceptive. It is an uncontrollable reaction. Corporate, governmental, and law enforcement organizations that use the equipment agree with its manufacturer's claims of 85 to 90 percent accuracy.

According to experts, VSA won't tell you who committed a crime, but it will tell you who *might* have done it—and who didn't do it. If an investigation is going in the right direction, VSA can verify that.

Harold Sagan wanted an answer for himself—one way or the other. Tim Bindner had to be pursued as a suspect or eliminated from the investigation. With no access to Bindner, but with tapes of Bindner responding to key questions, the detective decided to make use of the latest technology.

Sagan wondered if factors such as intelligence, or the ability to dissociate, could influence the results of a voice stress analysis. How bright the guy was wouldn't be an issue, Sagan was told. Dissociation? Nobody knew enough about it, but it could be a problem.

On March 22, 1996, Sagan received the results of the VSA. Two examiners had completed separate examinations of the taped material and were in agreement: The subject had shown deception when he said that he had not been in Fairfield on December 27, 1991, and that Nikki Campbell had not been in his car.

In the four and a half years since Harold Sagan had sat in his car at the foot of the Kolob Hills, he had worked other cases, cleared suspects, made arrests. He had watched as the same changes that were affecting other municipalities began to take their toll in the Fairfield police department. Fiscal reality required belt-tightening. Departmental policies and procedures became more rigid. Most of the changes made sense to Sagan, whose master's degree is in public administration. He had always believed in accountability. But the detective had never been comfortable with a regimented approach to criminal investigation—one that stifled creativity—and he could see that happening.

Sagan was two years away from what he chose to call "a change of careers." He didn't like the notion of retirement. He was a year and a dissertation away from becoming Dr. Harold Sagan.

And he knew that he would never let go of the Nikki Campbell case. In all the time that had passed, nothing had changed his resolve. A few of the Bay Area child cases had been solved. Dozens of suspects had been cleared in the unsolved cases.

Once again, the FBI had gone silent. Sagan knew that Larry Taylor and Tim Bezik had been tied up with a child abduction and homicide in Hanford, California, south of the Bay Area. Then there was the Richard Davis trial. But even after the death sentence had been handed down, Sagan's calls went unreturned.

Kim Swartz's idea of a standing task force on crimes against children—not a federal ad hoc group—held appeal. A regular exchange of information, the development of trust among local agencies, cooperation—all seemed attractive. The imagined barriers—the competition, the turf wars—separating law enforcement agencies in adjacent communities might just fall.

Then again, maybe that was wishful thinking.

Nothing in northern California is finished.

Millions of years ago, a great slab of the earth's surface slowly reared itself up from the sea and crushed itself into a docking position at the edge of the Sierra Mountains. The layers of land settled. The mountains continued to rise.

It was a gradual process—inconceivably slow, but inevitable. Whether it is the imperceptible shifting of the land or the explosive thrust of an earthquake, the terrain is constantly in motion

Always, there is more yet to happen.

This is a place always at the edge of its own apocalypse—whether from the pressures that build beneath the earth or from the stressors that accompany life in a fast and precarious lane.

Harold Sagan's investigation into the disappearance of Nikki Campbell isn't finished. It can't be. There is no statute of limitations on murder.

Besides, Sagan still has a suspect—a man he can't charge *or* clear.

Nothing is finished.

Years earlier, Mary Ellen O'Toole kept telling Sagan how intelligent Tim Bindner was—like the guy was some kind of genius. Maybe that's why the FBI gave up on him, the cop thought.

"He's very smart," Sagan said, "but he's not insurmountable. No one is."

Sagan worked his investigation, and he was patient.

48

FEBRUARY, 1996

Rosie Duncan enjoyed writing to her pen pals. The thirteen-year-old Walnut Creek junior high school student had even entered her name and address in some friendship books—usually small rectangles of construction paper stapled together and circulated among those who enjoy developing friendships by mail. So Rosie wasn't surprised when she received a letter from a seventeen-year-old Oakland girl who had found Rosie's name in one of the books.

The two girls had been exchanging letters for more than a month before police paid a visit to Rosie and her parents. Were they aware, sheriff's deputies asked, that "the Oakland girl" was really a forty-eight-year-old man?

They showed the Duncans a photograph of Timothy James Bindner. None of them had ever seen him before.

AFTERWORD

On May 2, 1997, the City of Fairfield agreed to settle Timothy Bindner's lawsuit. The Oakland man received $90,000; the city admitted no fault. Bindner's status as a suspect remains unchanged.

THE AMBER FOUNDATION
Kim Swartz, Founder and Executive Director
P.O. Box 565
Pinole, CA 94564-0565
24-hour hot line: 1-800-541-0777
Tax ID #: 94-3069460
California Tax #: CT 72480

The Amber Foundation is a nonprofit
organization staffed totally by volunteers. The
foundation is part of a growing national network
of organizations with the same mission: the
recovery of abducted children.

ABOUT THE AUTHOR

JOHN PHILPIN is a nationally renowned forensic psychologist—a profiler. His advice and opinions on violence and its aftermath have been sought by police, newspaper writers, TV producers, mental health professionals, private investigators, attorneys, and polygraph experts throughout the country.

Stalemate is the result of an ongoing dialogue between the author and the suspect, Timothy James Bindner.

John Philpin lives in Reading, Vermont, with his wife and son.